MW01199142

Music & Joy

Music & Joy

Lessons on the Good Life

DANIEL K. L. CHUA

Yale UNIVERSITY PRESS

New Haven and London

Yale University Press books may be purchased in quantity for
educational, business, or promotional use. For information,
please e-mail sales.press@yale.edu (U.S. office) or sales@yaleup
.co.uk (U.K. office).

Printed in the United States of America.

Library of Congress Control Number: 2023951678
ISBN 978-0-300-26421-0 (hardcover : alk. paper)

A catalogue record for this book is available from
the British Library.

This paper meets the requirements of ANSI/NISO Z39.48-1992
(Permanence of Paper).

10 9 8 7 6 5 4 3 2 1

For
Wee Hian and King Ling
Jennifer, Lucas, and Harrison

The joy of my inheritance

Contents

Part III: Unforced Rhythms

Part IV: A Good Measure

Preface

This book is a music lesson on the good life. *Music is joy* is its basic premise. To know music is to know joy.

Such knowledge is not the usual stuff of music lessons. I should know. As a professor of music, I teach music for a living, but music is not expected to teach us how to live. Just ask my students. They would tell you that their lives would be so much better without my class on music theory. Learning all those arcane concepts is not good for life: it is mostly good for an exam in music theory. So, far from teaching the good life, I may have taught my students how *not* to live well, since an exam-driven life is neither virtuous nor joyful. It's just sad. Thankfully, such a specialized course is only for the musically initiated. Few can enroll. For most people, such knowledge is too forbidding and so will do no harm. They are none the worse for their lack of music theory, but sadly, also none the wiser.

A music lesson on the good life, however, should impart wisdom to everyone. After all, there is no human culture without music. Music is a fact of life. It is everyday and everywhere. Its joys are all-inclusive. Everyone can enroll in this class. So a book that purports to be a music lesson on the good life would undermine its own premise if it were written only for the specialist. Music gives joy indiscriminately to whoever is there to receive it. You shouldn't need a crash course in music theory, let alone acquire sufficient musical literacy, to read this book. So come just as you are. Admittedly, you might see a snippet of music notation in the following pages; a fancy musical term may pop out from a paragraph or two. But fear not. With a little patience, there is nothing in the book that will exclude the ordinary reader from understanding what music has to teach us about joy. The lesson is for everyone.

In fact, being an expert might be more frustrating—and not just for the expert in music. Music and joy, as a subject, ranges widely across many disciplines. This book weaves different disciplinary threads together to create bold ideas with big narrative patterns. Skidding generally across its pages is the best way to cover such an expanse. The expert eye, on the other hand, might glisten when it sees a particular discipline surface from the text; a splash of philosophy, theology, sinology, or neuropsychology may lure the expert to dive beneath the general surface and fixate on arcane details. Such a pursuit, however, may weigh you down and lead to a labyrinth where wider perspectives are lost in the empty search for niche issues.

So carry your expertise lightly. All you really need on this journey is an open mind. Music and joy may not be a difficult lesson to pursue, but the relation between the two is a bit strange to accept. They make an odd couple. Music and joy may welcome everyone, but few would embrace them as a form of the good life. For most people, music is more about virtuosity than virtue. It concerns the adulation of great conductors and not the emulation of good conduct. Our listening habits are trained for easy consumption, not self-cultivation. Great hits rather than great joy top the charts for measuring music's ultimate value. So, ironically, the music we know may prevent us from understanding the lesson we need to learn. Its familiarity may clog our ears from hearing the good life, and close our minds from knowing its joy.

My task in this book is to persuade you to attend to a different music, even if it strains your ears and dazzles your eyes. This is a music so big that it may appear formless, disappearing beyond the horizon. The joy that vibrates in its tones may seem too vast to capture. You might be wondering what kind of music this might be. It's hard to say in a few words. A telescope aimed at the horizon will miss the point entirely; this is not a music you can grasp with an all-knowing gaze. Instead, imagine its definition as a voyage to foreign shores, where we will encounter strange beliefs and odd perspectives that will challenge our musical assumptions. On this journey, we will need to be charitable rather than critical in our engagement with these traditions, otherwise we will discover only how clever we are and miss out on the wisdom they might impart. As this is a lesson in *lived* knowledge, we will need to suspend judgment and believe all kinds of weird and fabulous things as if they are true. You might not ultimately commit to any of these truth-claims, but that's not the purpose of the journey. The point is to stretch your imagination and estrange your hearing to perceive something different. All that matters on this expedition is that you find in music the general condition for a way of life and a mode of being that leads to joy. If we arrive at this destination, then this book will be a lesson well learned.

Acknowledgments

Professors in the humanities tend to be lone rangers. We ride alone, spurring our brains to climb the heights of erudition. But it has not been possible to write this book alone. Music and joy cover a sprawling area of research too vast for a lone ranger to patrol. So I amassed a dream team of outstanding scholars to ride the range with me and guide my runaway thoughts in the right direction. I charmed and nagged these experts to talk to me, email me, Zoom me, supervise me, read my drafts, carry out research, locate sources, translate terms, notate examples, illustrate diagrams, perform scores, and edit chapters. It was a joy to work with them. I am not sure if all the neighing and mooing they've helped to herd into this book is music to their ears. So I will take responsibility for any cacophony that you hear; but any erudition that bedazzles you should also be credited to them. They are a brilliant team. Just mentioning their names here will not do justice to their contribution. So, as you read the roll call below, imagine a fancy fanfare and a shiny halo around their names. In no significant order:

Ellen Y. Zhang, Robert C. Roberts, Peng Yin, Jonathan W. Johnson (who also provided some charming illustrations for the book), Michael O'Connor, Yang Yuanzheng, Steve Gaultney, Rujing Huang,

Ryan McAnnally-Linz, Daniel Tsz-shing Lei (who recorded a Chinese folksong on the *dizi* to accompany my text), Henry Parks, Michael Puett, Youn Kim, Matthew Arndt, Julia Ronge, Miroslav Volf, Carol Harrison, Jing Wang, Egberto Bermúdez, Sheryl Chow, Elizabeth Margulis, Chan Hing-yan, Robert Sholl, Giorgio Biancorosso, MingJun Wilson, Mike Brownnutt, and Francis Su.

The last person on the list, the mathematician Francis Su, also makes a cameo appearance in the afterword where I describe the making of this book. Among other things, he serendipitously led me to Yale University Press. This book is no run-of-the-mill production and could have easily fallen between the cracks. It meshes together the ancient and modern world, Chinese wisdom and Christian thought, Beethoven and the blues, post-human methods and human flourishing, music theory and the practicalities of life in Hong Kong. The press has been visionary not only in agreeing to my far-ranging ideas but in trusting enough in the book's message to market the volume to a general readership. I am so grateful to the senior executive editor Jennifer Banks for making this book a possibility, and to her team for making it a reality. If the dream team herded my stray thoughts between these covers, the Yale team redistributed them in the public realm.

Finally, I would like to thank those who have supported the scholarly projects that have shaped many of the ideas in this book over the last ten years, in particular Peter McDonald and the McDonald Agape Foundation, Belinda Hung, and the Yale Center for Faith and Culture.

With all the good faith and goodwill invested in this book, I hope I have made good on my promise to deliver a complex book in a simple form that will bring joy to the lives of those who read it.

Music & Joy

I

Hard Questions

My music is not "nice."

—OLIVIER MESSIAEN

1

Is Music Joy?

The Ask

This book explores a simple question: Is music joy?

Nice. What's there not to like about such a benign question? But "nice" might just be its problem. In today's crisis-ridden world, people are not desperately seeking an answer to the question "Is music joy?" The world is in a state of existential crisis. Fear, not joy, defines our times. Terror and pandemic are rattling the nations. Division and delusion are wreaking havoc across the political spectrum, fomenting the conditions for social disintegration and nuclear warfare. And if the specter of blowing up the planet were not enough, it appears that our humdrum activities are causing irreversible climate change that not only imperils species diversity but will probably cause our own extinction. In this context, the question "Is music joy?" is hardly an urgent one. And besides, isn't the answer obvious? Almost everyone enjoys music. Clearly, music is joy. So why pursue the question further?

Because such an answer would, indeed, make the question superficial and inconsequential. Music would be nothing more than a bit of "auditory cheesecake," as the evolutionary psychologist Steven Pinker describes it.[1] Its joys would have no greater purpose than to tickle our ears with the occasional, if deliciously full-fat, thrill. Music is nice to have but hardly necessary to hear.

The philosopher Immanuel Kant held a similar view of music, although from the other end of the digestive tract. He compared the effect of music to intestinal massage. Music functions as a workout for our innards analogous to the benefits of a hearty laugh.[2] Enjoying it is like a physical reaction to a joke, amounting to nothing more than a giggle. In contemporary terms, music's joy is a laugh-out-loud emoji, something good for the bowels but barely eligible for what Kant regarded as the higher realms of thought—reason.

Underlying these arguments is a warning. Don't take music too seriously! Music may be pleasurable, but it would be a mistake to invest too much in its joy. It simply isn't worth it. As a professor of music in Hong Kong, I can sometimes see the anxiety caused by this view of music on the faces of parents as they bring their child to the university. It is as if they have lost their children to the Music Department. Through their silent smiles, I can hear their distraught brains shouting: "Why couldn't my daughter have chosen something useful like medicine, accountancy, or quantity surveying? Music was only supposed to be a nice bit of cultural capital to bedazzle other parents. Just because my child likes music does not mean that she should *study* it. Please, someone, rescue my child from the clutches of this evil music professor!" In Hong Kong, getting a real job with proper professional accreditation and a regular salary is the least you should do to honor your parents and help pay their mortgage. The pressure is so high in Asia that some of my students secretly take music courses while informing their parents that they are majoring in biochemistry. For them, music is indeed like cheesecake: a guilty pleasure.

Unless we are content with such a frivolous account of music, we should probably look beyond human pleasure as the answer to the question. Just because *we* enjoy music does not mean that we should determine its value, particularly when its joy is defined by our drives and appetites. If music is more than cheesecake, then it must mean more than something we consume and how that makes us feel. So, in order to grasp its significance, we may have to remove ourselves from the equation.

Far from being a nice question, "Is music joy?" turns out to have the nasty side effect of eliminating the human from the answer. This is a drastic procedure because it removes what we cherish most about music—ourselves. To delete the human element from music is like trying to erase the photographer from a selfie in order to see the object behind the subject. The difficulty here is not the obvious reason that we are unavoidably at the center of all human knowing; rather, our very knowledge of music today is in *selfie mode*. We assume a human-centric view of music.

In the West, this view has its roots in the birth of opera around 1600. The Renaissance humanists made music *human* (as humanists are wont to do), and opera came to symbolize this new status by promoting a new style of solo singing that followed the natural inflection of ordinary speech known as a recitative. In opera, to speak is to sing. Opera makes music human by aligning its tones to what the Renaissance humanists regarded as the very definition of our species—language. In the recitative, we literally imprint our identity on music by giving it our voice. In fact, the theory behind opera promotes the voice as the medium through which the self masters its environment. Speech should be sung, it argues, because words alone are ineffective in moving the audience; they need the emotive force of music to make their meanings felt. Music functions as the affective agency of the self with the power to influence the emotions of its hearers. Opera, then, is the musical selfie that puts humanity center stage.

In one of the earliest operas—Monteverdi's *L'Orfeo* (1607)—music is so self-conscious of its new identity that it materializes in human form to describe its powers. As the curtains rise, Musica sings: "I am music. With my sweet accents I can make every restless heart peaceful and inflame the coldest minds, now with anger, now with love." Today, we no longer need to be persuaded by Musica; we already believe in her humanizing powers. Humans *make* music. Its existence is dependent upon us. It is *for* us and *from* us and *in* us. It expresses us. It sounds like us. It is all about us. Its joys are in us. Like Musica, we are its incarnation.

One consequence of this human-centered context is that music aspires to become *great* music. Its greatest joys come in discrete pieces—our masterpieces. When the human is the measure of music, music becomes our *work* or our "opus" (to use the Latin term); music is our labor of expression, whether it's a piece of K-pop or a piece of bebop or a piece by Glazunov. So when we ask the question "Is music joy?" we invariably reach for our greatest hits for an answer. But great music does not make music great. It just makes humans sound great. Great music functions as a mirror for our narcissism and inflates our ego. But, in the magnitude of things, great works are just tiny little objects. They come in human sizes for our consumption. But this can make music less than great because in reality music is so much more than these beautifully packaged boxes of human culture. We need to think bigger. Our question requires us to sidestep the human and think out of the box. But how?

The Big Ask

Have you ever wanted music to stop? As a musicologist, I immerse myself in music every day. "Don't stop the music" should be my mantra. But there are just some days when I don't want to listen to any piece of music however great. You couldn't lure me with a Mozart piano concerto or a Joni Mitchell song. I just want silence. I want to isolate myself in an auditory vacuum and declutter my ears from sound. The composer John Cage is famous for composing four minutes and thirty-three seconds of seemingly no music in a piece entitled 4′33″. Aptly, this work was inspired by his attempt to hear the sound of silence. Cage put himself in an auditory vacuum—an anechoic chamber. To his surprise he discovered that there was no silence to be heard. Enclosed in the chamber, he could hear the operations of his nervous system and the circulation of his blood system producing two different frequencies. "Try as we might to make silence, we cannot," he reflected, because there is no escape from the rhythms of life.[3] We are part of the environment. Silence does not exist on our planet.

For Cage, music is everywhere all the time. It can't be put in a box. In fact, the title of Cage's 4′33″ underlines the boundless nature of music by questioning why music is divided into discrete pieces in the first place: Why 4′33″? That's just an arbitrary duration of time. And 4′33″ of what, exactly, since any *work* done by the composer is minimal if not nominal? 4′33″ cannot aspire to be a "great work," for Cage's masterpiece is a piece without a master. The human element is missing.

The content of the piece is often mistaken as silence, but as with Cage in the anechoic chamber, you cannot hear silence; when the soloist lifts the piano lid (or, in the orchestral version, when the conductor raises the baton), the audience hears itself listening. 4′33″ is an arbitrary slice of audience noise.

Except it is not noise. It is music. Everything in the environment, with all its contingent sounds—from the cough of someone in the front row to the hum of the air-conditioning—is music. Cage just puts a frame on a music that already exists, whether we humans make it happen or not. This is why a glance at the score should elicit a laugh (see figure 1); this frame—the only human contribution—is the most ridiculous aspect of the piece because it compartmentalizes what cannot be bounded. What is great in a great work is no longer applicable. 4′33″ underlines the smallness of our cultural habits. Cage lets music

Figure 1. John Cage: Score of 4′33″—Movement I.

out of the cage by framing the fact that we fail to listen to a greater music that is always already present.

Music is a matter of listening to what is given. Often, when we say we are "listening" to music we are merely paying lip service to our ears: we are not listening to music but consuming it. If we truly learn to listen, then music becomes a disclosure that cannot simply be consumed like cheesecake but begins to question our being. By eliminating the "work," music is no longer about us. It is no longer a mirror of our labor. It becomes a portal, a way of attending to the world. So maybe on those days when I want "silence," I am not escaping music; perhaps what I truly desire is to immerse myself in a music that is already everywhere in the world. Great music is great, of course (I've written many pages on its greatness), but a great work is not the basis for understanding music, let alone defining what music is. Human music is a subset of a music that is beyond the human. In fact, by attending to its own greatness, great music can tune out the world and shrink its joys. This may be why some days I just don't want to listen to any piece of music, however great. All I desire is a longer version of 4'33".

If we can learn to free music from its human enclosures, then we might give it the space to truly resonate. Undoubtedly, there is much to love about human music, but if can we lose it for just a moment in something bigger outside of our control, then we might begin to understand its existence more deeply. We might even learn to love it more.

This book, then, begins by letting go of our human-centric view of music in order to love music more. From this perspective, the critical word in the question "Is music joy?" is the one that connects music and joy: "is." It is a question of music's *being.* It is not about me or you or the music we make. We do not underwrite music's being. Joy connects with music without our species as the go-between. They can define each other without our feelings getting in the way. What this book explores, then, is a *fundamental* question: Is music's *very being* joy? Or, to turn the question around: Is joy defined by music?

From this perspective, the question becomes much bigger. If music *is* joy, then this terse little question opens out into a vast speculative space: the music that surrounds us is vibrating with joy. It has cosmic significance. The question redefines what music is, what joy is, and how their relationship shapes the world. Music would no longer be something we define but a condition of joy that ultimately defines us and the world. We would no longer make music; rather, music makes us; it en-joys us. When we listen to a music that is already given, the ethos of the cosmos and our place in the world comes into play. If the question is true, then music would be a disclosure of joy that changes everything precisely because it raises a fundamental question.

But everything would change only *if* music is joy. And this is a big *if*. After all, there is no obvious reason why music should be joy. The question may now be more consequential, but it also becomes a whole lot harder to answer. In fact, it is much harder to ask, especially in the narrow corridors of academia, where transcendent questions are deflated with a cynical pinprick. The question, with its big *if*, is too speculative and overblown. The risk of committing a fundamental error in answering this fundamental question is simply too high.

The "Don't Ask"

In today's intellectual climate, "Is music joy?" is a miserable research question destined for failure. The question only has two answers, either yes or no. And, in short, the answer is no.

No, music is not fundamentally joy. And the reasons are obvious:

1. Sad music exists. If sad music exists, then music cannot essentially be joy. The question is obviously pointless.
2. Not only does sad music exist, but music expressing all kinds of emotions exists. So why joy? Why not anger? Or love? Or terror? In fact, why even an emotion? The method is arbitrary.
3. And besides, music is too complex a phenomenon to be reduced to one emotion. To boil music down to an essence is too simple, too naïve, too one-dimensional. The method is flawed.
4. But there is an even bigger problem here: to reduce music to a single essence is to elevate it as a universal. Universals are dangerous. Not only are they tinged with unprovable metaphysical claims, they carry totalizing if not totalitarian overtones. And musicologists of all people should know better because for much of the nineteenth and twentieth centuries music used to be *the* universal art form. It was championed as the universal language, the condition toward which all the arts should aspire. But the only music that was valid for this absolute condition was a subset of Western classical music—it was even called "absolute music." But given our sensitivity to cultural diversity today, music can no longer be defined as a singular, absolute object that claims its universality by excluding difference. It is more correct today to speak of music in the plural as "musics." No one should speak of music as a single universal

phenomenon anymore. The method required by
the question is morally dubious and out of date.

5. Joy, too, is out of date. This term has long been
overtaken in academia by "happiness" research.
In the past, joy and happiness were often interchangeable terms. Today, happiness has its own
distinctive brand. There are many useful benefits
to being happy.

- Happiness is mindful; it has therapeutic
  value, focusing the mind to be in the moment amid the chaos of life.
- Happiness is measurable: it has a famous
  index—the happiness index—that can calibrate the well-being of nations.
- Happiness is modern; "the pursuit of happiness" is an engine of progress and independence: it is an unalienable right indelibly
  etched not only in the American Declaration
  of Independence, but in all who aspire to a
  vision of freedom. According to the philosopher John Stuart Mill, a liberal society should
  be founded on "the greatest happiness
  principle," which seeks the highest pleasure
  for the maximum number of people.

Mindful, measurable, and modern, happiness will
render music relevant and keep it up to date. In
contrast, joy seems like some mindless platitude
with premodern overtones—a word that an
endearing aunt might say over a cup of tea after a
delightful concert at the symphony: "My dear, one
finds Dvořák's Serenade such a joy, doesn't one?"
Compared to happiness, the word *joy* sounds
dated and morally shallow.

Arbitrary, flawed, and out of date, my research question should be abandoned. My book should end here.

THE END

But I have a better idea. Rather than end the book, I should punish the question for being so blatantly wrong-headed by pursuing the opposite question: Is music sad? Curiously, in today's intellectual climate, this question turns out to be both legitimate and very profound.

2

A Tragic Turn

A Sad Task

Music has been fundamentally sad for many years now in the West. Tragedy is its very being. Paradoxically, the proof of its tragic state is found in the most celebrated piece of joy on the planet: Beethoven's "Ode to Joy."

You would think that one of the greatest works in the Western canon would make a case for joy as the paradigm of music, but no: the explosion of joy in the finale of Beethoven's Ninth Symphony was thought to be utterly grotesque by some early commentators. The music critic Eduard Hanslick, quoting the theologian David Friedrich Strauss, described the last movement as an ugly head attached on an otherwise pristine torso. It is a monstrous end to a classically proportioned work.[1] Oversized and overwrought, its joy is as much a rupture as it is a rapture. So what kind of joy is this?

To answer this question, we need to return to the place where it all began—Beethoven's working desk. On its surface are three unrelated objects: a paperweight, an Egyptian inscription, and a tiny statue of the first consul of the Roman republic, Junius Lucius Brutus. Every day at his desk, Beethoven would see these three objects as he composed. They are just arbitrary things, collected at different times, no more than curiosities; and yet, on the flat surface of his desk, they are interconnected as emblems of the composer's creative vision. In particular, each object provides an insight into the kind of joy shaping Beethoven's compositional process and, most pertinently, the kind of joy animating the final movement of his last symphony. We are going to spend some time examining the "Ode to Joy" because if we listen to it with these objects in mind, we will hear the condition of modern joy and the reason why its music is necessarily sad. To know this joy is to understand why music is *not* joy.

Object Lessons

The statue—First, the bust of Brutus (see figure 2). Here is a man who famously executed his two sons without flinching as he founded the Roman republic. Take a long hard look at Brutus, because this is exactly what the statue seems to be doing to you. In this staring contest, you would definitely blink first. Here is a face that would seriously unnerve anyone with its implacable, impenetrable gaze.

In 1818, some five years before starting work on the Ninth, Beethoven imagined composing a choral symphony incorporating a Bacchanalian feast drunk on joy (rather than wine).[2] The "feast of Bacchus," as he noted to himself, was to emerge from a "pious hymn." However, when the Ninth Symphony premiered in 1824, the proposed hymn was canceled by something terrifyingly different. The final movement begins with a dissonant shriek known as the *Schreckensfanfare* (a fanfare of terror). It is a devastating blast that flattens everything within the vicinity of the symphony, rendering the music of the previous movements hopelessly inadequate in its wake. Indeed,

Figure 2. Bust of Junius
Lucius Brutus.

fragments from the earlier movements try to resurface as the
finale begins, but the fanfare's high-decibel rhythms hammer
them back into the ground.[3] Dense, dissonant, and deafeningly
loud, the *Schreckensfanfare* looms over the symphony as a sonic
wall of fear.

It is against this terror that human voices are mobilized
to declare a state of joy. "Friends, not these tones!" sings a solo
voice among the devastation: "Rather, let us strike up more
pleasant and more joyful ones."

"Joy!" he shouts.

"Joy!" the people respond.[4]

And so a "brotherhood" of joy is forged in the face of terror. This counterforce against terror is seen in the stony glare
of Brutus. If there is joy etched in his features, it can only be
one of austere resistance. Brutus, the founder of the Roman republic, was the face of the French Revolution when France

founded its First Republic. As a symbol of principled action, he was the model of an unmoved and immovable force against the ancien régime. In the Ninth Symphony, his stoic and un-yielding stature is the joy that withstands the assault of evil. And aptly, the form of the final movement is organized like a military campaign. The first thing that is required after the declaration of joy is a long march to gather the forces and unite the people. The famous "joy" theme is transformed into a re-cruiting song.[5] It begins with the same lone voice that had appealed for a different tone, but now it demands a different beat. In the distance, you hear the orchestra strike up the band from within its ranks, with the piccolo and contrabassoon im-itating a fife and drum. One man soon becomes an army as a chorus of people gather from far and wide, building momen-tum until the joyful throng becomes a stampede.[6] It is a coun-terpoint of pounding hooves. Richard Wagner astutely describes this force as "battle music."[7] With its martial rhythms and galloping drive, what had started out as a solitary march ends as a cavalry charge, speeding en masse with a joy that tramples over every obstacle in its path.[8] Brutus the immov-able becomes Brutus the unstoppable. This stampeding cho-rus is a foretaste of the frenzied celebration that will end the symphony, connecting the campaign to its final victory. As the movement draws toward the closing cadence, the march re-turns as a massive force, clattering with drums and cymbals.[9] This time around, it is faster, louder, and so much bigger. The brotherhood rises up as a noisy militia intoxicated with its own victory. The message is clear: the finale concludes with a blast of joy to counteract the initial shriek of terror.

What kind of joy is this? In the Ninth Symphony, joy turns out to be a defiant force that takes its stand on the bar-ricades. It befits the Promethean image of Beethoven, a com-poser who seizes fate by the throat to overcome adversity by sheer force of will. This is a *heroic* joy, the shout of a freedom

fighter raging against unsurmountable forces. What unites the
brotherhood in the symphony, then, is not so much joy itself
as a common enemy. In effect, Beethoven weaponizes joy. No
doubt the campaign in the symphony is a cause worth fight-
ing for. But at what cost? The fight—because it is *a fight*—scars
the virtue the work celebrates with the very evil it denounces.
In resisting terror, joy ends up imitating the enemy it fears.
Like Brutus, it too becomes cold, callous, and brutal. The final
victory in the closing measures of the symphony is no less terrifying than the opening fanfare. The movement may have
progressed from darkness to light, symbolized by the change
from the minor to the major mode, but the final blaze of glory
is just another sonic wall that replaces one oppressive force
with another.[10]

In the civilizing environment of a concert hall, this bar-
baric force is often lost. Beyond such polite society, however,
you can literally see the violence of the Ninth flashing on the
cinema screen because the final movement is often deployed
as a soundtrack for gratuitous scenes of carnage with multiple
explosions and crashing vehicles upended as a monument to
speed.[11] The trailer for the Hollywood blockbuster *A Good Day
to Die Hard* (2013), starring Bruce Willis as the Promethean
hero John McClane, brilliantly captures this force. The final
frenzy in Beethoven's "Ode to Joy" choreographs a firework
display of exuberant violence and explosive destruction armed
with a dazzling array of armored vehicles, careering helicopters,
and machine-gun fire (figure 3). The title of the movie says it
all: joy in the Ninth Symphony lives by dying hard.

The paperweight—This brings us to the second object on
Beethoven's desk: the paperweight (see figure 4)—or rather,
two identical paperweights cast in bronze, each depicting a
Cossack soldier galloping on horseback, wielding a spear, and
charging at speed. In the late eighteenth century, the Cossack

Figure 3. All guns blazing—from the trailer
of *A Good Day to Die Hard* (2013).

people were a military class within the Russian Empire. They
were highly feared by the Napoleonic army. If they were to fea-
ture in a Hollywood blockbuster, they would be the multitude
of extras in scenes of gratuitous carnage and high-speed
crashes. The two tiny representatives sitting on Beethoven's
desk kept watch over the composer's scores and sketches. Perhaps, while composing, Beethoven played with these two paperweights like toy soldiers in a war room. After all, his music
often glorifies war. The *Eroica* Symphony and the Fifth Symphony are narratives of military triumphs, and his propaganda
set-piece *Wellington's Victory* literally celebrates the defeat of
Napoleon with the noise of firearms. In fact, Beethoven's compositional strategies often resemble highly disciplined military formations. They are battle plans. Their ultimate purpose
is to charge over vast musical terrains in order to seize the final cadence as victory . . . which, of course, is exactly what the
Ninth Symphony does.

Figure 4. Beethoven's paperweight.

If Brutus represents the joy of resilience, then the paperweights represent the joy of rampage. It is as if the inner
strength of Brutus generates an outward force in these fero-
cious Cossacks. Their joy, captured in frozen animation, is the
exhilaration of speed and violence. "*Attack!*" is their jubilant
cry. The same command closes the Ninth Symphony, but instead of writing "attack" Beethoven gives the command to ac-
celerate: it marks the final charge to victory.[12] The closing
section is a military frenzy that routs out the enemy. Joy in
Beethoven's Ninth is the celebration of a destructive force. This
is why the philosopher Theodor W. Adorno claimed he could
hear in the composer's heroic works "the command to kill"
despite the celebratory noise of freedom.[13] This is a joy that
is most alive when it dices with death. It is as terrifying as it is
exhilarating, as violent as it is victorious, and as tribal as it
is total.

Contrary to its own claims, joy in the Ninth Symphony
does not exist unconditionally as a virtue that unites humanity. Rather, heroic joy is inherently violent because it is always

based on a threat. It requires a prior evil to react against in order to celebrate a virtue that merely replicates the evil it resists.[14] Joy may start from the command of a moral will (as seen
in the steely eyes of Brutus), but it ends with a rampage (as
seen in the charge of the Cossacks). The "Ode to Joy" turns
out to be an odious joy.

If concrete proof of its violence were needed, Wagner deployed the Ninth Symphony to incite insurrection during the
1848 Revolutions. His performances of the symphony so inspired the audience with political fervor that when fires broke
out in Dresden, a guard standing on the barricades expressed
his euphoria by shouting the opening lines of the "Ode to Joy"
to the composer: "schöner Götterfunken!" (beautiful divine
spark!). Joy's "divine spark" had set the city ablaze.

The inscription—Sadly, for Wagner, the spark was soon
snuffed out by reactionary forces. With the failure of the revolution, the disillusioned composer recast the joy of the symphony in a darker if more transcendent light. The Ninth
Symphony became a metaphysical revelation of doom. These
foreboding tones, however, are already promised by the third
item on Beethoven's desk—a piece of paper bearing an ancient
inscription from the temple of Saïs in Egypt (see figure 5). It
concerns the veil of the goddess Isis.

The inscription begins:

I am that which is.
I am all that has been and is and shall be.
No mortal man has lifted my veil.

These words reminded Beethoven that he was no mortal
man when composing at his desk. He believed his art had the
power to unveil metaphysical truths.[15] But such oracular powers can be deadly. After all, these mystical lines are a warning.

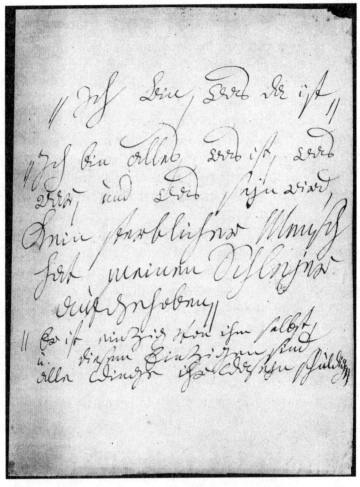

Figure 5. Egyptian inscription from the temple of Saïs copied by Beethoven and kept on his working desk: "Ich Bin, Was da ist / Ich bin alles, Was ist, Was / war, und Was seyn wird, / Kein sterblicher Mensch / hat meinen Schleyer / aufgehoben / Er ist einzig von ihm selbst, / u. diesem Einzigen sind / alle Dinge ihr Daseyn schuldig" [I am that which is: I am all that has been and is and shall be. No mortal man has lifted my veil. He is one—self existent. And to that One all things owe their being].

Friedrich Schiller, the poet of the "Ode to Joy," in the ballad "The Veiled Image of Isis" (1795) tells the tale of a young man who lifted the veil of the goddess only to be ruined by the knowledge of an unutterable truth that carried him to an early grave.

In the political context of 1848, the failure of the revolution was an early grave for the young Wagner. Something died inside him. He had styled himself as the heroic artist, but his futile crusade merely unveiled a terrifying truth: surrender is the only meaningful act in a future devoid of hope. The composer turned to the ideas of a philosopher who, according to Martin Heidegger, made "grumpiness" the principle for philosophizing the world—Arthur Schopenhauer. He made music "serious."[16] In fact, great music was called "serious music" on account of his philosophy. In his two-volume work of 1844, *The World as Will and Representation*, Schopenhauer extolled music as the deepest expression of cosmic reality, but this exaltation merely doomed music to his universal pessimism. Behind what the philosopher calls the "Veil of Maya" is a terrifying reality. However, the average mortal only sees the shroud of illusion. There is no access to the naked truth. But with music you can get close. Real close. To listen to music is to go beyond the veil and experience the most direct representation of an undifferentiated, impersonal cosmic will that drowns out our cries for individual meaning like the currents of a mighty symphonic river. The universe is a chaotic, unceasing, undifferentiated flow. Schopenhauer could hear in the symphonies of Beethoven this ineluctable force absorbing us into its unity as if we were mere dissonances resolving into the final cadence of the music.[17] The cosmic will is both fateful and fatal. In the face of this Primal Unity, resistance is futile. So, post-1848, the Ninth Symphony could no longer express the joy of victory for Wagner; music is now a consolation for an abandoned cause.[18]

But how can music in this gloomy state be joy?[19]

Wagner's melancholic vision is most joyfully articulated by his young admirer Friedrich Nietzsche in his first publication, *The Birth of Tragedy* (1872). Somehow, he gets Schopenhauer's philosophy to party . . . with a little help from Beethoven's Ninth Symphony. For Nietzsche, the choral finale is equivalent to a rave. In fact, he describes its joy as Beethoven had originally intended—as a "feast of Bacchus" (although Nietzsche uses the Greek name, Dionysius, instead of the Latin). However, under the shadow of Schopenhauer's gloomy philosophy, the drunken celebration is not going to affirm life as joy. Life is "nauseating," declares Nietzsche. There's no point struggling against this truth, he insists. Instead humanity must affirm its futility and celebrate the wisdom "to die soon." For Nietzsche, the Ninth Symphony parties in the face of death.[20] From this perspective, the terror of the *Schreckensfanfare* is no longer a force to resist but a fate to embrace. Its "musical dissonance" is to be affirmed as an existential condition, and its excess as a surge of vitality.[21] Humanity, then, should rise up in Dionysian frenzy and lose itself in revelry before Schopenhauer's cosmic will. In this way, terror becomes a rave, and joy is the drug that induces an ecstatic state of unity as our individual quest for meaning dissipates into a collective death-drive.[22] Nietzsche turns the tables on humanity: "die hard" becomes "die soon."

For Nietzsche, then, joy in the Ninth Symphony lives as an *art* of dying—what was known in the late medieval era as an *ars moriendi,* except that there is no salvation in this modern iteration. Toward the end of the symphony, when the chorus sings of the multitudes bowing down before their creator, Nietzsche imagines humanity embracing its own annihilation before a god indifferent to its existence. With the veil of Maya torn asunder, the philosopher inverts the image of the Promethean Beethoven: the heroic will no longer defines itself against a prior evil but surrenders before a transcendent will that absorbs humanity's hopeless struggle for identity into its being. So, if humanity wants joy, claims Nietzsche, it should stop striving to create its future like an artist; it should abandon itself as an artwork to a blind cosmic force, yielding its life to the whim of a higher creator.[23]

Ironically, in Nietzsche's rendition of the Ninth Symphony, Beethoven's anthem to humanity ultimately cancels humanity. To truly register the reality of the cosmic flux that engulfs us, we need to realize that it is best for us "not to be born, not to be, to be nothing." This is why the "second best" for us, asserts Nietzsche, is "to die soon."[24] Under these circumstances, music is both oracle and consolation for the philosopher. It unveils a cosmos that would be too horrifying to accept if it were not also a narcotic that numbs us to its revelation. Listening to the Ninth Symphony won't actually kill you, but it will give you a beautiful premonition of the best way to die . . . which, of course, is also the best way to live.

In this way, Nietzsche made the "Ode to Joy" the very being of music. But its essence is not joy. The title of Nietzsche's book makes this clear: *The Birth of Tragedy* is *Through the Spirit of Music*. If music is joy, then it is paradoxically a tragic joy. It is *fundamentally* sad even in its greatest moment of euphoria.

If music is oracular, as Beethoven claims, then Schopenhauer and Nietzsche are its philosophical high priests of doom. And their solemn tones have resonated all the way to the grumpy old men of philosophy in our postmodern times. Today, music remains a kind of sublime death wish.[25] Here, for example, is a quote from the philosopher Philippe Lacoue-Labarthe: "What moves me in music, then, is my own mourning."[26] If such a succinct formula for self-bereavement in music sounds insufficiently grumpy, here is a more elaborate lament from the father of postmodernism himself, Jean-François Lyotard: "Life laments its precariousness in an ever forgotten, anonymous death rattle. I maintain that music gets its beauties and emotions from the evocation of this condition of abandonment that is loud and mute, horrified, moist with a promiscuity without alterity."[27]

I am not exactly sure what this means, but it is definitely grumpy.

A Great Truth

The inscription on Beethoven's desk probably turned out to be more deadly than the composer had envisaged. What the Ninth Symphony reveals is the sad condition of modern joy. Like Brutus, it is a resilient force that only exists because it resists. Like the charging Cossack cast in bronze, it is a violent rampage that goes nowhere fast. And like the veil of Isis, behind its fabrication of joy, music reveals the truth of a meaningless abyss. In all three cases, joy thrives on death. Ironically, joy is profound only when it is underwritten by tragedy. So maybe we should heed the warning on Beethoven's desk and look away. No mortal should lift the veil of the "Ode to Joy" because what lies beyond its diaphanous surface is terrifying.

Understandably, some people get upset when they hear these terrible accusations against Beethoven's Ninth Symphony. The critique comes as a shock. Why would a professor of music seemingly denounce a masterpiece?

If it is any consolation, I will redeem the work by the end of the book; but for now, let's consider its claim to greatness. Beethoven's Ninth Symphony is undoubtedly a masterpiece. But if you recall, great works do not make music great; they just make humans sound great. So, inevitably, great music runs the risk of being all too human. If great music is a mirror of our humanity, then it is at its greatest when it is not merely a narcissistic projection; it needs to show us what we don't already see, something beyond our veil of self-delusion. What makes the Ninth Symphony great is precisely its revelation. It speaks the truth—a truth we fail to perceive because we only want to hear the best version of ourselves. We want the symphony to be an anthem for good; we want it to hymn the values of a humanity united by joy; we want the symphony to be the ultimate feel-good anthem—resilient, heroic, victorious. We want to be great.

And, indeed, the symphony has been deployed many times in this way. And that's fine. We should celebrate our human achievements. The problem is that these treasured moments are indiscriminate: they include the good, the bad, and the ugly. For example, the symphony was used to celebrate the fall of the Berlin Wall in 1989 and also to glorify Hitler on his birthday in 1942; its famous tune is not only the official anthem for the European Union, but was also the national anthem for the apartheid regime of what was formerly Rhodesia (now Zimbabwe). This is not simply a matter of cultural appropriation, as if the other side is always to blame. If the same joy in the same music is interchangeable under opposing regimes, then what unites humanity may not be as humane as we imagine. So let's take an honest look in the mirror. When we use the Ninth Symphony in such moments of unity, our joy may be no less tragic than the misery of those we have triumphed over; and our victories may be no less violent than the evil forces we oppose. The universal virtue we call "joy" merely masks a disturbing reality. What if the world is fundamentally violent and empty, and our joyful victories are nothing more than a futile struggle to survive chaos? What kind of joy inhabits this reality? What kind of music resonates in this world? Far from affirming joy, music reveals a tragic universe. Scarcity, brutality, and struggle are the meager resources for this frenzied celebration.[28] Ultimately, if inadvertently, Beethoven's Ninth Symphony questions the moral basis of joy and its relation to music. Perhaps Hanslick was right to hear the choral finale as a monstrous head that ruptures the beautiful body of an otherwise pristine work. The joy of the Ninth Symphony may be great, but it is definitely not nice.

A Sad End

Modern joy is ultimately tragic. And if music is the expressive vehicle of this tragedy, then my book is surely doomed. The philosophers of music from Nietzsche to Lyotard stand guard to secure its fate. It has not even been possible to rustle up the "Ode to Joy" as an anthem to bolster my cause without its violence ambushing my premise. In fact, it might be better for me to eat Pinker's auditory cheesecake than to swallow Schopenhauer's musical narcotic. At least my question would be true, if inconsequential. Just imagine the look on the faces of parents bringing prospective music students to me if I said: "Relax. Your child has chosen the right thing. There is nothing more important than studying music. It is vital for the future of our society. So, don't worry. Music will open the mind of your child to experience the terrifying truth of a meaningless life and how best to die soon."

It seems that joy in music is either too superficial or too profound for its own good. With the frivolity of cheesecake on one hand and a seriously sublime death wish on the other, it seems futile to pursue the question further. "Is music joy?" has already been answered not only in the negative, but by its opposite: music is sad.

II
Ancient Answers

I am convinced that joy exists.
—OLIVIER MESSIAEN

3
Reorientation

An Ancient Tour

We have a problem.

Part 1 of the book makes the obvious case for why my question is fundamentally wrong in every way. There is no angle from which to make it right: "Is music joy?" is methodologically flawed, philosophically sad, and socially irrelevant.

But this is not the real problem. Rather, the problem lies in what comes next. Part 2 of the book makes the case that my premise is fundamentally correct: music is joy. This is a disconcerting thought. Given the earlier objections, to make such a case points to a problem that is not so much about the question itself as the people asking the question. *We* are the problem because we can't see how the question might be relevant. We are blind to its meaning. So it is not the question that is wrong, but our context. The framework in which the earlier objections operate exclude a wider vision of music in which joy might be foundational. If this is the case, then there is clearly something amiss in our current thinking: the obvious arguments are only obvious because our minds are precluded from thinking otherwise. If music is joy, then we are not in the right place to know it.

So how do we see the question in the right context? We need to be in a different place, to go somewhere foreign, somewhere far from the familiar objects of the contemporary world that crowd our vision and clutter our minds. But where can we find a vantage point to squint pass the "obvious" blockages that preclude us from asking the question properly?

In part 2 we will embark on a speculative journey. It turns out that my out-of-date question is not out of date enough: "Is music joy?" is a question that seemingly only makes sense in the ancient world. We need a time machine to shake up our jaded concepts. So, to escape the familiar present, we will travel back to the distant past, and position our thinking in strange and fabulous lands full of ancient wisdom—China, Greece, Egypt, and Hippo Regius in North Africa.

Before we tour the ancient world, we need to prepare our minds for the new time zone. Strange ideas, made unfamiliar by the passage of time, require a suspension of judgment. Ancient beliefs are not "make-believe" but a way of life. To dismiss them out of hand as ideas that did not stand the test of time is to be a *modern* tourist in the worse sense of the term *modern,* as if our superior time zone distinguishes "us" from "them." We need to enter their world and suspend our own belief systems, otherwise we would learn nothing from ancient thinkers. So, as we engage with them, let's take them at their word. On our journey back, we might decide to filter out some of their cosmology, theology, mythology, or science, but hopefully, the strange encounters will estrange our own habits of thought and modify our lives in some way. So travel light, and leave some room for a few weighty souvenirs on our return.

The Character of Joy

We begin our journey by dialing back the clocks some twenty-four hundred years. Imagine yourself in ancient China. Our succinct question would have the opposite effect here: "Is music joy?" would not be worth asking—not because it is obviously false but because it is obviously true.

In Chinese, music is joy. This is because the character of joy is an indelible part of music. Quite literally. The word *music* in Classical Chinese is also the character "joy":

Although pronounced differently, the character *yuè* (樂—meaning music) is the same as the character *lè* (樂—meaning joy). Music and joy are in a *homographic* relationship—they look the same but sound different.[1] So every time you look at the character "music" in Chinese you also see "joy" (and vice versa). We could quibble over whether this homograph is merely coincidental, but both the Confucian and Daoist classics clearly equated the two meanings and aligned them with the Way (*Dao* 道).[2]

Although both traditions follow the Way, they are as divergent in their philosophical approach as yin is to yang. In Daoism, the Way describes the flow of the universe from which all things emerge; in Confucianism, it is an approach to a virtuous life wherein human institutions, from a humble family to the imperial court, are perfected through moral self-cultivation. Daoism is mystical and spontaneous; Confucianism ritualized and ordered. But in reality, as with the relation between yin and yang, each system interpenetrates the other, and it is

in seeking a balance between the two schools that the fullness
of joy is revealed in music.

Of the two traditions, Confucianism is the most musical:
its way of life is fundamentally one of "harmony." Unfortunately, the Confucian *Book of Music* is now lost, but some
scholars maintain that a version has been preserved in the
chapter on music in the *Book of Rites,* which announces: "Music
is joy."[3] This is reiterated in the book of *Xunzi,* attributed to
the third century BCE Confucian philosopher Xun Kuang. He
begins his discourse on music with the same declaration:
"Music is joy."[4] This joy is a human emotion (*qing* 情), but it is
not the kind of fleeting pleasure that we associate with our
drives and appetites today. Joy, for Xun Kuang, is more of a
disposition; or, in musical terms, it is "harmony" in the sense
that joy organizes our emotions and keeps them in order.[5] Joy
as music, then, is not so much a note as the relation between
notes: it is a complex state that is simultaneously felt and perceived, emotive and cognitive, reflexive and reflective. By keeping these elements in balance, joy leads us to the Way, guiding
us in the path of righteousness and benevolence. Conversely,
if we merely follow our instinctive desires, then "there will only
be confusion without joy."[6] According to the book of *Xunzi,*
without music regulating society with its joy, the moral order
would descend into chaos. We would lose the Way.

In many Chinese texts on music from 400–200 BCE, the
two terms—music and joy—were often assumed to be equivalent and interchangeable.[7] They shared the same "being,"
united as a principle that was not merely virtuously human but
musically cosmic. Joy was a music ordained by heaven. This
music was called "*great* music" (*dà yuè* 大樂) because—unlike
its counterpart today—it was literally great in both size and
significance.[8] It encompassed all things, and connected them
together. But most importantly, it functioned as a universal

balance that kept the world in order. "Music is the harmony of Heaven and Earth, and the attunement of *yin* and *yang,*" writes Lü Buwei (呂不韋) in his encyclopedic compilation of 239 BCE, *The Spring and Autumn Annals.* Humanity flourishes when it is tuned to this cosmic harmony, and joy is the result: "Jubilation is born of equilibrium, and equilibrium is born of the Dao."[9] So, the mutual association between music and joy wasn't just a nice bit of wordplay. It had massive consequences.

The Halls of Power

I discovered the significance of this in 2011 as a tourist in Beijing. I was visiting the Forbidden City, the former imperial center of government, with a rather unusual tour group—a motley assortment of music theorists from the West. In the academic world, Western music theorists are a rare and rarefied breed of intellectuals even in their native habitat: wandering the streets of Beijing, they seemed even more obscure and lost outside their natural environment. I had been invited to join the group in Beijing to share our wisdom at a music conservatory. But we soon discovered that our collective wisdom was pretty irrelevant outside of our tiny corner of academia. Music theory in China operated on a different wavelength to ours, with different questions and expectations. So our attempt at cultural exchange went awry. Our latest theories seemed pointless. Our specialized knowledge did not seem so special. In reality, our very distinguished group of professors probably amounted to nothing more than an insignificant speck of knowledge lost in translation and largely ignored in this bustling metropolis.

It certainly felt that way as we meandered through the palatial complex of the Forbidden City. After all, this is a forbidding place designed to overwhelm visitors with the power of imperial rule. It undulates like a mountain range with pavilions of splendor gleaming on the summits. But as we clambered up the steps from one great hall to another and read the inscriptions above their entrances, we soon realized that had we been music theorists in ancient China, we would have been considered the center of all knowledge. Our arcane theories and obtuse calculations would have been the pinnacle of wisdom. We were born too late! Had we existed just a few thousand years earlier, we would be imperial minsters, destined for the pavilions of power. Even the names inscribed above each of the great halls sounded like the subtitles of our books: The Pavilion of Preserving Harmony (*Bǎohé* 保和), The Pavilion of Central Harmony (*Zhōnghé* 中和), The Pavilion of Supreme Harmony (*Tàihé* 太和). Somehow, the Forbidden City seemed to be dedicated to us. It was all very flattering.

As you can see from their names, the three great halls in the Forbidden City are united by one term: harmony (*hé* 和 or in standard script 龢).

(standard script)   (variant inscribed above the great halls)

Harmony is the ultimate *form* of music. In the words of the three great halls: it is "preserving" (uniting), "central," and "supreme." In Confucian thought, the ultimate purpose of governance is to keep all things in perfect harmony.[10] But this cannot simply be given as an instant diktat. It is a Way. Hence, the Chinese character for harmony is also the character for tuning (*hé* 龢)—a way of finding the right relation between tones. The homograph *hé* sounds and looks the same, as if to connect the means to its end: to achieve harmony is a matter of attunement. It is about adjusting our emotions through our daily practices—the rites, customs, and formalities of everyday life—to resonate with the Way. When both are aligned, joy is made complete and harmony reigns supreme.

This is why the architectural plan of the Forbidden City positions music both at the center of imperial rule and as the fundamental structure of the cosmos (see figure 6).[11] When you enter its gates, you are symbolically enveloped by the architecture into a vast harmonic order. And resonating at its

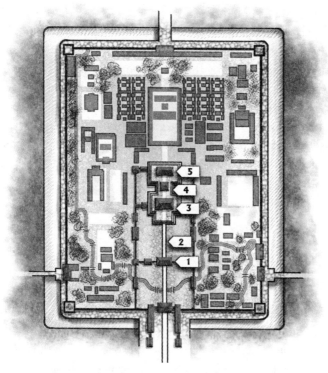

Figure 6. Plan of the Forbidden City: (1) Gate of Supreme Harmony; (2) Court of Supreme Harmony; (3) Pavilion of Supreme Harmony; (4) Pavilion of Central Harmony; (5) Pavilion of Preserved Harmony, Gate of Unified Harmony.

epicenter in the Pavilion of Supreme Harmony is the throne of the emperor. To have an audience with the emperor is to be in tune with the order of all things.

"Music is joy," then, is not simply a play on words in the Chinese language. It is a theory of everything. The entire universe and the governance of a vast empire was at stake in this homograph. So, as I stood in the Pavilion of Supreme Harmony surrounded by music theorists, I could feel the joy of music rushing to my head and its power tingling in my bones: somehow, in this very spot, the moral well-being of the entire universe had been entrusted to me!

So, what would a music theorist do under such epic circumstances? You might imagine that the first thing I'd need had I been employed by the palace would be a quiet, secluded study, lined with scholarly scrolls, for erudite contemplation and abstract calculation. But you would be wrong. Had I been the chief music theorist for the emperor, my first scholarly activity would be foraging. Forget the secluded study; I need a machete. My initial fieldwork would be far away in a bamboo forest.

The Emperor's New Tone

This research project dates back some four thousand years to 2697 BCE. Legend has it that the Yellow Emperor (Huangdi 黄帝) sent the scholar Ling Lun (伶倫) to the Ruanyu Mountains to cut and collect bamboo in the forest of the Xie Valley.[12] The task at hand was to find the perfect bamboo pipe to sound the fundamental pitch of the cosmos and so legitimize the rule of the new emperor. It was a tall order for what would only be a five-inch tube.[13] Nonetheless, the toot of this cheap little instrument was priceless: it would make the invisible cosmos audible. To blow into this pipe was to hear the winds of heaven blow across the hollows of the earth, harmonizing the two realms in one tone. It was both yin and yang, heaven and earth in harmony. Or, as the opening lines of Lü Buwei's chapter on "The Great Music" proclaims: "Far-off indeed are the origins of Music! It is born of standards and measures, and is rooted in the Great Unity. The Great Unity gives rise to the Two Forms, and the Two Forms give rise to yin and yang."[14]

In the forest of the Xie Valley, Ling Lun found the perfect bamboo and cut the section between the nodes in order to sound the new order. This pipe set the pitch from which all the other tones were to be calculated. From this standard pitch, Ling Lun measured a series of bamboo pipes to sound the notes of the scale by using the natural harmonics inherent in the initial tube. It made for beautiful mathematics, for the calculations were not only audible as a tuning system but visible as a geometry of pipes. The theory for measuring the length of each pipe is complex but, basically, by using the interval of the octave and fifth, the twelve tones of the tonal system could fan out in a series of well-proportioned flutes.[15] This is what "harmony" looked like in ancient China. To harmonize was to be in proportion; it was to be in tune. Unlike today, harmony was not the simultaneous sounding of multiple pitches, as in a chord, but a linear relation between notes, as in a melody. It was about being in proportion to a standard pitch. The bamboo pipe set the standard needed to be in tune with the universe.

To legitimize his set of pipes, Ling Lun calibrated each tone to the call of the *fenghuang*—the magical phoenix—whose rare appearance was an auspicious sign promising a harmonious reign for the Yellow Emperor. Ling Lun arranged the twelve pipes into two well-balanced groups, tuning six notes to the call of the female phoenix (yin) and six to the call of the male phoenix (yang).[16] Of course, the appearance of the phoenix undermines the veracity of the story, confining its truths to the realms of fiction. The story of Ling Lun and the Yellow Emperor operates as a founding myth; although the narrative may be mythical, it founded a practice. In accordance with the myth, each new emperor in China needed to find his personal tone—known as the "yellow bell"—to resonate across his kingdom. Without his new tone the emperor would be institutionally tone-deaf and cause his reign to go out of tune with heaven and earth, bringing discord to his people. A tuneless emperor would lose the "Mandate of Heaven" to govern. So when an emperor ascended to power, he would dispatch his noble "music theorist" to forage for the yellow bell in order to certify his rule.[17]

This concrete act was a critical task, for the recalibrated tone was literally a rule. Music, to recall Lü Buwei's proclamation, "is born of standards and measures" because the dimensions of the new pipe set the standard for measure, volume, and weight. The stick would standardize the length and volume, and by filling the hollow with sticky rice grains, the pipe would determine weight. So music was not merely a royal ritual that kept the courtiers in order: it regulated the entire economy of the kingdom in every dimension. The bamboo pipe was the ruler of the empire. Music was *really* the measure of all things. Hence, in another play on words, the bamboo pitch pipe (*lǜ* 律) doubled as the law (*lǜ* 律)—the *regulation*.

Since *lǜ*, as the standard pitch, was the law that tuned the harmonic system, it regulated a moral order. These regulations were virtuous because everything the pitch pipe measured was

in harmony: the yellow bell brought all things into a right relation. To be in tune, then, is to be in accord with the greater
pattern of the Dao. Everything, from the lunar cycles of the
calendar to the filial piety of each household, is measured by
music. In this sense, joy is defined as a way of life rather than
a momentary feeling; it is music not in the sense of a passing
pleasure, but as a permanent law. As Xun Kuang states: "Music
is unchanging harmony."[18]

Today, we seldom think of joy as a regulation. If anything,
joy should be unregulated. To *obey* joy is surely a performative contradiction. Joy should be out of order; it should sound
something like the frenzy that Nietzsche celebrates at the end
of Beethoven's Ninth Symphony—spontaneous, uninhibited,
energized, fast, and delirious. Clearly, joy in the Confucian tradition was very different from Nietzsche's joy. Nietzsche faced
a terrifying cosmos with intoxicated exuberance. He used joy
as a drug. The Chinese used joy as a stick and disciplined everything with it.

When we dial our thinking back some twenty-four hundred years to ancient China, music and joy become foreign
objects to us. Who would have imagined music and joy as a
five-inch measuring stick? The question "Is music joy?" is simply a different question in a context where the tuning of bamboo pipes was a form of mathematical modeling of joy's moral
influence in the universe. These measurements operated as a
kind of "restraining order" that kept excessive behavior at bay
through their perfectly balanced calibrations. To be moved by
music was to be unmoved by joy. In contrast to Nietzsche's
Dionysian frenzy, it was a state of "rest," a condition of composure.[19] To know joy, then, was literally to be composed by music.
It pulled you together, it formed your inner character, and it
tuned your being to the harmony of the natural order.

So, at the imperial palace, with its pavilions of harmonic order, the emperor hired musicians not so much for his entertainment as to cultivate moral authority. Given this significance, only a music that truly measured up to the task, known as *yayue* (雅樂), was used for the imperial rites. This music was highly regimented, with strict foursquare rhythms that choreographed the ritual movements in the vast open courtyards of the palace complex. Staging *yayue* was a form of spiritual discipline. Perfecting your moves was an exercise in virtue, an engagement in a harmonious order that might not be immediately apparent but was necessary to imagine in order to maintain social cohesion. In the Confucian tradition, practice makes perfect, turning learned virtues into spontaneous actions that literally "make" Way. Rites cleared the path for the good life to proceed.

Ultimately, joy in ancient China described a musical relation that brought all things into balance, upholding the moral integrity of the universe from the cycles of the moon to the political affairs of court. When the Confucian texts declared, "Music is joy," this homographic equivalence provided a cosmic image of ethical well-being at the center of self-governance and state governance. It was all very proper. We might call this relation between music and joy an "aesthetic propriety." It is aesthetic because it appeals to beauty as its authority; it concerns propriety because it relates to what is fitting as a way of life. In the Confucian rule book, then, beauty is predicated on a certain *fittingness* between things. To be in tune is to find the right fit. There is no excess. Nothing can be out of place. Since every note of the cosmos exists in a well-proportioned order, everything must align seamlessly with its harmony. Perfection depends on this relation. Or, as Confucius says: "It is from music that one's perfection is achieved."[20] To have joy is to have perfect pitch.

Surround Sound System

Before we reenter the time machine for our next thought journey, we should collect a few souvenirs from our visit to the Forbidden City and the Ruanyu Mountains. There are three items that we should keep with us on our travels:

1. A plastic replica of Ling Lun's bamboo pipe
2. A big yellow balloon from the Xie Valley
3. A shatterproof ruler from the Forbidden City

You will find that these three trinkets are intellectually very similar to souvenirs sold in other places on our tour—in Greece when we visit Pythagoras of Samos, in Egypt when we visit Clement of Alexandria, and in North Africa when we visit Augustine of Hippo. These items will come in handy for comparing ideas between the regions. So pack them carefully in your suitcase, although the balloon is admittedly a bit awkward to carry around.

Bamboo pipe: A replica of Ling Lun's bamboo pipe is shown in figure 7. As you can see, its shape imitates the wings of the phoenix. This traditional design is a reference to Ling Lun's magical adventures in the Ruanyu Mountains. The shape recalls the song of the *fenghuang* that tuned the original pipes. But there is a deeper symbolism. The wing-like design gestures to the wind that bears the phoenix aloft. In other words, the instrument points to the source of music. To blow across these pipes is to imitate the wind as it blows across the hollows of the earth.

As a souvenir of the founding myth, what lesson does this object teach us?[21] In ancient China, joy made for great music. But unlike great music today, it was great not because it was human but because it was nonhuman. In fact, it was

Figure 7. Bamboo pipes
known as *fengxiao* (鳳簫),
meaning "phoenix panpipe."

literally so *great* that it was barely audible to human ears. It
fluttered in the wind of heaven, it resonated as the great note
of the Dao, it was found among the bamboo groves and in the
call of mythical creatures. The bamboo pipe tells us that music
does not need humans to exist. It is always already there, in
and among the things that are prior to us, both animate and
inanimate, physical and metaphysical. Music surrounds us. It
precedes us. It surpasses us. It outlasts us.

So we humans don't get to "make" music first; rather,
music makes humans first. It measures us, forms us, composes
us, and tunes us. It keeps us from grasping the world as if it
were ours to possess and define. We cannot master its pieces;
instead, by tuning our being, music and joy embed humanity
as part of a larger cosmic scheme—a Way.

The German biologist Jakob von Uexküll, writing in the
early twentieth century, describes life on our planet as a symphony. The earth is composed of musical biospheres, or *Umwelten*. These are intricate contrapuntal relations created by the
co-evolution of living things in their particular environments.[22]
We are who we are in relation to the other things around us.

Uexküll's world resonates with the Confucian view of the cosmos: by setting the right tone in this symphony, humans can find their proper place as creatures in a finely tuned order. We need to finesse how we fit into this delicate and fragile ecosystem. Joy, then, is found in a decentered yet interconnected relationship with a harmony that is already around us. The plastic replica of Ling Lun's bamboo pipe reminds us to be in tune.

Yellow balloon: The second souvenir is the yellow balloon from the Xie Valley. Unfortunately, it has already popped. Oops! But the point was never the balloon. The key element here is the air inside it, released as the balloon zipped across the room, bringing a little bit of Xie Valley breeze to the stilted atmosphere of the modern world. We can't contain music. The balloon may have trapped the air in a location before it burst, but once the air escaped, the source of music has no fixed abode. Our second object is everywhere. So how do you hear a music that isn't here?

According to the Daoist philosopher Laozi, the Dao is "a great tone" too rarefied to grasp; it is like a square with no corners.[23] Being very great, ancient music is far too big to locate. Its rhythms are hidden in the lunar cycles and fluctuate with the changing seasons. Its joy isn't here or there. It is neither a particular feeling you experience nor one of many emotions that you can categorize and identify. Joy as music is a general disposition. It is a fundamental state, an order of being regardless of how we feel today or tomorrow. It is like the air we breathe. As such, it is everywhere and nowhere. It is nebulous and borderless, seamlessly traversing a universe where scientific and moral standards are inseparable, where natural and supernatural phenomena coexist, and where opposites are distinctly harmonious. We abide within this balanced order, integrated within its vast ecosystem. And it is precisely because we dwell within it that we have no position from which to take it all in.

How do you attend to a music that has no fixed abode? You do exactly what Ling Lun did: go foraging. Music can't be caught or simply bought like a balloon. Music has to be sought. It is about finding the Way. This is what the anthropologist Tim Ingold defines as wayfaring.[24] In the Chinese context, it is Dao-faring. There is no preexistent map with coordinates to pinpoint every dot of music, as with a score. Rather, finding music is an immersion into what we do not fully know: it is a tactile and emergent relation to our environment, in which we embark on improvised trails that crisscross the soundscape. Music is not a destination. To inhabit music is to track its fleeting appearance and go where the wind blows. It can be anywhere, anytime, anyway. Music, then, is fundamentally a disclosure. It reveals itself to those who seek to obey its call.

Shatterproof ruler: How do you obey music? The third and final item reminds us of its order: a ruler. We obey music because music rules. It has regulations. It is an authority, an external force. If it did not have authority, it would have nothing to disclose and there would be nothing to seek. If music rules, then listening to music is an act of conformity. Music is not a matter of self-expression in which we make the rules. Rather, music calls us to attention. It commands us to attend to the world. To be attentive is to listen to an underlying order of joy, however unruly the world might appear to be. It demands that we believe in the good and obey its order. If music rules, then to come under its authority is to have joy whatever the circumstance. It is shatterproof.

Obedience, then, is the beginning of joy. In fact, in the Confucian tradition, obedience is joyful—it a surrendering to a spontaneous rule. As a beautiful order, it can regulate without coercion. Its concrete manifestation in the length of a pipe is merely a figure that points to an ungraspable form. In this regard, we can learn something from Kant, despite his low view of music. Writing at the close of the eighteenth century, the philosopher describes our perception of beauty as the search for a law that we do not already know. This act of "reflective judgement," as Kant calls it, is a bit like wayfaring: there is no preconceived map or predetermined destination. Instead it seeks an undisclosed rule that we want to obey. After all, each piece of art is unique and requires a different journey. Joy lies in the discovery of this unique law.[25] If we scale this up from an artwork to the universe, we come close to what Confucius means by harmony. To seek joy is to incline your ear to an as yet undisclosed law in order to conform to its beauty. Finding this fit—this aesthetic propriety—is a discipline that harmonizes us to the nature of all things. Joy is the ruler of all.

To relate these three ancient objects to our modern world, let's connect Ling Lun with John Cage. When the Yellow Emperor sent Ling Lun to the Xie Valley, he gave him the same instructions as the score of John Cage's *4′33″*. Music isn't simply human. So, remove yourself from the center of the equation and listen to the environment. It is vast, but pay attention. Bend your ear to the bamboo forest. Inhabit its *Umwelt*. Seek its beauty. Obey its call. At first, you might think that there is no music there. But the score of nature isn't blank, just as the score of *4′33″* isn't silent. It is an invitation for our ears to forage in the environment and retune what we assume we know and discover a rule that has yet to be disclosed. If you listen attentively and track all that surrounds you, you will find a music beneath the seeming chaos that is the order of joy.

Be a Boar

When I returned to Hong Kong from Beijing, I found myself in a different relationship to my everyday environment. My identity as a music theorist was no longer grounded in my secluded office, where I would stare diligently at my computer, enveloped by the quiet hum of air-conditioning and guarded by a regiment of books. Hong Kong is often perceived as an urban jungle, but in fact most of Hong Kong is forested. It's a lush, undulating landscape, swirling with bamboo groves and knitted with the root systems of banyan trees that rise up from the ground like the organ pipes of a great cathedral. On my return from Beijing, I simply swapped one environment for the other. Music theory is now an outdoor activity: thinking music is trekking music. In fact, Igor Stravinsky once compared composition to foraging. "A composer improvises aimlessly the way an animal grubs about," he writes. "Both of them go grubbing about because they yield to a compulsion to seek things out."[26] As musical listeners we should attend to the world in the same way, sniffing around, grubbing about, grunting, digging, rummaging, trekking, and tracking all in the hope of stumbling across the "yellow bell."

I've yet to see a phoenix while walking in the hills of Hong Kong, but occasionally I would come across wild boars foraging in the bamboo groves. These plump and hairy creatures are both highly intelligent and very cute. They seem to have a permanent smile below their snouts, an expression I imagine to be a sign of contentment as they grub and rummage about. Maybe they are reincarnated music theorists from ancient China—a porky Ling Lun in search of the yellow bell. While contemplating these wild boars on my nature walks, I would have my 4′33″ of what joy must have been like thousands of years ago in this part of China when music theorists ruled the world.

4
Music by Numbers

Noise

Ancient Chinese music theory had a parallel universe in ancient Greece. Its founding myth was equally cosmic and fixated on keeping all things in proper proportion. As was the case with Ling Lun in a bamboo forest, the main protagonist of the myth, the philosopher and mathematician Pythagoras, found himself in an environment seemingly devoid of music. This environment, however, was a far cry from the breeze of fluttering phoenixes chirping among the bamboo groves of the Ruanyu Mountains. In ancient Greece, music theory was born from industrial noise; its founding myth was forged in a smithy.

Pythagoras's discovery of cosmic harmony, then, was less yin-yang than big bang. The story begins on an ordinary day in an ordinary place. The philosopher was going about his routine business in the city-state of Samos, which, back in the sixth century BCE, was an island bustling with cultural and commercial activity. As usual, he was deep in thought; he was pondering whether it was possible to measure sound in the same way he could measure an angle with a compass and ruler. While wandering the streets, the philosopher stopped at the smithy and heard the usual crackling of furnaces and cacophony of hammers. There were no musical instruments, musicians, or composers there, just blacksmiths doing what they normally do—banging metal loudly on anvils. But to his surprise, harmony struck his ears. Somehow, the hammers seemed to be playing music.[1]

In ancient Greece, the smithy was considered a source of noise pollution, resulting in one of the earliest known noise ordinances, dating from the sixth century BCE: the Urban Council of Sybaris ordered blacksmiths to reside outside the city walls.[2] The smithy, then, was the last place you'd expect to discover music. But this is precisely the point of the myth: the noise of this ancient industrial complex is the Pythagorean version of 4′33″. The metal workshop functions as the "empty score," creating an accidental space devoid of human intention for music to disclose itself through a nonhuman artefact: the hammer. Pythagoras heard a clang of consonances and dissonances booming from the smithy as different sized hammers were struck simultaneously against anvils. Intrigued by this blast of heavy metal, Pythagoras examined the hammers more closely (see figure 8).

There were five hammers: one was discarded as toneless, but he realized that the weight ratios between the other four different-sized hammerheads determined the music in his ear. The ratio of 2:1 (octave), 3:2 (fifth), and 4:3 (fourth) generated consonances, whereas the ratio of 9:8 (tone) produced a dissonance. It made for beautiful mathematics: the simpler the integer relationship the more harmonious the sound. Pythagoras arranged these harmonious ratios (1:2:3:4) into a geometric pattern composed of ten dots known as the tetractys

Figure 8. Harmoniously proportioned hammers.

$(1+2+3+4=10)$.[3] By stacking the four numbers, the ratios form an equilateral triangle.

Pythagoras surmised that beneath all the noise of the universe was an immovable and timeless structure—a music so engrained in the order of things that it had become too familiar for our ears to register. Everyday noise inhabits an inaudible music. Harmony, then, is the background hum of the cosmos, and noise is just a passing surface phenomenon. In Greek thought, this underlying order is called the *logos* (λόγος) of the universe—the creative principle that connects all things logically together. So for Pythagoras, music is a vital but tacit surround sound system in which we order our being. To en-*joy* music is to indwell its logic—the *logos*—and attune ourselves to its ratios.[4]

iPods

In Hong Kong today, it is the other way around: its inhabitants tune into noise. This might seem odd given the level of noise pollution in Hong Kong produced by urban construction. I live in a permanent bandwidth of high-decibel thumping and drilling equivalent to a pounding headache for the ear. But somehow for the residents of Hong Kong this noise is heard as a background hum in which music is a public nuisance. Noise is the Muzak of everyday life and music is noise pollution. To play music within earshot of another is to risk a noise complaint. And such complaints are common, since most of us in Hong Kong are packed like sardines in urban tin cans. Far from regulating society, as in the Confucian tradition, music is regulated by society. It is *ruled* an offense.

I first realized how serious a nuisance music was in Hong Kong when an application for a live band to ring in the New Year was granted by the Urban District Council on the condition that the event end at 11 p.m. Before we laugh at such petty bureaucracy, bear in mind that this ordinance points to a broader issue beyond the jurisdiction of Hong Kong—the privatization of listening. *Keep music to yourself!* is its rule. As with the ridiculous policy for the New Year celebrations, we are permitted to listen to music as long as it doesn't make any noise for anyone else.

Today, music lives in iPods.[5] "iPod" is an apt name for this device. It describes the self—the I—enclosed in a pod of music, preferably with active noise-canceling technology to isolate the experience. It is as if we want to live in sonic bubbles, floating like balloons in our personalized airspace. Our earbuds are earplugs; they isolate music in our head with a seal of silence. Under such conditions, music atomizes us, segregates us, disconnects us from the environment with silent partitions to sanitize our listening. It is precisely because music privatizes the self that we can no longer tolerate another person's music. It is noise. We may be commuting on the metro, for example, indifferent to the mechanical clattering of the train, but as soon as music seeps out from another commuter's earphone—however teeny and tinny that buzz might be—it is a disturbance. A nuisance. A noise.

In Hong Kong, the sound of construction is the hum of utility, the music of a booming economy. This trickling of money, clinking and clanking chaotically in the background, is the necessary condition of well-being in Hong Kong. It is the sound of joy. It is precisely because music is *unnecessary* in this economic order that it cannot be tolerated publicly as a permanent presence. In an iPodic society, music no longer relates us to a wider environment. It is a private pleasure, a commodity served on a plate of silence for personal consumption. It is about our taste, our identity, our playlist, our expressive individualism.[6] Music becomes an echo of the self with no wider resonance.[7]

Pythagoras's big-bang revelation at the forge puts our iPodic relation to music in question. Why should noise cancellation be the condition for music? It is as if silence functions as music's artificial life-support, disconnecting its rhythms from the noise of the outside world so it can breathe inside us. We end up becoming like the technology that isolates us—individual pods that segregate music from the environment. For Pythagoras, however, it is the other way round: music is not isolated from noise like random pods in an anarchic soundscape, but is enmeshed within noise as its underlying order. Our cosmos is *logos,* not chaos. So it is not the noise outside us that needs canceling, but the noise inside us that must conform to the music around us.

Music of the Spheres

How do you attune your being to the Pythagorean order? First, take a long piece of string. In the legend, Pythagoras's calculations at the smithy are mythical; the ratios are correct, but they work for strings, not for hammers. This was an immaterial point for ancient music theorists who carried out their calculations twanging a string on a device known as a monochord rather than wielding hammers to crunch their numbers (it was also much safer). In fact, the string became the symbol of the Pythagorean cosmos, vibrating as a long chain of being that connected everything in the universe. The hammer was just a founding metaphor—a big-bang theory to set "string theory" in motion. This obdurate and ugly object was the material portal through which Pythagoras heard a transcendent music that took leave of earthly matters to encircle the heavens as a series of immutable ratios vibrating from a cosmic string (see figure 9).

Known as "the music of the spheres," this celestial song topped the Western music theory charts for over two millennia. It was literally a number *one* smash hit. Music was totality, the singular universal all-inclusive set. Nothing was outside music. Everything was on its playlist. The music of the spheres was one giant iPod—or, rather, a "metaPod"—that enclosed everything in its harmonious geometry, from the rotation of

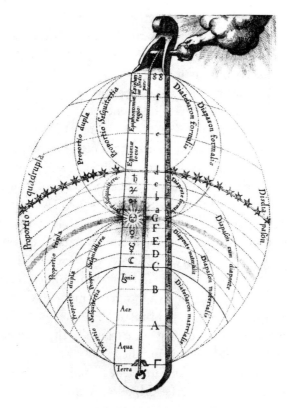

Figure 9. The music of the spheres vibrating as the
chain of being. A divine hand tunes the string of the cosmic
monochord that stretches from heaven to the earth to embrace
all the elements within the unity of its harmonic ratios.
(From Robert Fludd, *Utriusque Cosmi . . . Historia* [1617–19].)

the planets in the heavens to the circulation of fluids in the
body. So instead of atomizing humanity in silent bubbles,
music scaled humanity to the same celestial proportions in order to embed us in the universe. Humans were a microcosm
of the cosmic order. To be in tune with the cosmos was a matter

of synchronizing the movement of the soul with the movement of the heavens in order to maintain a beautifully tempered existence. The good life was therefore a *fitting* one that connected heaven and earth.

This relation was possible because the inaudible ratios emanating from the crystalline spheres of the heavens could be heard as vibrating ratios on the string of the monochord. Since these celestial ratios tuned the scales of the Greek modal system, terrestrial music composed from these modes could channel the power from above and affect the soul from below. We have access to the *logos* of the cosmos. Tweaking these modes therefore modulated human behavior. It was like a form of cosmic music therapy. Different tunings could temper moods, induce virtues, and curtail vices. In fact, it was said that Pythagoras could directly hear the celestial harmonies and so prescribe melodies in an appropriate mode to cure unruly emotions in his disciples.[8] Similarly, Plato advocated zoning laws not so much to remove noise from the city as to ban certain modes for fear of turning the mighty warriors of his *Republic* into effeminate and indolent men. The Lydian mode, known for its laxity, was forbidden. Only music tuned to brave, magnanimous, and temperate scales, such as the Dorian mode, were permitted. Such a society would be populated by beautifully tuned souls—brave, strong, just and, most important, moderate in balancing every element in harmony.[9]

Temperance—the virtue of balance—is the ultimate state of joy for Plato. In fact, it is quite literally a state: the city-state is in a "happy" state for Plato if temperance "runs through all the notes of the scale," organizing the different strata of society in harmony.[10] Think of the city as a well-tempered scale. Both high and low are bound by its proportions in order for reason to regulate the life of the republic. Ideally, in the perfect city-state, no one would lose their temper because temperance reflects the balance of a well-tempered cosmos. So to maintain good order, the guardians of the city, says Plato, "must lay the foundations of their fortress in music" and instruct the citizens in its theory. Without the music theorist imparting wisdom to all, lawlessness will invade the "state" of joy.[11] As in ancient China, governance is an exercise in music theory. It is about aesthetic fit—you need to attune yourself to the right mode to live rightly. Get your intonation right, and the harmony of the spheres will be a virtuous circle for you. Get it wrong, and you will be sucked into a vicious vortex of your own un-tuning.

In Plato's thought, the Pythagorean order became a vision of the good, true, and beautiful. *Kalon*—the word for the beautiful in Greek—is a multidimensional term. Its meaning includes the objective measure of the good exemplified in the harmonious proportion of the universe; it is the *ratio* of a *rational* life. To pursue wisdom is to travel the way of the beautiful, casting aside asymmetry to pursue the order of the cosmos that music discloses.[12] In fact, for Plato, music is only true when it transcends the material and temporal world of the senses as a cosmic ideal. Its ultimate task is not simply to educate the body and keep it in order; music should guide the intellect away from the visible toward the invisible realm of pure number, pure proportion, pure form, and pure reason.[13] Such beauty is the Mandate of Heaven for Plato's republic, bestowing harmony within its walls and joy to the state.[14]

As you might imagine, given such rarefied hearing, Plato did not hang out at the smithy. He classified blacksmiths with drunkards, madmen, and neighing horses. Of course, as far as town planning was concerned, blacksmiths were needed in the republic to keep the urban machinery in working order. Their manual labor, however, stands in contrast to the rarefied class of guardians who were tasked with bringing harmony to the

disorder.[15] All that noise and dirt of the smithy polluting the
urban environment merely clouded the reality of the good,
true, and beautiful that the guardians should exemplify and
propagate. Pythagoras in this regard could be seen as a model
guardian for Plato's perfectly governed society. He heard five
hammers at work in the blacksmith's yard, of which four
were in tune and the fifth one tuneless. He removed the fifth
hammer—the ugly, asymmetrical, disproportional object—
and pursued the intellectual joys of the other four hammers
to perfect his knowledge of the good life.[16] Noise is merely a
flickering shadow on the cave wall: music is the order that
brings reality to light. Given such good music, Greek life is
truly beautiful.

Souvenirs from Samos

We can't visit Plato's republic on our tour because it's fictional.
Pythagoras, on the other hand, philosophized in the city-state
of Samos. For a music theorist, this is a must-see tourist spot
in any tour of ancient history. On this island glittering in the
Aegean Sea, as in the Pavilion of Supreme Harmony that tow-
ered over Beijing, the moral well-being of the entire universe
was entrusted to a noble class of music theorists. And what a
universe it was! A postcard from ancient Samos would depict
a picture-perfect world undersigned by a mathematical equation so elegant that it could embrace everything true, good, and
beautiful. Book your place here in paradise, preferably next to
the hottest party in town—the smithy! So what souvenirs
should we purchase in Samos to add to the items we collected
in ancient China? If you recall we already have three objects—a
bamboo pipe, a yellow balloon, and a plastic ruler.

Given the significance of the smithy, the first souvenir to
add to the collection has to be a replica of one of the hammers

that banged Pythagoras's theory into shape. In the Greek myth, the blacksmith's hammer is equivalent to Ling Lun's bamboo pipe. Both objects have the same function: they sound out the universe as a nonhuman portal. Removing the human makes for truly great music. So bang that hammer! Make a big bang! For this reminds us how limited our understanding of music is today. A humanly controlled environment for music merely minimizes music as an isolated commodity; we only hear what we can enclose by silence, which is actually very little. But humans need to think big. Given the size of our most pressing concerns—our impact on the environment and the possibility of human extinction—a conception of music that reduces our hearing to atomized, autonomous pods precludes us from perceiving music's true greatness and significance. We would be trapped in a bubble, myopically nursing our expressive individualism. So let's burst it.

But notice how the hammer is repurposed by Pythagoras: a blunt, violent tool that normally gets things to fit by force discovers an aesthetic fit. Instead of forging form by coercion, it sounds out a rational order in terms of natural propriety. In other words, if we are to burst the bubble of the "iPodic self," it is not by the sheer force of the tool but by the sheer beauty of what the hammer discloses. It is beauty that pops the bubble.

Which brings us back to the balloon. If you recall, this souvenir, which fortuitously burst in transit, gestures to a music that has escaped its pod-like confines to become an invisible and inaudible essence with no fixed abode. Aptly, Pythagoras was said to have taught his disciples from behind a piece of fabric; he was heard and not seen, somewhat like a disembodied voice wafting from a loudspeaker or like the Wizard of Oz. In the same way, music in ancient Greece was a sound without a visible source—it had no fixed address, since it was the universal set in which all things are fixed. It simply surrounded us as a matrix of numbers. We live in it rather than locate it. So, to complement what's left of the balloon, we should buy a large sheet to cloak our voice, preferably a "fitted sheet" to ensure an aesthetic fit. The fabric reminds us that music does not emanate from a single source. It is not stored in a little pod. Rather, music is the fabric of space-time that wraps around us, embedding us in a universe that is our home. We dwell in music. It is our place to be. We may be disturbed by noise, but such chaos is not the ultimate nature of reality. To listen to music is to attend to a hidden order that folds around us.

The final object in our tour of Samos complements the shatterproof ruler we acquired in the Forbidden City. The rule of Pythagorean music theory was not so much a measuring stick as a vibrating string. The monochord verified the calculations that Pythagoras mythically forged at the smithy. So, the final souvenir from the island of Samos is a measuring tape from a local hardware store that we can stretch taut and twang loudly. These vibrations are the moving parts of the immutable numbers that order the universe. The music humans make on earth (the twang) are the ephemeral vibrations of an incorruptible music in the heavens (the numbers). As in ancient China, to rule the world is to measure it. These harmonic ratios formed an architecture of governance similar to the pavilions of the Forbidden City. Just as imperial authority emanates from an ethical tone that sets the standard for measurement, so Pythagorean ratios measured the good; the tetractys, like a triangular yin-yang symbol, expressed a geometric relation that kept the world in proportion; it was as beautiful as it was good because it was a perfectly balanced fit. The measuring tape, as with the ruler, reminds us that the entire cosmos is made to measure by music. It is the satisfaction of this inner rightness that forms the objective dimensions of joy. Music, then, is joy only in its measurable relation to everything. Music is not a personal pod that you carry around to style your identity with your subjectively constructed playlist; music is a relation to something greater out there in which your identity fits perfectly. To obey its rule is to be numbered among the most beautiful objects in the universe.

With a hammer to smash our small-mindedness, some fitted "sheet music" to unplug us from our iPodic habits, and a measuring tape to keep us in perfect proportion, we are now ready to leave Samos and wave goodbye to the harmonious blacksmiths. It was, as Pythagoras would have intended, a *perfect* visit. What could possibly be missing?

5

Event Organizer

Two Beginnings

Something is missing. Joy seems so well-tempered in the Pythagorean state that it borders on boredom. There are no surprises, no *WOW!* moments, no dynamic force to get its beautiful inertia moving. At least, not yet. It took a paradigm-shifting event to shake its regimented integers to life.

The advent of Christianity breathed a new sense of joy into the stiff and perfectly rigid cosmology of the tetractys. For its adherents, this new life was literally a resurrection—an Easter surprise. This joyous event in the form of a *bodily* resurrection in human *history* was also a surprising intervention in the ethereal and eternal order of the Pythagorean universe. As far as Hellenistic thought was concerned, the corporeal and temporal should have degraded the purity of joy, but somehow the Christian gospel, in all its sordid materiality, reanimated the great music that ordered the cosmos with something even greater. Or, as the Christmas angels declared: "Behold! I bring you good tidings of *great* joy."[1] This announcement of "great joy" should be heard as the intrusion of Messianic time disturbing the timeless numerology of great music. It was a collision of Jewish and Hellenistic thought: joy as historical fulfillment and music as an immovable order fused to create the paradox of the eternal moment.

History was never an essential condition of a cosmos measured by perfect integers. Such an elegant universe just is. Its timeless ratios held all things in proportion. This equilibrium was its joy. Such perfection functioned as a universal set in which subsets might interact, but nothing would change the set itself, let alone add to it. It was perfect, after all. So when the Christmas angels declared the arrival of a greater joy, it could only be considered a miraculous intervention in a Pythagorean cosmos. Joy, in all its incalculable magnitude, disrupted the timeless measurements of the cosmos with what the philosopher Alain Badiou would call an "event"—something that breaks in from beyond the universal set to reconfigure its order. The gospel, in Badiou's terminology, is "supernumerary," something in excess to what can be counted in the oneness of the universe.[2] With the event punching a hole from the outside into the Pythagorean order, what was mathematically perfect was made even better; its beautifully proportioned ratios were made *good* with a completely new tuning that moved the universe and caused it to sing for joy. Christ, to play on Badiou's term, is the *"event" organizer* who got the Pythagorean cosmos to truly party. Suddenly, with the event of Christ, the endless rotation of the universe was given a different spin. It was nothing less than a conversion.

The significance of the new temporality for a numerical universe was momentous. Events have beginnings, and "In the beginning . . ." happens twice in the Bible—in the book of Genesis in the Old Testament and in the Gospel of John in the New Testament:

In the beginning God created the heavens and the earth. (Genesis 1:1)

In the beginning was the Word. (John 1:1)

The two great temporalities of joy in the Christian narrative are creation and new creation. Genesis 1 announces the "first" beginning, in which God makes all things. John 1 adds the "second" beginning, in which God enters the world he has made, not to make new things but to make all things new. The first creative event begins with the divine words: "Let there be light." The second event is the light itself coming in person as the Word: "the true light that gives light to everyone" enters the world as the Word made flesh in order to redeem the world.[3] And as we shall see, each event has its own song in the Bible— the song of creation and the song of salvation.

The Pythagorean universe, in contrast, has no beginning. Founded on the number one, it is always eternally there. Greek mathematics had yet to incorporate the concept of zero from Indian mathematics into its equations to calculate the possibility of a creation from nothing. So, despite the hammer, there was no big bang. The beginning never happened. It took Christian thought to reimagine the Pythagorean universe where God himself is the smithy wielding the hammer "in the beginning" to set the world in motion.

In her book of visions *Scivias*, the abbess Hildegard of Bingen (1098–1179 CE), writing in the twelfth century, envisioned the creation of the universe as a fiery and noisy act within a metal workshop, with God functioning as both the flame and hammer. In fact, having three persons in one came in handy; as a Trinitarian being, the Holy Spirit could fan the fire of God the Father, while Christ banged the cosmos into being as if shaping copper on an anvil; with blow after blow, the hammer sent sparks into the atmosphere until heaven and earth were perfected by the hand of the divine workman.[4] It was a glittering and sparkling spectacle—less divine sweat than dazzling splendor.

In Hildegard's vision, Jesus is at work "in the beginning" because John's Gospel places Christ retrospectively into the

Genesis account: He is the creative Word through whom everything came into being: "In the beginning was the Word, and the Word was with God, and the Word was God. *He was with God in the beginning.* Through him all things were made. Without him nothing was made that has been made" (John 1:1–3).

The abbess not only described her mystical revelation of creation in words, but illustrated it as an image (see figure 10).[5] Her attempt to illuminate the prologue of John's Gospel resulted in what appears to be a giant lollipop set on fire. It illustrates how creation happens twice in Christian theology: the account in Genesis dominates the top half of the page, and the account in John's Gospel fills the bottom half. The image is to be read from the top down.

Figure 10. Hildegard of Bingen's vision of creation
and new creation in the *Scivias*.

The blazing circle symbolizes the Trinity in eternal communion. Notice how this fiery disc is positioned not only at the top of the page, but in front of the frame and just beyond the border as if to indicate that it exists outside the frame of time. However, the stick on which the circle is attached enters the frame, burrowing into a clump of formless matter at the center of the image: it represents a sudden bolt of lightning bursting forth from eternity into the world. This flame is a flash *in time,* through which Christ, the Word of God, forges the universe into existence: "Let there be light."

At the bottom of the page, new creation—the event of salvation that splits human history "before" and "after" Christ in the Christian calendar—mirrors the first creation. But it is not an exact reflection: the blazing circle is now half hidden because salvation in Hildegard's vision rises like the dawn. This beginning is not a new world but a new day, as if the bottom of the page were the horizon for the emergence of a new temporality. This sunrise radiates the same light as that of the blazing circle, but it now appears behind the frame and within its border. The second "beginning" is folded inside time and framed within the material world, for the flame that flashes forth is now in human form—the Word incarnate: "The Word became flesh and made his dwelling among us. We have seen his glory, the glory of the one and only Son, who came from the Father, full of grace and truth" (John 1:14).

From out of the fiery disc, a luminous Jesus appears in the flesh with a halo of flames piercing the darkness above him. Christ, explains Hildegard, dispels the darkness through his death and resurrection, and returns to the glory of Father with an even greater brilliance full of immeasurable joy.[6] The narrative comes full circle: the disc at the top and the one at the bottom should ultimately coalesce, as the joy of Trinitarian communion embraces the joy of new creation.

In the *Scivias,* joy is the culmination of an epic narrative of salvation. But we do not need to get to heaven to experience this joy; it is already staring straight at us in Hildegard's illumination. The image is itself new creation at work on earth. The abbess, who was famously known as the Sybil of the Rhine, had no intention of recording this vision in a book, let alone for posterity. Women in the twelfth century were not expected to write or assume prophetic authority. This vibrant image of creation and new creation was not meant to be. It took an "event" to change a seemingly changeless order. In 1141, at the age of forty-two, Hildegard received what she believed to be a divine instruction to write down all she could "see and hear."[7] In her account of this particular vision, Hildegard is commanded by a celestial voice "not to be timid" but to speak out, even though she regards herself as an untaught woman, "trodden on by the masculine sex."[8] So what we "see and hear" in her vision of new creation in the *Scivias* is itself a new creation: it is nothing less than a new voice soaring above the patriarchal institutions of the high Middle Ages. Indeed, the *Scivias* itself is unique in its time: to capture what she could "see and hear," Hildegard fashioned a multi-sensory work, commandeering the arts of illumination, music, drama, and poetry to breathe new life into a familiar message.

In particular, it is the joy of music that animates its pages. The *Scivias* constantly references songs of jubilation. Had the abbess been given the technology to record sound in conveying her visions, we would hear the harmony of "timbrels and harps and all kinds of music burst forth" at the end of her account of creation and salvation.[9] The *Scivias,* however, does not only describe music; it is itself musical. Hildegard was a prolific composer of ecstatic chants, and the book is interspersed with her liturgical songs.[10] So to add to the multimedia experience, it would be fitting to imagine a medley of her elaborate melodies forming the soundtrack for the images and text of the *Scivias*.

In fact, music, for Hildegard, is the very means of making the joy of heaven incarnate on earth. Music for her is the intersection of time and eternity: to sing on earth is to resonate with the endless song of heaven, renewing each moment as an ever-present event. This relation is akin to the image of the blazing lollipop with its fiery rod connecting heaven and earth, except that the disk is no longer the abstract and somewhat vacant blaze that existed before time. In the final pages of the *Scivias,* where Hildegard describes the end of time and the fullness of salvation history, the concentric rings are populated by the whole hierarchy of heaven, with the redeemed joining the choir of angels in jubilation. As with Beethoven's Ninth Symphony, Hildegard's vision in the *Scivias* culminates in a singing community of joy. Her finale, entitled the "Symphony of the Blessed," is literally composed of different hymns harmonizing together as one celestial "song of rejoicing."[11]

In the Christ-event, time has changed the cosmic harmony of eternity with a symphonic narrative that now includes humanity in the communion of heaven. Joy in the Pythagorean cosmos is not only the order of creation rationalized by numbers but the event of re-creation animated by a songful people.

Following the Star

In Hildegard's theology, music is the joy that radiates across the cosmos and extends through history from the beginning of creation to its redemptive culmination. It was a relatively standard view in medieval Europe, despite her extraordinary vision. But in what sense is music joy in the biblical narrative of creation and new creation? After all, music does not figure in the creation account in Genesis. There are no Pythagorean numbers or some cosmic "OM," as in the dharmic religions, to structure the creative process. The poetic text that opens Genesis may have been chanted, but that does not directly link music to creation. Joy is also absent from the account. There are no songs of jubilation. Joy may be implied obliquely in the six-fold affirmation of the goodness of creation that punctuates the end of each day's work—"And God saw that it was good [*kalon*]"—but an explicit relation between music and joy informing early Christian theology has to be pieced together from scattered references elsewhere in the Bible.[12]

In the Hebrew scriptures, the book of Proverbs portrays joy in the figure of Wisdom. Wisdom accompanies God in creating the world. She functions as God's craftsman, imbuing joy into everything that is made. Unsurprisingly, given joy's propensity for measurement in the ancient world, Wisdom's main task is to be a ruler. She measures and marks out the foundations of the earth. As with Confucian and Pythagorean thought, the goodness of the created order in the Hebrew scriptures is defined as a fitting one. Joy is based on right relationships; it takes delight in how the world should be. Hence, Wisdom's co-creative process with God seems to be more play than work, for Wisdom is "filled with delight, day after day," as the universe is formed, "rejoicing always in the LORD's presence, rejoicing in his whole world and delighting in humankind."[13] Wisdom, then, not only creates the world but celebrates its goodness. According to the Hebrew scriptures, joy is the sound of wisdom in creation.

With the advent of the gospel, early Christian writers identified Wisdom as Christ. In the New Testament, it is Christ who accompanies God in creation, and it is through Christ that all things are made.[14] When John's Gospel opens with the declaration "In the beginning was the Word," the Greek term

translated as "Word" (*logos*) is a conflation of Greek philosophy and Jewish thought. It is both reason and wisdom. In this
logos, the principle of order that holds the Greek cosmos together is identified with the person of Wisdom in the Hebrew
scriptures through whom all things were made. And since the
Greek cosmos is inherently musical, to capture the meaning
of *logos* in John's Gospel, the term has to resonate with the musical order of Pythagoras as well as with the divine joy of
Wisdom. So, in the beginning, music is joy.

Given this temporality, joy is no longer just a number
fixed in the heavens; it is a musical rhythm that weaves heaven
and earth together from the beginning to the end of time. In
other words, Jesus, as Wisdom, does not simply measure the
universe in the beginning; he himself is the melodious measure
who keeps the universe in proportion. As with the identification of Wisdom with Christ, this musical understanding stems
from the scriptural tradition of Jewish thought. In the Hebrew
Bible, the book of Job describes the creation of the earth as a
celestial song of joy: the stars sang while the angels responded
with shouts of elation. It was a kind of interstellar call and response: "Where were you when I laid the Earth's foundation?"
asks God of Job. "Who marked off its dimensions? . . . Who
stretched a measuring line across it . . . while the morning stars
sang in chorus and the angels shouted for joy?"[15] As with the
cosmology of Confucius and Pythagoras, music, joy, and
measurement are intertwined with the celestial bodies as the
founding order of the universe. The morning stars provided
the music that measured creation.

In the New Testament, the morning star mentioned in
the book of Job reappears to conclude what it started: instead
of being the opening measure of creation, it becomes the final
measure of history. Just flip to the end of the Bible. In the closing chapter, where the end of history is anticipated with the

return of Jesus in the book of Revelation, Christ is called the "bright morning star."[16] Christian commentators therefore inserted the Christ who shines at the end of time back to the beginning of time. He bookends the entire biblical narrative. Christ is the leading light in the star-studded choir of creation and the "superstar" that will stage its end. As the morning star, Jesus not only sings creation into being; he is still singing and has yet to sound the final cadence as all creation waits for the culmination of salvation history.[17]

A Blueprint for a Temple

What exactly is God measuring and making in singing creation and new creation into being? The Hebrew Bible is dotted with detailed and seemingly tedious lists of measurements. However, these are not cosmic numbers derived from the harmonic proportions of a string or pipe: they are only cosmic inasmuch as the dimensions form a blueprint for the construction of a temple or tabernacle in which the God of the universe is to reside. The music hammered out in creation measures the foundation of the earth in order for our planet to become a habitation for the divine. Creation is a building project in which humans are appointed as priestly project managers on a construction site.

In the New Testament, the new creation instigated by the Christ-event is also a temple project. The prologue of John's Gospel states: "The Word became flesh and made his dwelling among us": the term translated as "dwelling" is literally "tabernacle." Christ is the new blueprint, or the cornerstone, for a new temple. He is the new measure—the Dao, as the Chinese Bible translates *logos*—of a new kingdom. Music, in this sense, is a form of sacred architecture. As in ancient China, music is a site for a throne. As with Confucius and Pythagoras, in

Jewish and Christian theology music is a meeting place between heaven and earth. But unlike Pythagoras, who divided spirit from matter, in this account music does not articulate them as separate realms. Instead, music delineates a sacred space where heaven and earth indwell each other. Joy is the music where God and creation meet. It is where eternity inhabits the moment.

Piecing together the theology of music and joy through the biblical account of creation and new creation is a necessary detour to prepare for our visit to North Africa, where we will encounter Clement of Alexandria and Augustine of Hippo. Both writers assume the Pythagorean cosmos to be the scientific structure of reality for their theology of joy, in which time is inserted into eternity. As with Hildegard's blazing lollipop, music encircles the created order as an endless orbit and bursts into human history as a paradigm-shifting intrusion. The universe is a temple measured by music and filled with music. This is a song that is both transcendent and immanent, both beyond us and with us, holding all things together. The balance is less a proportion than a paradox, where seemingly opposite conditions coexist as a new order: not merely time and eternity, but matter and spirt, motion and rest, earth and heaven, obedience and freedom, suffering and joy. If Pythagoras's postcard from Samos seemed too picture-perfect, if its idyll was too distant and its numbers too aloof, then listen up to the new music of the gospel: joy is not only cosmic—it's about to get close and personal.

6

New Song

A Special Administrative Region

Hong Kong is a paradox: when I arrived from London to the University of Hong Kong in 2008, the region seemed perfectly balanced between autonomy and integration. In 1997, the British handed its colony back to China. At that time both sides agreed that Hong Kong would be a "special administrative region," a unique balance of what the Chinese premier Deng Xiaoping called "one country, two systems": for fifty years after unification with China, there would be two different orbits in one universal set. China and Hong Kong would retain their own systems of governance, with Hong Kong operating autonomously within the "foreign" environment to which it belonged: it was an improbable politics of yin and yang.

And yet in 2008, this balancing act seemed possible. Hong Kong was like an experimental lab, bubbling with a unique combination of elements that promised the possibility of change within the region without violence. This tiny corner of China was, in its own way, a modern Shangri-La, a paradise of paradoxes: simultaneously rude and deferential, East and West, high- and low-tech, densely urban yet mostly rural, bound by red-tape yet free in spirit, believing in democracy within a communist regime. In 2008, with Beijing's Summer Olympics displaying China's best self on the international stage, Hong Kong's paradoxical existence was rich with possibilities. Of course, it was far from perfect and an untested ideal, but something about its imperfect mixture was pure joy.

The gospel is like a special administrative region in a Pythagorean realm, a paradox of one cosmos with two systems. This alternative kingdom, which Jesus compared to an inconspicuous mustard seed, is an experimental lab of redemption, breathing a different tune across the cosmos, not so much to overrun its rule but to permeate it with a paradoxical mixture of elements—a compound of God made man, or a kingdom that is "on earth as it is in heaven." The gospel, then, is a seed rather than a structure; it is a catalyst for change in a static cosmos, causing the Pythagorean universal to fluctuate with a different vibe.

The second-century theologian Clement of Alexandria (c. 150–215 CE) was among the first to hear this alternative tune quivering in the Pythagorean universe. At the time, Alexandria was a bustling metropolis. Like Hong Kong, it was a heady mix of identities, a trading port whose well-heeled and well-versed inhabitants also traded ideas. Located in Egypt, founded by Alexander the Great but now under Roman rule, it was the center of Hellenistic learning, Christian scholarship, and Jewish thought. Clement wove these different cultures together to communicate with his audience. In doing so, his vision of the cosmos begins with a multicultural song.

Close and Personal

In his *Exhortation to the Pagans* (*Protrepticus*), Clement describes Christ—the Word of God—as the singing *logos*. The "pagans" to whom Clement addresses his *Exhortation* are the

Greeks. Clement was raised in the pagan religions of the Hellenistic world; so when the theologian arrived in Alexandria around 180 CE, he put his extensive knowledge of Greek philosophy and cultic practices to good use. His strategy for bringing the pagans to faith was to denounce their cultic practices and use Greek philosophy as a forerunner to the truth: just as Jewish wisdom pointed to Christ, so Hellenistic thought foreshadowed the gospel.

The opening chapter of the *Exhortation* is a Pythagorean fanfare. "In the beginning was the *Logos*" and that Word, states Clement, "composed the entire creation into a melodious order, and tuned into concert the discord of the elements, that the whole world might be in harmony with it."[1] Clement reconfigures Pythagoras's universe by *personalizing* its abstract numbers with Christ. There is one universe, but it now has two systems: number and person. Truth is not just a numerical ratio writ large in the heavens but a musical *logos* who became flesh. Given these extreme scales, music is necessarily a paradox. It is a cosmic equation that is intimately personal.

So to be in harmony with the world is not simply to be in the right ratio as a number in a perfectly tuned universe. Those Pythagorean calculations now require an affective commitment to the order of creation because there is a person behind the numbers. As Clement declares: the creator of the universe loves the world "and takes delight only in the salvation of humanity."[2] This is why the *logos* sings. What is fitting is given a voice; the *ratio*-nality of the universe becomes a well-measured love song. To capture this paradox, Clement plays on the Greek word *nomos*, which can mean either "law" or "melody." However, there is no need to choose. In Clement's *Exhortation*, *nomos* means both: the *logos* is an objective law and a personal melody. It is both ratio and song, timeless and timely.[3]

With Christ as the singing *logos,* the order of the cosmos
is no longer passive but relational. The love song seeks an answer. Joy, in this sense, is antiphonal: it is predicated on a call
and response. If the *logos* sings, then all creation sings. After
all, everything made through the *logos* bears the notation of
the divine song. Music is ingrained in creation. So for Clement, everything has its own melody, whether it's a chirping
grasshopper or a seemingly silent rock. In fact, Clement, elab-
orating on his wordplay on "nomos," describes the world as
"auto-*nomos*": it functions as a self-given (auto) melody (nomos).[4] The world is its own musical jurisdiction—a special administrative region. Our planet, then, sings *freely* within the
greater harmony of the *logos.* When rightly aligned, this counterpoint produces a music of universal praise that celebrates
the sheer goodness of being. Ultimately, harmony, for Clement, is doxology.

The gospel elevates the Pythagorean system to the highest form of worship. But this upside has a flip side. The downer
in the high calling of creation is an abyss previously unknown in the well-tempered universe of Pythagoras. Whereas
for Plato, humanity goes out of tune because the soul forgets
its initial form and merely has to recall the original instructions to retune itself, for Clement humanity is permanently un-
strung by sin.[5] The tuning peg has not so much slipped as
gone missing, leaving humanity "untunable" and vulnerable
to all manner of loose and lurid sounds. Discord has entered
the cosmos; so, instead of joining a symphony of joy, humans
are lured by a different song that grates against the good in
creation. Sin also sings. Its song is an existential threat.

Within the Christian framework, the immutable backdrop of the Pythagorean cosmos becomes a stage for an epic
drama in which the creator writes himself into the plot as the
"true champion" on the world stage.[6] The *logos* who sings cre-

ation into being returns to his creation in order to retune the *discord* of a fallen world. The *logos* literally becomes human in order to resolve the dissonance. So what was a distant music comes near. Christ, who composed the universe before time, in becoming flesh, enters the universe in time as a *new song* in a double act of creation and new creation. The commitment of the *logos* to the created order is not simply personal: it is now *close* and personal.

Reason and Magic

For pagans well-versed in Greek thought, a singing Jesus healing the world would not be particularly shocking. Singing deities in human form are a dime a dozen in the ancient world. In making Christ music incarnate, Clement merely places him in a long line of musical deities in Greek mythology, of which Bacchus and Orpheus are the most celebrated. Bacchus is wild and a bit of a party animal, whereas Orpheus is suave, with a charming voice; but their expressions of music, for all their difference, unite as an overpowering force that can send you into ecstasy. For Clement, however, these musical deities are not to be celebrated: they are the source of the pagan practices that he denounces as sinful. It is precisely the musical powers of Orpheus and Bacchus that result in the un-tuning of humanity.

Clearly, Clement has to distinguish Christ the God-man from the demigods of Greek mythology. The difference between them turns out to be a fundamental divide in the history of music, a running battle between two forces jostling for supremacy: reason and magic. They function like magnetic poles, causing the moral compass of music to spin wildly throughout is history. It is about the power of music. Does music enhance you or enchant you? Does it liberate you or possess you? For Clement, true joy is found in reason, whereas magic is a fake and ultimately a fatal attraction. Reason is represented by Pythagoras; his ratios will temper your being. Magic is represented by Orpheus; his voice will seduce your ear. So where does Christ, the singing *logos,* fit in this opposition?

Christ fits neither. Or rather, in Clement's theology, Christ is the incarnation of the former in the guise of the latter: he is *logos* made flesh, the reason of the universe in person. He is both number and song. He bears the objective truth of Pythagoras, but communicates it with the personal charm of Orpheus. This combination, however, should not be construed as some hybrid, as if Christ is an amalgam of magic and reason. For Clement, Christ represents a completely new paradigm that transcends both elements.

Greek mythology is populated with demigods who wield music as magic. The *Exhortation* opens with two examples: Amphion and Arion. Amphion rebuilds the walls of Thebes by playing his lyre to levitate stones; and Arion lures dolphins with his song to rescue himself from certain death by pirates at sea. In these seemingly innocuous tales, music is used to charm inanimate objects and tame wild animals. In other fables, music even has power over death. Orpheus not only tames beasts, but famously persuades the gods to give up the dead from Hades with his singing. With the allure of his voice, he charms his way into the underworld to save his beloved, Eurydice, from the clutches of hell.

Ironically, these myths do not play out against the musical backdrop of a Pythagorean cosmos; they depict a tragic universe predicated on the necessity of violence and sacrifice. In Greek mythology, magic is tragic. Orpheus's fate, for example, is already sealed by the gods of Hades even as they permit his music to charm their ears. It appears, at first, that Orpheus has persuaded the gods to allow him to rescue his beloved. But they permit Orpheus to lead Eurydice out of Hades only on the condition that he does not look back at her, knowing that he is destined to fail. So there is no hope in hell, only the conditions for losing his beloved to a second death more tragic than the first, for this time it is executed by Orpheus himself: he looks back at her, their eyes meet, and she vanishes back into the underworld. Ultimately, Orpheus's song merely anaesthetizes the pain of a tragic order.

Similarly, Amphion rebuilds the city of Thebes with the magic of his lyre and usurps the throne of the city, but his generational line is cursed. His demise is a complex tale of jealousy and revenge, but in outline, his wife angers the gods, all his children are murdered as a result, and, in despair, Amphion is driven to suicide. His music may be charming, but it does not change a violent order. Magic remains tragic.

For Clement, such sorcery is the idolatrous underbelly of music's joyful order. These charming tales are idolatrous precisely because they are charming. Music as enchantment is not an attunement toward the good but an enticement by another power. As magical influence, music is ultimately a form of tyranny and deceit, claims Clement.[7] It controls objects and beings; its pleasures are a ploy to deprive humanity of reason and seduce the will. Such joy is not an obedience but an addiction. This is the difference between music as moral freedom and music as irresistible lure. To obey music—to measure up to its rule of joy—is to exercise your freedom through the use of reason; to be enticed by music is to lose your freedom, as if controlled by an external force. Like an enchanted animal or levitating rock, it makes you less than human. True music is therefore measure, not magic. You obey its science rather than succumb to its spell.[8]

Fast-forward to modernity: the same battle still rages between reason and magic. The pagan rites denounced by

Clement are precisely the practices associated with the cults
of Orpheus and Bacchus that were celebrated at the birth of
Western opera around 1600 and in Nietzsche's *Birth of Tragedy,* published in 1872 to celebrate Wagner's music dramas. In
both accounts, music deprives humanity of rational will. Opera is Orphic: its earliest manifestations are not only about
Orpheus—as in Monteverdi's *L'Orfeo*—they try to imitate
Orpheus in using music to manipulate the emotions of those
under its power. Musica, if you recall, works her magic as a
spell over her hearers. She literally en-*chants* them. Joy is a seduction. In Nietzsche's *Birth of Tragedy,* joy is Bacchanalian
(or, to use the Greek term, Dionysian): music functions as a
metaphysical narcotic that induces a state of frenzied worship
before the face of terror. Music is a magic potion that anesthe-
tizes the pain with ecstasy. In both cases, music is at best delusional, like the myths themselves, and at worse demonic—a
power that possesses you.

In contrast to an idolatrous music, Christ, exhorts Clement, is the truth, the Word, the very wisdom of God. In this
case, music is not an illusion, a delusion, or an opiate to escape
reality. Christ does not possess the power of music as if it were
some mysterious force to bedazzle his hearers in a tragic cosmos. Rather, as *logos,* he *is* music. He *is* the nature of reality—
the rational principle of the created order. Creation, then, is
not some enchanted world under the spell of music populated
with magical beings, but an anti-tragic order that reflects the
image of its maker, who *is* music. Music is the underlying *logos*
that makes reality good.

So far so Pythagorean. For Clement, the *logos* holds all
things in the universe together in equilibrium; its ratios are the
measure of joy. And, true to its Pythagorean origins, these proportions are so beautifully balanced that they are motionless,

free from the pull of uneven forces that might destabilize reason from obeying the law. "As rational beings," writes Clement, "we [humans] must tune ourselves temperately," like a string that is neither too taut nor too loose.[9] We need to be "just right" in order to resonate in a universe predicated on keeping all things just right. The harmony of the *logos,* claims Clement, is neither tuned to the Dorian mode, which Plato extolled for its bellicose effect; nor is it tuned to the Lydian mode, which Plato banned from his republic for its moral laxity.[10] That would be "just wrong." Harmony is found in their blending. Joy is an all-inclusive state of "rest," an unperturbed place of fullness and clarity where the well-tuned human will can live rightly.[11] Clement's message is clear: stay calm and believe in Jesus.

But a Pythagorean cosmos can only go so far. At some point, its rationality needs a reality check.

Taming the Beast

By 2014, after six years in Hong Kong, I sensed that the harmonious joy of "one country, two systems" was unraveling as a lie. Social injustice, income inequality, the indifference of the ruling class, and the visionless bureaucracy of officials created the conditions for social and political dissonance. The Dorian mode with its bellicose effect was permeating society, and the "1 percent" that luxuriated in the wealth of the region had all the complacency of the Lydian mode. Without an all-inclusive state of "rest," choosing wisely and living virtuously was proving impossible. It felt as if yin and yang were grating against each other like tectonic plates. A society known for its propriety was about to experience an Orphic effect and plunge into a Bacchanalian frenzy. Hong Kong, touted as the experimental

lab for the future of the region, lost its reason and was no longer able to govern itself. It fell under a tragic spell and became
untamable.

What happens when a society goes out of tune? If the
universe is violent—as in the myths of Orpheus and Bacchus—
then that's just the nature of reality. Music might be a consolation, but it won't make a difference to a violent order. But a
well-tuned cosmos would also be useless under such circumstances. Both the Pythagorean and Confucian systems preclude anything truly new from happening. "Music," states the
book of *Xunzi,* "is unchanging harmony."[12] Similarly, Plato for-
bade musical innovation in his republic because to change the
law of music would shake the foundations of the state.[13] Pythagorean and Confucian theories of music simply assume that
joy is a preordained order; we conform to its unchanging rule.
So if Hong Kong is unraveling, the solution would be to excise
the unfitting elements and impose the former order because
nothing can change.

Clement also believed in a preordained order, but its joy
is fundamentally incomplete. The fullness of joy is only possible with radical intervention because there is an irrational
number—sin—among the perfect integers of the Pythagorean
cosmos that threatens to detune the entire system.[14] Sin, by
definition, is disobedience. Given a rule, sin is bent on breaking it. In biblical language, it is a fatal condition that turns a
sound heart into a stony one.[15] As far as Clement is concerned,
humans are worse off than the boulders that Amphion har-
nessed with the power of his lyre to build the wall of Thebes:
our stony hearts are too cold to be moved by his music. We
humans are senseless blocks, hardened against the truth. In
fact, our obdurate nature refuses to bend to its law. Orpheus
may have tamed wild animals with music, writes Clement, but
humanity has proved itself to be an untamable beast. The or-

der of music cannot domesticate the feral instinct of sin. We are too wild for the *nomos* of the cosmos—its melody cannot tune us and its law can only condemn us.[16] We are simply "unfit" for the world.

Clearly, in Clement's theology, humanity cannot hold a tune or stay in tune. And yet, his solution is not to eradicate our species. Our absence may restore a flawless system, but the world would be less perfect as a result: something would be missing. What is required is not a subtraction to maintain a changeless order but an addition that changes the calculations. Or, to return to Badiou's concept of the event, something "supernumerary" outside the universal set of Pythagorean numbers needs to break in as a new equation for joy.

For Clement, salvation history is the radical intervention that completes joy in the act of new creation: the *logos,* who existed before time to create the world, enters time to re-create it. In this sense, the Christ-event is the revelation of the true Orpheus, not because this God-man sings better or performs greater magic than his mythical counterpart, but because Christ is the song itself in person; and as the incarnation of the *logos,* he has the authority to create something new in the world and change the nature of reality. Christ, then, does not enchant the world; he renews it. So ultimately, joy is not a fixed tuning for Clement. It's an improvisation, an unending song, a melody in progress, a theme undergoing new creation. This is why Clement renames Christ "the *new* song." The song promises radical change. "See how mighty is the new song!" he declares. "It has made humans out of stones, and humans out of wild beasts."[17]

Clement is aware that he is preaching a paradox. As he admits, the *logos* is an ancient tune that existed before the creation of the world. The *logos* cannot change because it is timeless. So what exactly is "new" about this new song?

What has changed is the medium. The song enters the world as *an instrument.* In the event of the incarnation, Christ, the universal melody, becomes a concrete particularity. The song is new as a material object. The medium is literally—if not physically—the message. In Pythagorean terms, Christ is not simply the *logos* of a rational order, but the hammer through which that order is made known. Or in terms of the Dao, he is like Ling Lun's bamboo pipe, through which the Holy Spirit sounds a new order. As song, he is fully God; and as instrument, he is fully human. Christ is the union of song and instrument—the paradox who mediates God and humanity. Christ, then, models a new humanity as an instrument through which the eternal song is sounded anew.

In Greek philosophy, such a contamination of spirit and matter would be unacceptable. Pythagoras's banged-up hammers are supposed to point away from the corruptible world toward the immaterial realm of ideal numbers. Clement, however, has turned the process on its head: the transcendent order has materialized on earth as the divine tool. But there is something even more scandalous at play: the medium is not simply the materialization of the message—it's a multimedia collaboration with the created order.

At first, Clement's explanation appears fairly standard: Clement describes humans as a microcosm of the Pythagorean order. But if music, as divine *logos,* can be scaled down in the incarnation as an instrument, then humans can be made in the likeness of Christ. We, too, become "beautiful breathing instrument[s]"—a medium for new creation.[18] So there's a whole orchestra on earth! And Christ is the concert master who collaborates with us by teaching us how to play the new song. This is the shock of the new in Clement's musical theology of salvation: humanity is brought into a unique co-creative process, duetting with Christ as an instrument of praise. The *logos* is no longer a music above that we attune to; rather, it is in us as a music that instructs us; and it is with us as a music that accompanies us. Humans participate in a relation of joy with the *logos*, not only obeying the divine law like tamed animals, but freely improvising the new in creation like Christ himself. Obedience, then, is not a matter of law but of joy. It is not an unbending conformity to what is given but a responsive creativity to give. In terms of the word *nomos*, it is less a rule we keep than a melody we invent. In this duet, we are instruments of the new song, adding something of our imperfect selves to its melodious measure. The perfection of joy is premised not on a high fidelity to the *logos* but on a co-creativity with the *logos*. There are no spectators in the theater of praise, only partakers, making the perfectly good in creation absolutely great in salvation.

What does this orchestra look like on earth? As a "beautiful breathing instrument," says Clement, humans are a harp that sounds the new order, a pipe through which the Spirit of God breathes, and a temple in which God lives. It's a strange assemblage of parts for a new humanity, made of strings, tubes, and stone blocks! Perhaps Clement is upcycling the fable of Amphion, turning its senseless stones into living ones. In this retelling, the boulders are not magically levitated by some outside force to build a wall; rather, humans are *autonomous* self-assembling blocks, powered from within by the music of the *logos*, to form a portable temple "to receive the Lord."[19] Music, in this sense, is moving architecture for the presence of God.

If you recall, in the Hebrew scriptures, measurements often pertain to the building of the temple. As with the Pythagorean cosmos, this building is a measure of joy; its proportions hold all things in order. In the New Testament, this temple is transfigured into "living stones" founded on Christ the cornerstone; it is no longer a fixed proportion but a fluid population that fills the earth. There is no building to measure. The only measure is the song that resounds in an ever-changing flow. This is why for Clement there can be no musical instruments except the human instrument—the voice—because the living stones that form the temple are also the music that fills the temple with songs of praise. As an ever-new song, it is always a song in progress in which humanity, in concert with the whole of creation, participates in the completion of joy.

Being an Instrument

Before we leave Egypt, let's head to the local bazaar in Alexandria for some souvenirs. So, what should we buy in this bustling metropolis to remind us of the relation between music and joy? It's hard to find anything significant. Clement has so radicalized the Pythagorean cosmos with joy that there are no appropriate souvenirs. There is no-*thing* to purchase because we humans are the "thing" that has been purchased in the Christ-event—we are literally *redeemed,* bought with a price. Ideally, then, the item from Egypt that we should collect alongside our souvenirs from China and Greece is "us." Humanity is the equivalent of the bamboo pipe and the hammer. But it would be pointless to lug a cardboard cutout of ourselves on our travels since we already carry ourselves around. We are not a cheap replica of the real thing, but the very object itself through which joy is made complete in the universe. In other words, we humans, as a tool, become the "nonhuman" object of ancient music. We are the instruments that open a portal beyond our human limits to a truly great harmony. Perhaps as a "living stone" fit for a temple of joy we could pick up a rock to remind us that we are human objects rather than human subjects called into relation by the *logos* of the universe.

Our souvenir from Alexandria raises a fundamental question: What does it mean to be a musical instrument? There is a critical difference between being an *instrument* and being *instrumental*. Humans are often accused of having an instrumental relation with the world. It is an impersonal and indifferent relation. We use reason as a tool—an instrument—to manipulate the environment remotely in order make the world the way we want it. In exercising an instrumental reason, humans are not themselves instruments but rational agents that operate the tool. We are subjects that control the world rather than objects within the world. We are reason at work. But if humans are tools, we become an instrument through which reason—the *logos*—operates. Our co-creative duet with the *logos* ensures that we are the means—the instrument— through which joy materializes. Reason works through us. It is a personal commitment oriented toward the good. But if we see ourselves as the self-sufficient embodiment of reason, then we are no longer a means but an end, and music would cease to be joy because it would just be deployed for our instrumental purposes.

The difference between being an instrument and being instrumental is the difference between "being real" and "faking it" for Clement. If music is an extension of our instrumental reason, then music will be a replica of ourselves: it becomes human, or rather a cardboard cutout of our humanity. Clement would call this doppelgänger an idol because it prevents us from seeing reality. As with Orpheus, music would just be an expansion of our power; we might even believe that we can manipulate Hades to give up its dead, but our belief is delusional. Its joy would be a cheap imitation of the real thing. Its end, declares Clement, is ultimately violent, tragic, and meaningless.

On the other hand, making humans the *tool* ensures that music is enacted through us not as fake goods but as good works. In fact, being an instrument was precisely how musicians defined themselves for over a thousand years in Christendom. For Hildegard of Bingen in the twelfth century or the seventeenth-century music theorist Andreas Werckmeister (1645–1706), who was one of the last proponents of the Pythagorean system, humans are the tools of God.[20] By being an instrument, says Clement, humanity can be taught how to play music not only by the *logos* but with the *logos* in order to enhance the harmony of the world. We are engaged in a co-creative improvisation, making joy a renewable energy source that sustains the planet. Humanity, then, becomes the instrument through which the created order is constantly made new through a doxological relationship with God. As such, jubilation governs the very integrity of the universe, for humans are the channel though which a divine song brings joy to completion.

Do You Hear the People Sing?

I could hear people singing in the streets. It sounded like the stirrings of a revolution. A few months earlier, I was sitting in my office when my colleague from the law faculty knocked on the door. We had been working on a new course. He came to say that the course would have to be delayed because a plan for civil disobedience that he had published in a book had suddenly gained traction, and he would now have to lead it. I'd had no idea that he was an activist. He seemed a little too unassuming and dorky to lead a protest. But clearly, the tectonic plates of "one country, two systems" had fractured and he was about to leverage the gap for greater democracy. He assured me that this protest would come in love and peace. Indeed, "love and peace" would be the slogan. It was reassuring. Perhaps joy would be completed in the process, I thought to myself. I would soon hear joyful singing in the streets, reenacting the revolutionary tune from the musical adaptation of Victor Hugo's *Les Misérables:* "Do you hear the people sing?"

7

Baptism

The Ladder

Clement reimagined the Pythagorean cosmos with a new song. He gave its eternal order a nudge in time. Two centuries later, Augustine of Hippo (354–430 CE) experienced a similar transfiguration of Pythagorean music theory in his conversion to Christianity: he infused the static numbers of the harmonic universe with a divine rhythm, imbuing time with a providential dimension.

Perhaps this added dimension was inspired by Augustine's own conversion: it was musically providential. He heard a tune—not so much a new song as an everyday ditty wafting from a nearby house. At the time, Augustine was in a state of spiritual turmoil, paralyzed by his remorse for sins that he could neither shake off nor bear to give up. He had gone into a small garden to be alone with his tears when, quite unexpectedly, he heard music. It was the "the voice of some boy or girl singing over and over again—'Pick it up and read, pick it up and read.'" This innocent song, probably nothing more than a child's game, broke through the turmoil. Its repeated lines in Latin, "Tolle lege, tolle lege," became the vehicle for a divine rhythm to penetrate Augustine's heart and animate his soul. Somehow, this ordinary tune opened up his spiritual ears so that he could no longer resist the irresistible call of God. Augustine understood this ditty as a command to find a Bible, *pick it up,* open a page at random, *and read.* In doing so, his eyes fell on these words from St. Paul's Epistle to the Romans:

> Not in dissipation and drunkenness, nor in debauchery and lewdness, nor in arguing and jealousy; but put on the Lord Jesus Christ, and make no provision for the flesh or the gratification of your desire.[1]

These words changed Augustine's life. The experience also changed his theory of music. Augustine's conversion was not only musical, it also coincided with his work on music theory. In line with the verse from the Epistle to the Romans, this was a theory designed to keep music sober and free from fleshly gratification in order for it to be clothed with his new-found joy.[2]

Augustine began work on his six-volume treatise, *De musica,* as he prepared for baptism in Milan in 387 CE under Bishop Ambrose, and completed the work a few years later after returning to his childhood home in Hippo Regius in Roman North Africa. His tuneful conversion led to an intensely musical baptism. Drenched not only with holy water but uncontrollable tears of joy, Augustine found himself immediately transformed into the very instrument of worship that Clement describes in his *Exhortation.* In his *Confessions,* Augustine recalls how, in the days following his baptism, the sweetness of salvation flooded through him and overflowed as a torrent of song. "How copiously I wept at your hymns and canticles," he confesses to God, "how intensely was I moved by the lovely

harmonies of your singing church!" The young convert found
himself in a symphony of jubilation in which the joy of heaven
and earth overwhelmed his ears and coursed through his being, distilling truth in his heart and calling forth praise from
his lips.[3] Bishop Ambrose, a composer of hymns and the pio-
neer of antiphonal singing (where the congregation sings in alternating groups), established conditions of joy in his church
that would leave an indelible mark in *De musica*. The congregation in Milan was a "multivoiced instrument," as Clement
might say. It was a living temple. Its joy was a palpable microcosm of divine reality. And Augustine wanted to capture this
reality in his treatise.

    De musica can almost be read as symbol of conversion.
Augustine famously defined music as "the science of measuring
well" (*Musica est scientia bene modulandi*).[4] And true to form,
he did a lot of measuring in *De musica*. In fact, the tape measure
from Samos and the plastic ruler from Beijing would come in
handy for anyone reading through the first five volumes of
De musica, because Augustine's idea of music theory was to
unwind the harmonic ratios into linear rhythms: instead of
measuring the geometry of space, he measured the process of
time. As a professor of rhetoric in Milan, Augustine was well
versed in the notion of rhythm as a source of eloquence in poetic speech. In *De musica*, the numbers of the tetractys (1, 2, 3,
and 4), from which all harmonious ratios are derived, form the
basis for the metrical patterns that should keep poetic verse in
proportion.[5] It was all about numbers because to move well is
to measure well. Music theory ensured an aesthetic fit between
rhythm and syllables. Admittedly, the arid application of Pythagorean numbers to poetic meter—or syllabic feet (*plodus*)—
makes reading the first five books of *De musica* somewhat of
a plod. But suddenly, in the sixth book, joy breaks through the
pedestrian content, as if music theory itself has been baptized

by Ambrose. In the final volume, *De musica* is bathed in a theology of music inspired by Ambrose's hymn *Deus creator omnium* (God the Creator of All Things). The first five books were simply a preparation for baptism, which casts the dry calculations of the earlier volumes in the light of the new creation.

In book 6, Augustine declares that God, the creator of all things, is music.[6] Akin to the musical *logos* of Clement, this eternal and immutable source sings creation into existence, bestowing a melodious measure on the entire cosmos. Everything is number. Nothing exists without number, for Christ, the *logos* through whom all things are made, is the personification of number.[7] And what a lot of numbers there are!—ranging from the corporeal to the incorporeal realms of creation. There are numbers resonating in the body, numbers perceived by the soul, numbers stored in the memory, numbers analyzed by reason. The qualities of these numbers are arranged in ascending order, with the materiality of sound at the bottom and the eternal numbers of Pythagorean harmony at the top.

The final book of *De musica*, then, functions as a ladder ascending from the mutable realms of the senses to the eternal realms of reason where music, in its numerical perfection, is declared "the hymn of the universe" (*carmen uniuersitatis*).[8] This hymn is Wisdom herself, the *logos* of God. As numbers in motion, music reveals with each temporal step "the higher secrets of truth," elevating human reason toward divine wisdom. "Along this path," writes Augustine, "Wisdom pleasantly reveals herself, and in every step of providence meets those who love her."[9] In Augustine's hands, music theory becomes an act of love—a desire for Wisdom that is as disciplined in its measurement as it is effusive in its praise. It describes an affective ascent from motion to rest—from time to eternity. It is a movement of body and mind toward a divine symphony of jubilation that declares by its very order the goodness and greatness of God.

Given this transcendental ladder, any passing pleasure that music gives on earth only finds its joy when it ascends toward its highest immutable state—in God himself. Ambrose's hymn—*Deus creator omnium*—is a microcosmic embodiment of this theology. As music, it expresses the numerical rhythm of the universe; as liturgy, it contemplates a God who is the creator of that universe; as a hymn, it orientates the creature toward its source of joy. It is a musical ladder that leads us upward, rung by rung, number by number, from sense to reason.[10] At its highest level, the hymn of Ambrose rhymes with "the hymn of the universe," and so transports the singer through this doxological relationship from the physical to the transcendental realm where the affective dimension of joy finds its rest in an unchanging state of joy in God.[11] Music is not simply "the science of measuring well." By the sixth book, music is joy.

Good Grief

Augustine probably completed *De musica* around the time he moved to Hippo (now Annaba in Algeria), where he was ordained a priest and later bishop.[12] The treatise was not only a well-tempered work but a well-traveled one. It was written on the hoof, carried around by the theologian for over five years, from Milan, where Augustine was baptized, then to Ostia, where he set sail to his family estate at Thagaste in North Africa, before ending up on the shelf of his library in Hippo around 391.[13]

Given the ascending structure of *De musica*, I imagine that Augustine would have placed his six volumes regally on the top shelf of his new library, requiring a ladder to access the work's rarefied musings. The volumes would certainly have taken pride of place in the library as among the first books on the shelf; and they must have had a special place in his heart as souvenirs of a momentous period of change in his life.

Speaking of souvenirs, we might as well sneak into Augustine's library in Hippo and grab the ladder as a memento from Africa. Augustine probably won't miss it because, if you examine the ladder, it is broken. A rung is missing. So let's just take it and stash it in our luggage as an allegorical object to help us read *De musica*.

De musica takes us on an upward trajectory. Its step-by-step ascent, however, doesn't get very far before humanity stumbles, breaks a rung, and falls off the ladder. The fall, the original sin of Adam passed on as a congenital flaw, as far as Augustine is concerned, means that, as a species, we slip up every time in our musical elevation toward joy.[14] There is an impasse—a gap. The missing rung appears to divide *De musica* into two realms: a lower temporal realm of corruptible matter and a higher eternal order. Unfortunately, the use of Pythagorean music theory, where earthly music is merely a shadow of celestial music, only serves to accentuate this illusion of duality. But this would be a massive misunderstanding. Pythagorean numbers impose themselves top down on the material realm, as opposed to Augustine's ascent, which deliberately clambers up the ladder.[15] For Augustine, it is just a missing rung and not a divide between good (ideals) and bad (matter). There is nothing the matter with matter, either in creation or salvation. Its transient and mutable quality is just its material condition. In fact, since God created matter from nothing, its transience is the condition for a co-creative relation of shaping a world that is constantly coming into

existence.[16] Augustine's ladder from the temporal to the transcendent is predicated not on a duality but on a propriety—
an ordering of what to love.[17]

Here is the problem. Music is the science of measuring
well. A fallen humanity, however, is incapable of measuring
well. In fact, it measures things really badly. If God is music,
the ultimate measure from whom all things are made, then humanity in its fallen state cannot measure up to its rule. In the
first five books of *De musica*, meter orders the beauty of poetry;
music gives verse its metrical form. The problem that Augustine points to in volume 6 is humanity's propensity for monosyllabic pleasures. We habitually fail to find the groove and
grasp the meter because we are fixated on a single syllable, says
Augustine, attaching our worship to a meaningless sound
with no comprehension of the poem. In itself, the syllable may
be beautiful, but in our monosyllabic fetish, we have made the
temporal and mutable our *only* joy—we have turned music
into what Augustine calls an object of "carnal pleasure."[18] Lost
in the sensual joy of its beauty, and distracted by its immediate temporality, we devote our energies to this object, seeking
a release from our irrational existence, as if the only things to
live for are a few disordered syllables. A music without truth
is a condition for idolatry, for we make what is temporal and
mutable into gods. Such joy is of no value because God, the
creator of all things good, has been replaced by man, the creator
of all things cheap; we have taken what is good in creation and
subtracted the good to make our own impoverished world.
According to Augustine, nothing but human pride holds this
crumpled universe together, which is to say that *nothing* holds
it together, since pride for Augustine is just the puffed-up
posturing of an empty ego.[19] Without God sustaining the universe, pride merely reverses the process of creation from nothing back to nothing.

This is why *De musica*, for all its rhythmic technicalities, carries an underlying message that not only reflects Augustine's conversion but is a call to conversion: "repent and be baptized" is its New Testament mandate.[20] Only when our love is rightly ordered can humanity measure well. With Christ as the missing rung, we can ascend the ladder and direct our joys toward the immutable and eternal.[21] Earthly music is not so much a "delight of the senses" as "a delight through the senses" in which the carnal undergoes a conversion from lust to love as we gaze upward.[22] Recall the command in the Epistle to the Romans that transformed Augustine on the day of his conversion: "Put on the Lord Jesus Christ, and make no provision for the flesh or the gratification of your desire." The temporal and the mutable only find their meaning when oriented toward what does not change, yielding a more complex, complete, and permanent joy. The love of the higher realm will order the love of the lower realm, just as the knowledge of poetic meter will make sense of the single syllable, enabling us to appreciate its significance. The lower rungs of the ladder are the means to a higher end, not ends in themselves.[23]

How do you hear a ladder? If you recall, harmony in the ancient world runs in sequence like a tune and not in parallel like a chord. The notes may not sound simultaneously, but each step of a tune has to be remembered and anticipated for time to be coherent. You don't forget a step just because you've moved on to the next level; and the next rung is not some leap in the dark but is always anticipated. Every step remains in play in order for it to be in tune and in time with all the other steps as you fix your gaze upward. The ascent—indeed, time itself—is not strictly linear for Augustine: it is consonant, bringing the past, present, and future into a complex relation between rhythm and resonance.

The ladder, then, is an allegory of the interrelationship between the temporal and the immutable. As such, these are not easy steps to take. The movement from one distinct level to another is one of difference and interaction, as well as conflict and mediation, as the temporal and immutable intermingle. In this interval of time, the main thing is to keep going with the end in mind—to keep in step with providence and with joy itself. What is "fitting" for Augustine is the moment-to-moment situation in which we seek God's purposes; what is "beautiful" is the final melody composed of all the "fitting" moments by the immutable creator for our eternal enjoyment.[24] Joy is the movement from the fitting to the beautiful. And as with all the ancient thinkers we have considered, its ultimate form is an eternal disposition, a motionless state balanced at the still point of a changing world; or, in this case, at the top of the ladder. In Augustine's terms, it is a state of "rest" in our restless wanderings.[25] Music as moving numbers stops as a cadence at the top of the ladder; that cadence, in concluding a beautiful melody, structures the ascent.

We can take Augustine's life as an allegory of this interrelationship between the temporal and immutable. If we open the window into his life during the time he was writing *De musica,* we see a person in turmoil, uprooted, upended, in perpetual motion and wracked with extreme emotions: his conversion, his baptism, his return to Africa, the complete loss of family with the death of his mother in Ostia and then his son in Thagaste, the sale of his family estate, and his calling to Hippo—all this occurred in just five years. The temporal, mutable, and corruptible were very real conditions as Augustine pondered the constancy of joy through music. Joy is not the cancellation of the lower realms, as if their temporal expressions have to be denied for a higher purpose: joy is the interpenetration of the unchanging in the midst of change, an interjection of the motionless in the motions of being human, a companion through suffering. It is a complex, multilayered rhythm, a music that echoes the sacrament of baptism itself.

Augustine's baptism took place on Easter Vigil on April 24–25, 387 in the hours between sunset and sunrise that mark the interval between Christ's death and resurrection. The rhythm of joy is precisely at this interface where night and day, death and life react and interact. It is an ascent to eternal life. We do not know if Ambrose's hymn was sung at Augustine's baptism, but its day-night imagery of creation would have bestowed a symbolic resonance in this moment of new creation.[26]

Deus creator omnium	God, creator of all things,
polique rector,	And governor of the world,
vestiens	clothing
diem decoro lumine,	The day in decorous light
noctem soporis gratia.	And the night in gift of sleep.[27]

We do know, however, that *Deus creator omnium* was the song that sustained Augustine during one of the darkest moments of his life a year after his baptism. As Augustine was about to embark for Africa, his mother, who was traveling with him, died, sending his soul into inner turmoil, made worse by the formal façade of self-control that he had to maintain in front of his companions. A fake repose made his turmoil inconsolable. Even a bath—a secular baptism—could not wash away his sorrow. His restless condition was only stilled after a divine yet mundane gift of a good night's sleep, as prescribed in Ambrose's hymn: he awoke, regenerated, as if from an Easter Vigil, recalling the opening verse of *Deus creator omnium*. It was only after this gift that his grief found release in tears of sorrow and solace in God's unchanging grace.[28] As Ambrose puts it in *Deus creator omnium*, in voicing a harmony of praise,

Augustine experienced a "night that shines back in faith," and a joy within the "nocturnal gloom." The message is clear: however dark the night might be, there is a "night that shines" because ultimately God, the creator of all things, is light. Or, in the terms of *De musica,* God is music, and the jarring noise around us will harmonize under his providential timing. *De musica* may be built with abstract numbers structured in an ascending order, but Ambrose's hymn is not an abstraction. It was very real for Augustine. And yet, it climbs this ladder, rung by rung, number by number. This is not some conjectural, intellectual assent but an experiential and providential ascent. Joy is lived in the interrelationship between the temporal and immutable.

Augustine calls this tension from one step to another the "interval." In this movement, joy is not annulled by suffering; it transcends suffering as it seeks the higher rung. Given the vicissitudes of life, this motion is less a straightforward ascent than a rhythm, undulating from beat to beat. It does not grasp the totality, but is a form of "wayfaring," searching for the next step in proportion to the last.[29] Its ups and downs, its death and resurrection, ascend tentatively, interval by interval, as a providential motion toward rest. Joy is lived as an undulating melody that boldly entrusts itself to a fitting cadence that will make all things beautiful in time.[30] Augustine's ladder is firmly planted here on earth so that in singing we might turn our hearts to the created order and find our joy in its creator.

Balanced Steps

Having taken Augustine's ladder from his library as a souvenir, we might ask how it fits in our motley collection of objects. The rungs of the ladder remind us that life is a rhythm ordered by the "steps of providence"; its way upward, like the

Dao or the co-creative improvisation of the *logos,* is a form of wayfaring. Rhythm is something that is sought rather than caught. This temporal movement within the eternal order of harmony enables seemingly imperfect moments of pain to inhabit its passing intervals. Restlessness is integral to rest, and its measure can only be theorized as rhythm rather than tuning. If we are to duet with the *logos,* as Clement instructs us, then time, measured by the movement of desire toward the good, is the emergent property of joy's equilibrium: we are moving toward rest. Augustine supplements what is often left unsaid in the perfectly balanced systems of the Dao or the tetractys: the restless and sometimes disoriented condition of wayfaring is part of what it means to follow the curved line between yin and yang, or to cross over from one ratio of the tetractys to another. These are the critical moments that require us to keep balance and not fall off the ladder. Joy is hard: rest, as in modern mechanics, requires *work* to curb our natural motion.

We will return to Augustine and the question of suffering as a component of joy in music later in the book. But we need to leave now because we have stayed too long in Hippo. It's 430 CE, and the Vandals have laid siege to the city and will burn it to the ground. Thankfully, Augustine's library will survive. But, with the Roman Empire teetering on the brink of collapse and the end of the ancient world in sight, we had better grab the ladder and make a dash for our time machine.

8

Going through Customs

Debriefing

We have now come to the end of our musical tour of ancient times that brought us to China, Greece, Egypt, and a sea crossing from Milan to Hippo, with a medieval detour along the Rhine to visit Hildegard in Bingen. It was, I hope, a mindboggling excursion, riddled with fabulous tales and strange ideas. But before we return to the twenty-first century, we should go through customs, survey our odd collection of souvenirs, and pause for a debriefing on the relation between music and joy.

If we examine our assortment of relics, clearly ancient music would not pass through customs today as music: a bamboo tube, a hammer, a plastic ruler, a measuring tape, a broken ladder, a fitted sheet, a burst balloon, and a rock are not things we normally associate with music. Of course, in Alexandria we also collected ourselves as a memento of music. But even here, despite our similarity to human-centered music, we have become unfamiliar to ourselves as something no different from the other artefacts in our collection. We are a thing, a tool, just another object rather than a human subject. Such an unfamiliar self would not be carrying portable headphones on board the time machine to isolate our being in a sonic capsule to nurture our expressive individualism.

In ancient times, music is not something we possess, compose, or define. It is given as an order—a *nomos* both in the sense of a command and an arrangement—in which everything is related. Music inhabits a world of objects, independent of human perception. This is why its founding objects are found objects. They are already out there in the world, operating as its ruler, both in the sense of a measure and a sovereign. Since music is everything, it is truly great. It is the ecosystem of the entire universe, a co-evolutionary co-creative counterpoint that harmonizes all things from the chirp of a grasshopper to the motion of the planets. As creatures in this ecosystem, we may be moved by music, but music itself does not move; it is something prior to us that currently surrounds us and will one day outlast us. As number, ratio, and measure, it is nonnegotiable and unchangeable. In this sense, humans do not make music—there is nothing to invent. We can only seek it and obey its regulations. To listen *to* it is to listen *for* it. After all, it is unlocatable, veiled like a riddle that is not so much a secret as a device to separate passive consumers from seekers of truth. To listen to music is to incline our being toward the unknown, waiting for a disclosure—like Ling Lun foraging in the bamboo groves, or Pythagoras examining the hammers in a smithy, or Augustine on Easter Vigil—in hope that some unexpected portal will open out into a vast universe in which truth is revealed in all its glory. Music is ultimate reality. It is God, truth, wisdom, Dao, *logos,* reason, the Mandate of Heaven. This is why to listen to music is an act of obedience, inseparable from moral, social, and environmental responsibilities. To listen to music is to be entangled in everything yet ordered by the source of everything.

Ancient music is hardly recognizable today. What about joy? Joy, in the ancient world, would be equally alien today because it was music. As music, it is also the order of everything: joy is to be in tune with the universe. The atomistic, instantaneous, high-speed joy of the modern world, consumed as a quick fix to disconnect us from the pressure of existence, would not be certified as joy at all by the ancients. It would be classified as pleasure in the same category as a narcotic or cheesecake. Unlike the frenzy of Beethoven's Ninth Symphony, ancient joy is slow music: so slow that it is more or less motionless. To enjoy music is to take time until there is no time. Hence joy is not ultimately an *emotion* because it has no motion: it is an immovable disposition located at the still point of music. Joy is found in an all-inclusive harmony that holds all things in balance. It is a well-tempered tuning, devoid of extremes, characterized by a sobriety and a propriety that is ascetic in its fittingness and aesthetic in its orderliness. It is a relation, a proportion, a ratio, a measure, a rule; it is an absolute, not so much a quantity as a quality that is fixed by the immutable relations of music. A universe in which music is joy is not just an order but a commitment to an order. Joy is sought but cannot be grasped. It demands an obedience in an environment beyond our control. Joy sacralizes the cosmos, protecting its spaces from being plundered and consumed; it turns our vision toward a harmony that is more than the sum of the parts. To claim that music is joy is to give joy a permanent structure in a universe that, like the stars in the heavens, is supposed to orientate the earthly traveler along the path of the good life.

Goodbye

So, it is with some sadness that I return to the buzz of the modern world. I will miss Confucius, Pythagoras, Hildegard, Clement, and Augustine. They were all so different yet united in their sense for joy and love of music. Still, something in me wants to leave. Don't get me wrong. They are perfectly nice people. Yet, admittedly, it is somewhat of a relief to be getting back to our own times. Music may be joy in the ancient world, but it is a very inconvenient joy compared to the convenience of the modern world. It is so exacting, so dutiful, and takes itself far too seriously. All that accounting and measuring and ascending. It's exhausting just thinking about it. And besides, it's a tad too lofty, if not too elitist, for its own good. Such rarefied thought seemingly demotes everyday music making to some form of lower-class activity. Perhaps it's better for me to ditch the dutiful joy of the past and bag some *duty-free* joy for our return. It would be less taxing and more consumable. So, as we board the time machine, I'm going to insert my noise-canceling earbuds, disconnect my being from my surroundings, and relax in my iPodic capsule.

III

Unforced Rhythms

I am convinced that joy exists, convinced that the invisible exists more than the visible.

—OLIVIER MESSIAEN

9
Retrofitting Ancient Music

All Change

In the ancient world, music *was* joy. But *is* it joy? Is music joy *today*? For the question to have any relevance, the virtuous relation between music and joy has to be a practical proposition *now* and not some antiquated idea *then*. Can we retrofit ancient music to the engine of the modern world and still make it speed off in a plume of joy?

Sadly, the answer is no. Why? Because everything has changed. Music has changed. Joy has changed. Science has changed. Dialing back the clock won't change anything. For all their eternal insights, our ancient music theorists would appear antiquated today in a world that no longer requires their well-proportioned Zimmer frame to steady its changing motions.

Let's examine these changes.

First, *music has changed*. No one is going to download Pythagoras's greatest hits on their iPod because they are inaudible, immaterial, and timeless—which, basically, removes everything that makes music music today. Even if you turn your volume knob all the way up to 11, Pythagoras is not going to rock. Today, music is real, not ideal.

There have been modern attempts to make the ideal real. In 2002, the Divine Music Administration at the Temple of Heaven in the Forbidden City was reestablished to revive Confucian ritual music. Had I known earlier, I would have applied for my dream job as Chief Imperial Music Theorist of all China. I could have abandoned my books to go foraging for the yellow bell to sound the Mandate of Heaven for the politburo of the Communist Party. But times have changed. It turns out that the task these days is more a matter of reinventing national identity than discovering cosmic joy.

For some officials, the reconstruction of ritual music was a revelation: it sounded horrible. But this should not be surprising. A mandate from heaven is not nice music: it is measured music, only fitting for the ruling elite. The music, after all, was used as a ruler. So, unsurprisingly, if you download a historically informed performance of imperial ritual music on your iPod it would sound something like a ruler: the music is composed of long, loud, unbending notes in unison, all of the same length. Finding joy in such music might be a case of the emperor's new tones, clothing its modern proponents with an ancient virtue that only they can hear. For everyone else, such an arcane reenactment might bring some joy as a tourist curiosity, but it is unlikely to go viral as a cosmic mandate.[1]

Second, *joy has changed.* To imagine joy as a strict and rigid ruler keeping us in line with the cosmos sounds a bit grim for today's hedonistic society. A ruler seems less like an instrument of pleasure than a stern implement to smack your backside precisely because you were having too much fun breaking the rules. So, ancient joy isn't going to be much of a laugh. It is too well-behaved to hang out with the spontaneous, extreme, pleasure-seeking joy that characterizes our times. Such joy is not under God, the good, or the Mandate of Heaven for its orientation. Today, joy is mostly a momentary thrill, awesome in its intensity and total in its self-containment. But its "totally awesome" nature is neither total nor awesome in the ancient sense. Modern joy is tiny and consumable, like a concentrated pill of pleasure.

Such tiny joy has a big brother in the modern world that might be more comparable to the size and scope of its ancient counterpart. The "Gross National Happiness Index" (GNHI), endorsed by the United Nations in 2011, is truly gross. It is a modern, shiny joy with big crunchy numbers to calibrate our global well-being. Originally proposed by Bhutan in 2008 as a countermeasure to the Gross Domestic Product (GDP), the GNHI ranks nations according to an aggregate of various measures of happiness. As such, its numbers are diametrically opposed to the ancient conceptions of joy. What we might call the "Great Cosmic Joy Index" of the ancient world is an absolute measure and not some sliding scale to calibrate the happy state of nations. Great cosmic joy was total, objective, and measured by music, whereas gross domestic happiness is piecemeal, relative, and measured by surveys that record whatever feels good (or not) under the yearly grind of the GDP machine. In fact, the Great Cosmic Joy Index—at least for ancient China—was not opposed to GDP but was its very instrument, measuring, weighing, and counting its gross domestic products in each imperial cycle. Today (2023), on a scale 0–10, China ranks 5.8 on the happiness index, which seems nicely balanced in the middle; but in the ancient past the figure was always and only 10 (if measured on the current scale) because that was the length predetermined by the bamboo pipe. Such a perfect score is a pipe dream in a volatile, data-driven market of subjective happiness. No one will be dancing to this ancient tune or laughing all the way to the China Bank of Supreme Harmony to count their happiness.

Finally, *science has changed*. It no longer employs music theorists to speculate on the laws of the cosmos. They have been banished to the quiet corners of academia, talking to themselves on the coherence of a tiny canon of "great" works. The universe is not their score because the universe clearly isn't a theory of harmony. Compared to the space-bending, time-bending, and mind-bending theory of relativity and the eleven dimensions of string theory, a cosmos of four simple integers holding everything in perfect proportion seems naïve, if not ridiculous. Science still deploys numbers to model the universe, of course, but everything no longer adds up to 1. Although, ironically, it seems that the ancients were right on a micro-level, since quantum leaps actually jump in simple ratios in a similar way to Pythagorean ratios, and the amplitude of quantum waves adds up to 1.[2] But this merely proves how wrong they were in being right. They were peering down their microscope the wrong way.

By far the greatest change since antiquity is the categorization of these elements into three separate domains. It is not only music that is isolated in a bubble today. Science and joy are also segregated in different spheres, one for "facts" and the other for "values." They are no longer integrated with music into a form of knowledge that governs the cosmos. Each has gone its separate way, with its own specific behavioral cultures and methods of assessment. They have disengaged from the whole into isolated pockets of knowledge in pursuit of modern progress.

So, times have changed. In fact, *time* has changed. Time is no longer full of music but is now drained of substance. What was harmonic has become what Benedict Anderson calls "empty, homogeneous time" in which time has no significance in itself but functions like a vacant container in which arbitrary events happen.[3] It is precisely because time is frictionless and featureless that things can freely separate; music, joy, and science need no longer relate and can form their own independent spheres and jurisdictions. If time is flat and empty, then there is nothing given that is proper to it. There is no need for anything to fit. There is no need to be in tune. There is no need to connect. So there is no need to put music and joy back together again. For me to reconfigure the ancient resonance between music, joy, and science today would be out of time with our "empty, homogeneous" times.

So my question—"Is music joy?"—is still a big problem. Confucius, Pythagoras, Clement, and Augustine may have my back but, despite being such a formidable panel of experts, they can't hold up my question under the strain of the contemporary world.

Is there anything we can retrieve from antiquity? Unfortunately, all the ideas we collected from the distant past represent the wrong customs for modern life. They are useless for defining music today. The bamboo pipe, the hammer, the ruler . . . these objects are just relics. But what about us? We cleverly smuggled a tool-like version of ourselves from Alexandria inside our bodies. Can some aspect of this ancient custom between music and joy be transported to the present within our very lives?

Lost Goods

One way to facilitate this life-size export is to imagine Augustine or Confucius living in our time. Their formality might seem a bit quaint for the modern world to live by. Joy, after all, was very proper back then, with all its aesthetic fit and polish. You can sense its orderly conduct in the pages of Augustine's

1/5
Overall Quality based on 27 ratings

Augustine O. Hippo
Professor in the Rhetoric Department

0%   **4.5**
Would take again   Level of Difficulty

Professor Augustine's Top Tags
LECTURE HEAVY   VERY BORING
CLEAR GRADING CRITERIA
RELAPSES INTO LATIN   AVOID

December 16, 2020

I mistook the class on ancient music for Greek life. Total mistake. Admittedly, Professor Augustine lectures in a toga, but the class is mind-numbingly boring. Professor Augustine's teaching style is prim and proper, to say the least, punctuated by long formal silences which become even longer when he waits for the class to answer his seemingly rhetorical questions. The lectures are like a formal interrogation, with a barrage of pedantic questions that only have four correct answers – literally one, two, three, or four. But, somehow, I always guess the wrong number for whatever metrical feet he is obsessing about. Then he will say something weird in long and short syllables and ask "does this not sound more proper to you?". If you must go to a music theory class, take Professor Chua's course instead – it is totally awesome and an easy pass.

Figure 11. Rate My Professors—Professor Augustine's course in ancient music theory.

De musica. The polite dialogue between master and student might have been appropriate in 400 CE. In the twenty-first century, this would be regarded as too formal, if not somewhat pedantic. St. Augustine would get a low teaching evaluation score on RateMyProfessors.com (see figure 11).

Universities today are places for open-minded and opened-collared informalities. When I was a music professor in London, my students called me "Dan" and their emails usually just called me "Hi." When they passed me in the corridors they might casually call out, "Hey!" but mostly they would call out nothing. However, when I arrived in Hong Kong, I was surprised to find my status in society formally elevated: a professor is really somebody here. Everyone treated me with deference and called me properly by my title. I was no longer a monosyllabic object—"Dan," "hi," or "hey." Students would invite me as their VIP guest to speak at the Music Society, dressing up in suits in honor of my presence. When I passed them in the corridor, they seemed to lower their heads and reverently address me as "Professor Chua." In lectures, they would hang on my every word as if I were St. Augustine in *De musica*. I felt I was in some kind of time warp.

Today, the vestiges of past behaviors often seem like quaint formalities that no longer hold true. But, as Confucius might point out, such social rituals are less about authenticity than role-playing in order to cultivate virtues for a harmonious social order. The philosopher Theodor W. Adorno maintains that such examples of etiquette, although remnants of past truths, have not outlived their value in the present. They are not just social niceties but repositories for lost "goods." They remind us of values we have lost.[4] This is particularly true in Hong Kong, where some Confucian practices still operate in modern society, such as the burning of ritual objects to care for the dead. Relatives of the deceased purchase paper replicas of things that might be useful in the afterlife—everything from rice cookers and false teeth to Gucci handbags. By burning these items, the paper replica will pass over into the afterlife as the real thing. Of course, no one believes this to be true; it's just a custom, and yet this ancient formality demonstrates a respect for ancestors and family relationships that would otherwise be lost in the modern metropolis. The deference of students for their professors is also a vestige of a Confucian culture: it is a remnant of an ancient respect for learning. It may seem somewhat awkward in a modern university, but the propriety points to a lost "good."

Similarly, when ancient writers equated music and joy, they were not simply playing with numbers to satisfy their minds with abstract calculations; it was a practice, a form of the good life that supported an affective and moral structure. Joy was an act of obedience that led to freedom. These three words—joy, obedience, freedom—would not normally belong together today but crystallized in music they made perfect sense in antiquity: music was the measure that ordered their relation. Admittedly, the calculations that underwrote the good life were wrong by today's scientific standards, but joy and music still provided a genuine structure for a balanced and integrated lifestyle. The numbers may be erroneous, but the good life was real.

So, for the moment, let's treat these values as "lost goods." Whether you want to believe in Jesus, follow the Dao, or fortify your courage with the Dorian mode is up to you. But if you decide to keep a distance, you can still pursue the good these traditions promise and consider ways in which ancient wisdom can speak to the contemporary world. Otherwise, our modern blinkers will preclude us from seeing any good, and we can never learn from the past in our blind belief in progress—and joy and music will be nothing more than superficial pleasures in our lives.

So, the questions we need to explore if we are to retrofit ancient values into modern music are about life. In what sense can joy be a *form* of living articulated by music as a way of being in the world today? Can a past practice, like an outmoded form of etiquette, still hold some value today as a "lost good" despite all the changes? Can joy return as the harmony of the good life?

A Retrofitted Life

Part 3 of this book attempts to retrieve an ancient lifestyle for the modern world, in the hope of arriving at the best of both worlds. We are not playing off one against the other: we are retrofitting them together.

This is no easy task. Retrofitting ancient joy to the musical present is complex and fiddly, for there are many moving parts, some of which are missing. First, we need to source the "lost goods" of ancient joy. Then we must modernize these practices without losing their distinctly cosmic, nonhuman, and formal relations. At the same time, retrofitting ancient joy cannot simply be an awkward nod to outmoded customs; these vestiges of the past have to be rewired to form a finely tuned engine, recustomized for the speed of modern life. They need to be scientifically measurable, musically analyzable, and joyfully livable by today's standards.

Each aspect of this task—the scientific, musical, and moral—is difficult enough to execute, but the most complex procedure involves fitting these dimensions perfectly together to form a new universe. To simplify the process, let's break the task down into three "easy" steps:

1. Retrofit ancient joy to modern living.
2. Retrofit ancient music theory to modern music.
3. Connect the two retrofitted objects—joy and music—to modern science and reposition them in the cosmos.

If any of these three stages fail, then the high-risk task will derail and result in no gain. But if all this works out, then music becomes a virtuous way of being in the world. The ancient universe will be back on track in modern times. And music will be joy *today*.

10

Facial Recognition

Step 1: *Retrofit ancient joy to modern living.*

Face Book

In the past, joy was measured by music and cosmology. Today, it is measured by psychology and neuroscience because joy is more a state of mind than the state of the cosmos. In current psychology, joy (or happiness) is one of six basic emotions famously identified by neuroscientist Paul Ekman in the early 1970s: joy, anger, disgust, fear, sadness, and surprise. These six are the primary colors of emotions that we mix and match to express our feelings.[1] Aptly, the idea of categorizing these primary affects can be traced back to the Confucian *Book of Rites*, which describes how ritual and music should regulate human emotions.[2] In the book, each basic emotion, of which there are also six, has a particular sound:

Sorrow	—sharp, fading away
Pleasure	—slow and gentle
Joy	—exclamatory and soon disappears
Anger	—coarse and fierce

Respect   —straightforward and humble
Love   —harmonious and soft[3]

The key, however, is not to define these emotions but to keep them in balance. These diverse sounds need to be in harmony; they need to be in a state of joy. Joy is therefore both inside and outside the system; it is an underlying fabric that is also folded within as one of the six basic emotions (see figure 12). In modern terms, ancient joy is not merely an emotion but a form of "emotional intelligence" that manages our affective reactions.

Unlike in ancient China, the modern basic emotions are tied to neither ritual nor music since they are innate reflexive behaviors hardwired in the nervous system, designed for evolutionary survival rather than social etiquette. They are not heard but seen, showing up automatically in our facial

Figure 12. Joy, like a Moebius strip, is both outside
and inside the system.

muscles as indicators of a primary emotional state. They are
emojis rather than sounds.

Joy	—😀
Anger	—😠
Disgust	—🤢
Fear	—😨
Sadness	—😞
Surprise	—😲

Ekman's claim is that these emotions are not culturally
specific but intrinsically human; they are etched on our faces
whether you are a tribal chief isolated in the jungles of Papua
New Guinea or a college student lost in the high-tech jungle
of Tokyo. In this sense, joy is universal. Everyone experiences
joy. Even some nonhumans, like my dog. I am convinced that
my poodle, Chong Fay, has learned to smile and could be included in Ekman's test for facial cues (see figure 13). In any
case, in neuropsychology, his tail wagging is equivalent to a
human smile. Joy is universally canine.

So joy is universal—at least for humans and dogs. But for
modern joy to truly resonate with its cosmic counterpart in the
ancient world, it would need to be more than one of six universal emotions; it would have to function as a universal set
for these emotions. Joy needs to be distinct as an overarching
virtue to regulate our emotional well-being.

Of these six emotions, joy is the only positive one, and
has attracted the least research among psychologists for whom
anger, disgust, fear, sadness, and surprise seem to be more
pressing social concerns. Joy, in this sense, is unique. Its posi-
tivity puts a brave smile on our survival instincts. Fun, strong,
and attractive, joy has a voracious appetite for fitness. It wants
more of the good stuff to feed its evolutionary lust. In contrast,

Figure 13. Universal facial expressions of the six basic emotions
(after Ekman).

surprise is shocking; and anger, disgust, fear, and sadness are
forms of emotional distress and expressions of frustration.
They are repulsive, withdrawing their affections in their impetus for self-preservation. As the only positive emotion, can
joy be differentiated as a higher-order emotion, regulating the
other affects as a form of "emotional intelligence"?

Possibly. Neuroscience can't put a finger on joy's where-
abouts. It turns out that joy is not simply a discrete emotion.
It is all over the place, neither here nor there. Unlike for anger,

grief, or fear, neuroscientists have not found a specific center in the brain for joy. Pleasure does have specific locations in the brain, but these "pleasure centers" and "hedonistic hotspots" are related to addiction, appetite, and sexual drive; they loop in self-affirming cycles of liking, wanting, and learning how to get more of the same. These reward circuits may contribute to joyful emotions but are hardly the only stimuli for their expression. They are not the same, which is why, in the *Book of Rites,* pleasure and joy are categorized as different emotional states.

In contrast to pleasure, joy seems to be distributed across the central nervous system. It is a complex coordination rather than a particular location because virtues have no moral centers in the brain.[4] In fact, as the psychologist Sylvan Tomkins notes, whereas excitement can be self-induced, joy cannot exist autonomously within the self.[5] You can't just make it happen by yourself. Joy is not a location because it is a *relation*—a relation that transcends the self. It is an outward gesture, an ecstatic connection rather than a static loop: as such, it is not so much a reward circuit as a circuit breaker that directs its pleasure to another object.

It is this rerouting that puts joy on a virtuous journey. All the primary emotions have objects, but joy is unique in that its object does not repel the emotion back in frustration or shock: joy reaches out to locate its satisfaction in its object. What *takes place* is therefore always a dis-*place*ment—an outward movement toward a connection. "Joy," writes the theologian Miroslav Volf, "is the emotional attunement between the self and the world."[6] Or as the moral philosopher Robert C. Roberts puts it: joy "is not a sensation, but a delight in the way the world is."[7] This could be cosmic or mundane, metaphysical or circumstantial.[8] Whatever the scale, joy needs to find satisfaction in the object of concern. This relation defines joy as a basic and open structure. "Joy is *as simple and as unspecified as an emotion type can get*," writes Roberts. "Its structure is: *something satisfies a concern of mine*."[9] This outward relation ensures that joy is not an emotion that can be mastered, pinned down, or possessed; it has to be discovered as a kind of surprise or serendipitous "fit," resulting in a harmonious feeling. As a fitting relation, modern joy begins to resemble the aesthetic propriety of ancient joy. There is an element of permanence about this relation because it is not primarily founded on pleasure, which is a momentary satiation of desire. However ephemeral the initial delight, the "fit" does not disappear once it is satisfied. As long as the fit is a right-relation, joy always remains.

Survival of the Fitting

In evolutionary terms, we might call this "the survival of the fitting." The neuroscientist Antonio Damasio describes this evolutionary fittingness as "survival with well-being"; the evolutionary goal of life, he claims, is not merely to survive but to positively thrive.[10] If joy is founded on fittingness, then the origin of joy is simple. It is a self-regulating system to maintain stability. It is nascent in any state of *homeostasis*. For Damasio, this is evident in the simplest life form: a single-cell organism automatically detects and reacts to changes in its environment to regulate its life. This is basic chemistry—a tiny code of conduct scribbled within a cell to maximize equilibrium. Writ large in humans, joy is homeostasis as virtue. Its attunement with the world stems from the same need that every organism has to balance, measure, regulate, and modulate the relation with their surroundings in order to live efficiently.[11] Arriving at joy is simply a matter of climbing up what Damasio describes as an evolutionary tree with progressively more elaborate networks branching from its trunk (see figure 14).

It is an ascent from automatic reactions to volitional actions, beginning with reflexes, immune responses, and metabolic balancing; then to pain and pleasure circuits; and from appetites and drives to emotions; then from emotions to feelings, which are mental sensors of our emotions; and from feelings to reason and ethics, where desires become concerns. At the top of the tree, neural psychology branches out into moral psychology, and here joy flowers as a virtue.[12]

Figure 14. The Homeostasis Tree of Life (after Damasio).

Once at the top, the neural maps "associated with joy signify states of equilibrium for the organism," claims Damasio. "Joyous states signify optimum physiological coordination and smooth running of the operations of life."[13] As a treetop feeling, joy is a mental realization and not just an emotion: it is a reflection on our homeostatic condition. It is not so much the sensation of pleasure itself as an overview, "like a score composed in the key of pleasure." Joy in this very modern sense is not dissimilar to joy in its very ancient sense: the neural map has replaced the cosmic map, but its networks are equally harmonious and balanced, and it is defined as a disposition rather than simply an emotion. Damasio's ascent would only constitute the first few rungs of Augustine's ladder (God does not perch at the top of Damasio's tree), but he still describes joy as a progression toward perfection. To move toward greater perfection is to arrive at "greater functional harmony."[14] Joy is an evolutionary orientation, the condition to which life aspires.

The perspective of moral psychology arrives at a similar conclusion as neuropsychology. For Roberts, joy is a universal set for the play of positive emotions. Its basic and open structure ensures that it is not only an emotion but also an emotion found in other emotions. In fact, Roberts claims that joy is so unbounded that its form is open to any content or concern. Joy is "the general form of positive emotions," he writes; it is the underlying relational framework in which positive emotions operate. For example:

Hope is joy in future prospects.
Triumph is joy in winning.
Relief is joy in the termination of adversity.
Pride is joy in the excellence of something associated with oneself.[15]

Such positive emotions—hope, triumph, relief, pride—are specific forms of joy; they are subsets of a general emotion. To speculate further, as a general form, joy could play a coordinating role in connecting different emotions in harmony. Its openness is an inclusive system. It is not only atop the evolutionary tree as the purpose of homeostasis, it is also a root system to regulate the flow of positive emotions.

In this sense, modern joy operates as a kind of emotional intelligence that not only regulates our actions and reactions but constantly opens itself out to modulate and modify our relations to the larger rhythms of life. Joy is a higher-order relation and a persistently open structure capable of including everything under its measure of well-being. As expressed in the Confucian *Book of Rites,* joy is a universal emotion that is both inside and outside the system, participating with the other basic emotions and keeping them in balance.

Conspicuous Consumption

There seems to be some promising chemistry between ancient and modern joy: Ekman paints joy as a universal; Damasio elevates joy as a state of equilibrium; and Roberts defines joy as an open form and a harmonious fit. Retrofitting ancient joy to these modern concepts should be relatively simple. But something is not quite right. There is a moral problem, an awkward fit: modern joy is not *intrinsically* virtuous.

Joy may be a harmonious fit for Roberts, but he is merely describing a psychological state. There is nothing necessarily virtuous about this harmony. Both Roberts and Ekman, for example, include *schadenfreude* as a form of joy; delighting in the pain of another may feel good but it is not particularly virtuous. Or, worse still, satisfaction could be had from the success of some dastardly plan to blow up the Houses of Parliament in London. Such glee would still constitute joy in Robert's definition, but would fail to live up to its ancient definition. Even Damasio's evolutionary tree, designed to blossom with joy, could ultimately bear bad fruit because there is no moral trellis to guide its growth. There is nothing to prevent joy going rotten, despite its virtuous aspirations. In its modern form, joy is a kind of free-floating homeostasis in search of balance. It is an open form with no moral boundaries. To acquire moral value, its structure would have to be oriented toward an *external* good.[16] Or, in keeping with our arboreal metaphor, something outside its own system—the soil or the sun, for example—would need to regulate its roots and shoots if joy is to bear good fruit.

This was unnecessary in the ancient world because joy was not a tree but an entire ecosystem. And the name of the ecosystem was music. Joy was intrinsically virtuous because music was joy. It was not a psychological state but the moral order of the universe: cosmic harmony guaranteed the good with its well-tempered ratios regulating the psychology of joy. In such a system, bad joy would be inconceivable.

Nothing demonstrates this ancient-modern divide more pertinently than the neuropsychology of music today, which precludes the possibility of joy as a virtue. Consumer materialism seems to have colluded with scientific materialism to reduce the question of joy in music to pure pleasure. Music is gratifying rather than well-tempered. Its consumption results in a momentary thrill verified experimentally as a dose of dopamine in the brain. The pleasure of music is simply the amplification of the reward circuits in the limbic region, creating an appetite for good vibrations rather than the good life.[17] Even when measured by the notches on Damasio's tree, music does not get very far up the trunk, preferring to perch on the lower branches of appetites and drives. Getting to the top to chirp among the buds of joy is too much of a moral aspiration for neurobiological sensibilities: the body should remain morally neutral—it's just matter animated by chemical reactions.

Not surprisingly, given the reliance on opiates, there is a certain affinity between neuropsychology and Nietzsche's drug-induced aesthetics of music. In fact, music psychology often shares the same pessimism as the *Birth of Tragedy*; it merely exchanges Nietzschean metaphysics for Darwinian evolution. Instead of reveling in frenzy before the Primal Unity, the joy of music, according to the cognitive psychologist David Huron, is a dance of survival before primordial fear: "it is nature's knee-jerk pessimism that provides the engines for much of music's emotional power," he states, "including feelings of joy and elation."[18] The pleasure we gain from music is less a function of joy than the by-product of the other primal emotions hardwired as survival instincts in the brain, in particular, fear and surprise. "The surprise facial expression," Huron astutely observes, "is the same as the one for horror."[19] Why? Because life is precarious. Who knows what might suddenly befall us from behind or pounce at us from around the corner? Our physiological responses to danger—fight, flight, or freeze—are the basis for an "aesthetics of pessimism," speculates Huron. The mechanism of anticipation and vigilance needed to survive an unpredictable future is the same mechanism at play in music: danger results in a state of heightened excitement, escape results in a sense of relief. In music, the release of opiates under such conditions is sublimated as a taste of "sweet anticipation." So, next time at a concert when your spine tingles with chills, or when you inhale in surprise, or when your jaw drops open in awe—remember that your distant ancestors felt the same way when chased by a rampaging mammoth.[20]

In much of neuropsychology, music is simply a by-product of evolution. Ironically, Darwin, instead of following his own *Origin of Species,* explains music in terms of sexual selection; in this case, music is a mating call—its attraction enables the perpetuation of the species.[21] Huron, following Darwin's *Origin of Species,* reduces it to natural selection: music arises from our survival instinct—its heightened reactions enable the preservation of the species. In both cases, music is a sublimation of primal mechanisms, the innocuous leftovers of some distant biologically conditioned behavior. There is likely some truth in all this, but Huron's speculative account is one-dimensional. If the *only* explanation for music is the human reaction to a violently random environment, then music can give no insight into the world around us because the environment itself is devoid of music. There is no harmony in a precarious and chaotic universe.[22]

So, according to neuropsychology, music today is *not* joy. It confuses pleasure with joy. And its pleasure, if anything, is the opposite of joy: the sublimation of fear. Music, then, is not much of an ally in the modern world for joy's virtuous well-being. Does this matter? Why bother? Surely, as modern humans, we have outgrown music's moralizing tones by now. Why would the modern world need ancient joy to castigate its moral behavior, given its undoubted advances today?

As an example, we need only look at our anxiety over climate change for an answer. If life is simply about adaptation and pleasure, and if our environment is just stuff for our survival instincts to overcome and exploit, then we will likely destroy our planet in demonstrating our evolutionary fitness.[23] Instead of being instruments of a greater harmony, we elevate our reason as an instrumental force to beat the chaos around us into whatever shape we want. That's a homicidal rather than homeostatic relationship: we end up killing the planet, if not ourselves, with our very survival skills. If music arises solely from fear rather than joy, then domination and destruction underwrite its existence. And if the pleasure of music is merely some kind of adrenalin rush, then its vision of the future will only last as long as a momentary thrill. Pleasure, in this sense, is short term; joy, in contrast, is long term because it is a disposition toward harmony. The future of the planet needs joy if we are to survive.

So to salvage our attempt to retrofit ancient joy to modern living, we need to inject some virtue into the system. But given the fundamental opposition between modern and ancient definitions of joy in this regard, we need to try something highly speculative: a thought experiment to reorientate neuropsychology toward ancient virtues.

Beautiful Prospects

In this experiment, we will bring back two modern thinkers, the biologist Jakob von Uexküll and the philosopher Immanuel Kant, who last appeared in the chapter on Confucian and Daoist concepts of music. Their modern ideas, if you recall, resonated with the "great music" of ancient Chinese cosmology. Uexküll's evolutionary model was musical, echoing the cosmic harmony of ancient China; and Kant's model of knowledge was aesthetic, echoing the Way as a search for fittingness.

If music is to blossom at the top of Damasio's evolutionary tree, then there needs to be more than self-preservation pruning its branches. Homeostasis may concern survival, but for Damasio, it is also about harmony. Fitness does not preclude fittingness: rather, life constantly adjusts its feel for a harmonious habitat, seeking an optimal balance in a complex, dynamic, fine-tuned, interconnected system. Evolution, in this sense, is co-creative rather than simply adaptive. It is more attuned to the musical model of Uexküll than Darwin's model of survival. For Uexküll "every organism . . . is a melody that sings itself."[24] Its song is reminiscent of Clement's *logos* duetting in counterpoint with the environment. Each organism engages in a co-evolutionary improvisation with its surroundings, creating a biosphere of sensory perceptions unique to itself. Uexküll imagines these self-enclosed worlds— or *Umwelten*—as an orchestra of different organisms interconnecting their melodies. After all, the word *organism* is derived from the Greek word for instrument, *organon*.[25] When the organisms play together, evolution is symphonic and the music it makes is an orchestral ecosystem.[26]

By imagining music as a purposive system at work everywhere in the environment, Uexküll has transposed the music of the spheres to the music of the biospheres. We can't hear this music in full since each self-enclosed world is a unique sensory experience made for a particular organism, but we can imagine the underlying point of Uexküll's musical analogies: life is beautiful. Its laws are intricately tuned *like* harmony. It is co-evolutionary *like* counterpoint. It is purposeful *like* a melodic line. So primal fear is not the sole engine of evolution; there is also something beautiful about it. Although in itself this may not be virtuous, given the ancient triangulation of the good, true, and beautiful, perhaps there is some mileage in retrofitting the beautiful to the moral- and neuropsychology of joy as described in the work of Roberts and Damasio.[27]

Kant calls the process of judging something to be beautiful an act of "reflective judgement." It is a cognitive process that searches for what is uniquely harmonious in the object of attention.[28] In seeking a harmonious fit, a reflective judgement is akin to Roberts's description of joy as a "something [that] satisfies a concern of mine." Beauty, as with joy, is the pursuit of what is "fitting."

A reflective judgment is also an open exploration; there are no preconceived ideas in its search for what makes an object beautiful. In this sense, it resonates with Damasio's description of joy as a process of homeostasis. Beauty and joy both seek an optimal balance between the individual and the environment, a harmony between content and form. A reflective judgment, then, incorporates the psychological mechanisms of joy outlined by both Roberts and Damasio. Beauty, from this perspective, can stand in for virtue in the attempt at retrofitting ancient joy into modern thought.

According to Kant, there are two main requirements in judging something to be beautiful. First, it needs to be an unforced fit. Imagine a painting by Cézanne—perhaps a scene of Mont Saint-Victoire in Aix-en-Provence. The artwork is unique. Its technique is innovative. We cannot simply force some predetermined concept to capture its beauty. Rather, we have to seek out the concept from the artwork itself. This process could frustrate us ("I don't get it!"), but it could equally satisfy us as a harmonious discovery ("Wow! That's beautiful!"). Joy is the serendipitous discovery of this unforced fit; it celebrates a relation that is just right. If we scale the object from a landscape painting to an actual landscape (what Kant calls "natural beauty"), then the environment can be seen as something beautiful. It may not be metaphysically beautiful, as in Augustine's "hymn of the universe," but it could be a finely tuned ecology, as in Uexküll's *Umwelt*. Joy takes delights in such a world.

The second requirement is distance. Delighting in the beautiful, for Kant, is only possible if the attention directed toward the object of concern is "*disinterested*." To be disinterested in something is to keep your distance: we are required to stay away because the object is not to be used or abused for our own desires. If the relationship is one of *interest*, then the object would be something useful to own and consume rather than beautiful to behold and respect.[29] For the neuroscientist Anjan Chatterjee, the notion of disinterested attention is to *like* something without *wanting* it.[30] It simultaneously stimulates and disables our hedonistic hotspots. This is why joy is not a reward circuit that is addicted to pleasure: it is a circuit breaker that prevents liking from wanting. So it is not simply an appetite but a cognitive *disposition*. It is not primarily a reaction but a reflection—a reflective judgment.[31] So, to regard the world as beautiful, we must distance ourselves from the temptation to exploit it for our own desires, and search instead for its hidden order. Our planet is not a piece of real estate to invest in so that we can gain interest; it is an object that teaches us to divest our interest in order to seek the beautiful.[32] Natural beauty, in arresting our attention, demands an obedience of *dis*interest.

Perhaps joy today can recover its virtuous past by delighting in the beautiful. Music, in this regard, might teach us anew how to rejoice in the world. This, of course, may involve thrilling and chilling moments, as Huron suggests, but joy is more than the flushes that pulsate through our bodies: it is a cognitive delight in discovering how things are put together in right relation. To perceive beauty is to see how the world should be. And since this is a cognitive process rather than an automatic reaction, joy can be learned. Its desires can be trained, and its perceptions refined. We can be experts in joy.[33] John Cage's 4′33″, in this sense, is a training manual to teach us to hear beauty in what is already around us, however mundane or even ugly it may seem. It puts an aesthetic frame over the environment, then invites us to pay attention to the soundscape as *music*. In this frame, we are like one of Uexküll's organisms—an *organon*—tending and attending to the melodies around us, in symphony with our environment, and in search of relationships that are inviolably beautiful.

Darwin, in his later years, regretted his failure to cultivate his brain in appreciating music. Somehow, after the age of thirty, a part of his brain had atrophied, resulting in "a loss of happiness" because neither poetry nor music gave him any joy. He speculated that this lack "may possibly be injurious to the intellect, and more probably to the moral character, by enfeebling the emotional part of our nature." His mind, in other words, was robbed of moral joy. If he could live his life again, he said, he would learn music. In this respect, Darwin wanted to be Uexküll.[34]

Pain in the Brain

Training the brain to be an expert in joy is not necessarily pleasurable. Disinterested joy is a form of delayed gratification. As a circuit breaker, joy is a pain in the brain: it draws boundaries, sets limits, denies access, reroutes concepts, and creates distance—all for the sake of upholding the beautiful.

Joy is paradoxically painful: to like something without wanting it is a cognitive dissonance. Pleasure, on the other hand, is painless—at least, as far as the philosopher Jeremy Bentham (1747–1832) is concerned. In the late eighteenth century, he defined optimal happiness as a quantitative measure, with pain at the negative end of the scale and pleasure at the positive end. The moral task, for Bentham, is to provide the greatest pleasure for the maximum number of people. It is about sliding your moral actions as far as possible to the happy end of the scale—away from pain and toward pleasure.[35]

A joy oriented toward beauty, however, takes no pleasure in unalloyed happiness. Pain and pleasure are not polar opposites because joy has a feel for something greater. Joy always senses something more beautiful just beyond the horizon. There is a purposeful trajectory at work, even if the final outcome is as yet undisclosed. In searching for an unforced fit, joy's openness can receive sensations both of pain and of pleasure and keep them in play. In fact, without this tension, joy's moral value would simply snap.

It is this high pain threshold that distinguishes joy from other associated modes that are subsets of joy. Pleasure is a momentary sensation; it lives positively in the present as a circuit of reward and defines itself negatively against the circuit of punishment. As such, pleasure cannot bear pain; it is at the wrong end of Bentham's sliding scale. Similarly, happiness has to be happy to be happy. Its index is diminished by sadness. But paradoxically, joy can incorporate sadness and pain yet remain joyful; it is a permanent disposition, whatever the circumstances. This is true in many religious traditions, particularly in Christianity, where some of the most terrifying and miserable forms of suffering—imprisonment, torture, persecution, and martyrdom—can be counted as "pure joy," including Christ's crucifixion.[36] Joy is not a brave face or the relief of escaping danger. It is a way of seeing the world beautifully, a felt strength founded on something greater, beyond the self, toward a fittingness that overrides even a truly horrific death.

But even a less horrifying propositional structure, such as "Hope is joy in future prospects," implies that despite an unhappy present there is an underlying structure of joy. In fact, since joy is a relationship, hope can only be built on joy's fittingness with something bigger and better out there that is "for us." This something can range from the most mundane to the most transcendent of relationships—the loyalty of a dog, the beauty of nature, the comradery of friends, the love of a mother, the goodness of humankind, the order of the universe, the providence of God. It just depends on the scale of the *Umwelt* you inhabit. This "something bigger out there" (of whatever size) is joy's cosmic dimension. It puts a smile on your face, despite miserable circumstances, and regulates your emotions to prevent total despair. But unlike Ekman's smile, it is not just an automatic reaction: it is a reflective action.

Rope Bridge

The task in this chapter was to bridge ancient joy with its modern counterpart. Admittedly, we made a ropy bridge, frayed and somewhat stretched in places, in the attempt to intertwine psychology, neuroscience, and evolutionary theories with the cosmic harmony of Confucius and Pythagoras. Still, in crossing over from the ancient to the modern world, we managed to create some sympathetic vibrations to keep both worlds in sync. Joy's modern definition can sound something like the harmonious workings of the ancient cosmos.

Branching out at the top of Damasio's tree, joy is a measure that regulates our being; it is ingrained in nature as a form of homeostasis that attunes us with our environment, bringing us into a fitting balance. It is an all-inclusive harmony, an open form, a universal set, a higher-order relation oriented toward the beautiful. It is not a fleeting feeling of pleasure but a permanent principle of order that seeks a fittingness not simply to survive but to flourish. As a form of training, there are rules to obey in being joyful.

Modern joy may not share the calculations that kept the ancient cosmos intact, but it can maintain aspects of the good, true, and beautiful as a form of life today. Such joy can exist this side of modernity without dragging the metaphysical machinery of the ancient world across the bridge. What remains may seem somewhat quaint compared to our investment in a hedonistic economy, but joy's ancient currency has not outlived its value today. What appears as a form of etiquette may in fact be hardwired in evolution to break the pleasure circuits of hedonism in order for life to fully function.

11

Counting to One

Step 2: *Retrofit ancient music theory to modern music.*

Real Music

In the previous chapter, joy found a bridge between its past and present states, despite the vast chasm of time. Neuropsychology was able to map joy as a basic emotion onto a cosmic virtue and put a smiley face on ancient forms of propriety. This means that we can text a happy-face emoji to Confucius and he would give it a thumbs-up 👍. Ancient conceptions of joy, then, can be retrofitted onto the modern engine of joy and zoom into the future.

But can this joyride be music? Modern joy may connect with its distant ancestor, but if the ancient equation between music and joy is to have any relevance today, then music would need a modern makeover: its present state needs to be joy. So, there is no point reconstructing the inaudible and numerical music of ancient wisdom as a metaphor or analogy. For this question to be meaningful, music has to be real. It must operate in time and make a recognizable sound. It needs to function as discrete pieces that physically vibrate rather than as cosmic ratios that metaphysically emanate. It should sound like Bach or Beyoncé rather than a thud from a hammer, a toot from a tube, or a twang from a string . . . or just nothing at all. And if it is to have any cosmic resonance with modern science, it needs to get relative with Einstein and move in space-time rather than stay absolute with Pythagoras and fixate on timeless proportions.

Music theory today no longer operates under the cosmic geometry of Pythagoras. It analyzes real music—like Bach or Beyoncé. But, strangely, despite the collapse of the musical cosmos, music theory has not been able to shake off its Pythagorean past and still finds itself in the rut ordained by its former orbits. Old habits die hard, particularly after two thousand years of ingrained thought. Today, music theory continues to be fixated on harmony. This is understandable since most music in the modern world is harmonic. Whether you play Bach or Beyoncé, chords matter. So there is nothing inherently wrong with this focus. The question for music theory is whether harmony is the *basis* of music. This belief could simply be an outdated custom. Today, what remains of the Pythagorean system are the mechanics of harmony without its virtues. The analysis of chords are facts without value, forms without content, functions without wisdom. So if we are to equate music with joy today, we need to ask two further questions:

1. Is music harmony?
2. Is harmony joy?

These are *fundamental* questions. So it is not a matter of mapping emotions to music, because what sounds joyful varies for different times and in different cultures. Our modern ears, for example, are too distant from antiquity to distinguish the emotional difference between the Lydian and Dorian mode. Today in the Hindustani tradition, there are similar modes called *ragas,* which are associated with various moods. But unless you are trained in Indian classical music, you are unlikely to distinguish with any certainty a happy raga from an angry one.[1] However, you are likely to hear both ragas as harmonious. Harmony is about how the components of music relate and hold themselves together. It is less a question of feeling than of coherence. So the question "Is harmony joy?" is not about joy as a harmonious feeling expressed in a certain type of music within a particular culture but whether harmony is joy's essential definition in any music across all cultures. Similarly, the question "Is music harmony?" is not asking whether harmony is an aspect of music (which it obviously is) but whether harmony is music's irreducible being. If the answer to either of these questions is no, then we have a problem. My question, which has just taken one step forward in the realm of neural and moral psychology, would have to take two steps back in the realm of music theory.

In this chapter, we begin with the second question: Is harmony joy?

Harmony—Ancient and Modern

Harmony is an ambiguous word. Before we explore its ramifications for joy, we need to keep in mind its different definitions as we toggle back and forth between the ancient and modern world.

In the ancient world, harmony is tuning. It is a linear relationship. Picture a musical scale as a vertical line composed of dots. The intervals between the dots are fixed at the correct ratios. As tuning, the distance between the dots do not move; but once activated as a melody, the dots are mobile, sliding horizontally in time as a linear pattern. Harmony is about joining the dots of the melody together by relating each note to the correct ratio and, in the Chinese system, with the standard pitch (the yellow bell). As a tuning system, harmony is fixed as a timeless, theoretical order for the play of melodies.[2]

In the modern world, harmony is the simultaneous combination of pitches. Tuning is simply assumed as the fixed system for a dynamic process. The process is both vertical and linear in that the laws of harmony enable simultaneously sounding notes to progress in time. It is about counterpoint and chord progressions, the movement of intervals and triads in synchrony.

In both the ancient and modern world, harmonic theory is the rational law of coherence between pitches: harmony guarantees the unity of music. It is about getting the tone right. Hence, in the ancient world, it was the musical synonym for the beautiful and, as such, the basis for joy. But is harmony really joy?

One Singular Sensation

Pythagoras's harmonic theory is beautiful because it emanates from a single number: one. There is *one* harmony, *one* string, and *one* rule in the cosmos. Similarly, in the Confucian tradition, music is *one* Way, *one* pipe, *one* measure, and *one* yellow bell. Joy, in this harmonious context, is the one singular sensation of the universe. It can happily regulate all things and keep humanity in balance within the created order. This works perfectly as long as the universe remains infinite. The infinite ensures that the harmonic order is ungraspable by human hands. In this scenario, humans are merely tools within a system operated by harmonic forces that are beyond their reach. We are, to return to Clement's analogy, "breathing instruments" in a cosmic symphony. Or, in the terms of Chinese cosmology, the Dao is a "great sound" incommensurate with any human scale; it has no form for us to grasp yet conditions our mode of being.[3] The one is beyond us.

However, such a singular conception of harmony can go horribly wrong. Left unregulated, this "singularity" is as much a black hole that sucks everything into its gravitational grasp as it is a totality that orders the motion of the cosmos. In the wrong hands, the mathematical elegance designed to keep all things in proportion can mask a violent concentration of power around which everything is forced to rotate. Harmony, in such cases, becomes authoritarian: there is just one ring to rule them all. It is about force rather than fit.

If beauty is an unforced fit, then harmony is not always beautiful. It may appear magnificent, especially when power is on display, but the splendor often belies the violence beneath the order. Nowhere is this more dramatically demonstrated than at the Teatro Mediceo in Florence. In 1589, a lavish theatrical spectacular known as an *intermedi* was staged by the architect and engineer Bernardo Buontalenti to commemorate the marriage of Christine of Lorraine to the grand duke Ferdinando I de Medici. Joy in all its splendor was to be celebrated. And music was to be the conduit for such joy. The opening scene pictures the harmony of spheres descending to earth to bless the happy couple. But in Buontalenti's design, the cosmic choir is no longer an infinite joy that surrounds us: it is staged in linear perspective (see figure 15).

On Buontalenti's scenic backdrop, the harmony of the cosmos—personified as rows of beautiful women receding toward the vanishing point—is contained in a geometrical space. Their curvaceous bodies and flowing dresses hide a grid-like structure emanating from a single point that locks the women in place. Harmony is no longer in ratio but in perspective, caught as an object within a rigid container for the

Figure 15. Keeping the cosmic order in perspective: Bernardo Buontalenti's design for the first *intermedi* of *La pelligrina* of 1589—Harmony Descends to Earth.

human eye to observe. And who should be enthroned at the viewpoint facing the backdrop at the opposite end of the theater than the sovereign himself: Ferdinando I de Medici. The theater was designed so that the linear coordinates of perspectival space converge in the singular vision of the duke (see figure 16). He sees it all, as if the cosmos is framed by the proscenium stage and trapped behind a glass wall. From vanishing point to viewpoint, the harmonious order is under the *super*-vision of the sovereign's eye. Infinity (the vanishing point) is in his hands. He rules with a godlike, all-powerful grasp. The message is clear. He is the One.

It only takes a slight shift of perspective to turn the rule of joy into the rule of fear. Music is no longer harmonious the moment humanity goes from being an instrument that duets with the cosmos to a sovereign who plays the cosmos as an

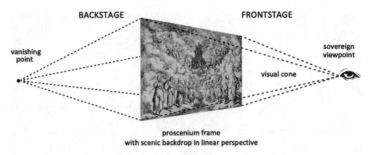

Figure 16. Sovereign vision in perspective.

instrument of power. Once the force of character becomes a
force of will, the virtuous circle becomes a vicious one. So it
turns out that ancient joy, despite it claims to permanence, is
a volatile and highly precarious act precisely because it has to
be so perfectly balanced to be in harmony. If you look up at
the ancient cosmos, harmony is ordered like a circus where joy
teeters dangerously on a single string with only a five-inch
bamboo pole to balance itself.

So, as a system of governance, joy's pristine rule is prone
to human corruption. In this sense, the Teatro Mediceo in
Florence realizes what is already latent in the Pavilion of Supreme Harmony in Beijing. Stagecraft and statecraft are one:
the harmonious form, because it converges on a single point,
is simultaneously an architecture of coercion. The Mandate of
Heaven, if transferred into the wrong hands, will stiffen into
a counterfeit harmony with concrete measures. And joy's melodious measure will be replaced by an external law that only
fits by force.

Music versus Music

The problem is inherently musical. What is most feared in the
harmonic order is, strangely, music itself. In both the Confucian and the Pythagorean traditions, harmonic theory was

designed to regulate the power of music, for fear that it could unbalance society. Music turns out to be the symptom for which it is the cure. Why does Clement of Alexandria prescribe the music of the *logos* to tame the music of Orpheus? Because music is a wild animal that needs to be sedated by reason lest its unruly emotions cause people to run amok. Similarly, for Plato, the wrong tuning would result in moral laxity: society would be ungovernable due to the seduction of the wrong music. Confucius elevated the refined music of court ritual to suppress the vulgar music of the masses, for fear that music's lack of discipline would bring disorder to society. In theological form, an unruly music could profane the order of worship with all manner of sensual delights that would lead to licentious and idolatrous practices of self-expression. In all these cases, music's excess has to be reined in by the calculation of numbers to provide some conceptual grip on the uncontrollable emotions that music might induce in the unwary listener. Music's speculative theory was therefore a spiritual exercise that enabled the mind to discipline the body by dematerializing music's physical effects into timeless truths of the universe.

In these cases, there is a thin line that separates good and bad harmonic theory. Both sides attempt to balance the books to arrive at the number one. Properly conceived, harmony is an obedience that leads to freedom: it is joy. Badly conceived, harmony is a controlling force that limits freedom: it is power. Such power can be joyful, but for all the wrong reasons: its pleasures derive from an obsession with management, regulations, administration, and organization. We might call this an ascetic joy, a killjoy kind of joy for control freaks. Under such conditions, harmony becomes a pathology, a compulsive disorder for order, the reasoning of an unbalanced mind to maintain balance. Joy, under the rule of one, is therefore fragile, always on the brink of flipping over into its very opposite—fear.[4]

So, to return to the central question in the chapter "Is harmony joy?" the answer is yes and no. It flips and flops. It depends on how you count. You might think there is not much to count. Just say "one" and you're done. Game over. It is just like linear perspective: you see it all in an instant. One.

But this is not how the ancient world counted. If you look at the yin-yang symbol, unity is a relation between two elements: "one" is composed of two different but interlocking sides. Similarly, in the arithmetic of ancient Greece, the smallest number is two because one is their combination and therefore not a number but a relation of unity. Music is counted as one only as a ratio of two numbers. Christianity goes one step further: it does not take two to dance but three. The One is triune. God is a self-sufficient relation of joy, a three-in-one dance of Father, Son, and Holy Spirit, with an infinite capacity to include humanity in its celebrations. In ancient thought, then, one is irreducibly plural. It is uncountable. Infinite. Ungraspable. It is not a zero-sum game, where winner takes it all—that would be fractional and factional.

Chinese Abacus

Ancient arithmetic no longer holds true today. One is no longer plural. It is not properly harmonic. It is a monophonic order. Of course, the concept was always prone to collapse, but now it is hard to conceive of its order in any other dimension than its flattened state. Today, "one" is all or nothing.

Take Hong Kong, for example. "One" rules the region today. As I write, a national security law has been imposed to police Hong Kong. The authorities regard it as a necessary force to keep order after the protests and riots that wracked the region and defaced the city. One law, zero tolerance, no deviance. The one law keeps everyone aligned. It is a silent order in which counting aloud is not necessary because the total is always one. There is nothing to calculate. It is all or nothing.

This is not the way I remember Hong Kong. When I visited Hong Kong as a child in the 1970s, counting was not silent. It was noisy. I was fascinated by the use of the Chinese abacus in the shops; it would make a clickety-clack sound, as fingers deftly shuttled beads back and forth as if the teller were playing a lyre (see figure 17). This ancient machine was like a digital computer of the analogue kind, using fingers as the digits to account for the assemblage of things that I brought to the counter, which were usually cheap objects like the souvenirs collected on our tour of the ancient world: plastic rulers, measuring tapes, balloons, colorful whistles, and kazoos. Counting was a rhythm, a fingering that just kept adding and adding, theoretically to infinity but limited by the money in my pocket. But now counting has no rhythm in Hong Kong because it only has one click: the total.

How did Hong arrive at total rule? In 2014, the Occupy Central movement took the streets of Hong Kong in an act of civil disobedience, blocking the traffic in its demand for democratic reform. It came "in love and peace," as my colleague promised. Students formed the main body for the blockade, setting up camp on the highways and byways. Being Hong

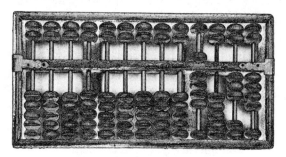

Figure 17. Chinese abacus.

Kong students with immaculate etiquette, their protest was very polite and rather proper. It was harmonious in a very Confucian way. Their activism was as deferential in their request for political change as the way they lowered their heads in the corridors and addressed me as "Professor Chua." For a brief moment, they created a well-tempered society: a homeostasis of joy. It was not simply the sense of comradery or their unity of purpose that was utopian: it was their propriety. The protestors were so harmoniously organized that they obeyed the "Keep off the grass" signs in public spaces, tidied up their own mess, recycled their waste, set up placards apologizing for any inconvenience caused, redirected traffic, attended tutorials in makeshift tents, and diligently completed their homework. Their sense of community was a self-regulating system negotiating an environment in flux, as obedient in its civil disobedience as yin is to yang.

Today, hardly anyone recalls this utopian moment because it was just a moment. Harmony is fragile, always on the brink of chaos. The organizers of Occupy Central placed the students on the front line and left them to fend for themselves, claiming that the future belonged to them. So the students just held the line. The Hong Kong authorities refused to dialogue and played the waiting game to deflower their political innocence. They simply watched the students morph to become more like them. With every police offensive, they became more intransigent, more aggressive, more militant in their reaction. Perhaps the governing authority knew that it would only triumph if the students could be made into their image as masters of power and so unleash the violence beneath their propriety. You become like those you oppose, which is why binary oppositions are seldom yin and yang despite their diametrical differences: they are just yin and yin in conflict.

Predictably, the protest descended into a chaos, and with each subsequent iteration became more violent and self-destructive until the movement was neither governable nor self-sustaining. It all came to a head in the final months of 2019, when a tone-deaf government played all the wrong political notes and unleashed social dissonance on an unprecedented scale, culminating in the siege of several universities. As the protests escalated, what had started as a nonviolent movement became a leaderless organization of students addicted to street-battle tactics as if they were playing a live video game. Their ideals may have been admirable, but the moral high ground had been lost: the students had to be *the One* in the same way that the authorities were already the One. A Hong Kong anthem was cobbled together to vie dissonantly against China's national anthem. The political spectrum was reduced to two colors—either yellow or blue. All or nothing was the demand.[5] "Independence!" was the cry. But in a zero-sum game, two "ones" cannot coexist: only the winner takes it all. And today the winner has taken it all. Everything has been taken from the students. "Harmony" has finally been restored. One prevails. But it is a joyless order.

Is harmony a joyful order? Yes and no. It is too volatile. Given such uncertainty, perhaps the best way to count should not be "harmonic." And besides, after a while, no one listens to its joy because it is as unsustainable in its perfection as it is inaudible in its execution. In practice, power is a zero-sum game. Modern harmony is not a joyful order in the ancient sense. It no longer knows how to count. So perhaps joy can be accounted for differently by music today. Instead of tuning its scale in accordance with an eternal harmony, why not give it a more mundane clickety-clack sound, akin to the rattle of an abacus?

12

Counting to Two

Step 3: *Connect joy and music to modern science and reposition them in the cosmos.*

The Other Side

If the answer to the question "Is harmony joy?" is uncertain, then what about the other question, "Is music harmony?" Is that answer also uncertain? After all, we have already noted that music is a house divided: harmony regulates music's unruly undertones to uphold its laws as the fundamental principles for music's being. Music imposes an order on itself, as if it were trying to cure its own recalcitrant symptoms with a measure of discipline. So it is only by establishing the law that harmony lays claim to be the foundation of music. But in its quest for a foundational order, harmony risks hardening its laws into a coercive structure, turning its joy into fear. If music is joy, then harmony is not its sure foundation. It is too shaky and, given how we count to one today, too risky. We need an alternative order for joy, a music that is not fundamentally harmony.

The alternative may be hiding in plain sight. After all, what exactly is the "music" on the other side of the law that harmony regulates? Is this seemingly improper element—this "other" of harmony—more basic than harmony? If harmony has to regulate a rogue music, isn't this "other" prior to harmony?

To find out, here is a thought experiment: imagine music without harmony. This would be a music without any tuning. There would be no melodies to whistle, or chords to strum, or notes to sing. If this is possible to imagine, then harmony is not fundamental for music to exist. So did you hear anything? A drum? Tap dancing? A rap? Bamboo chimes? Music does not need harmony to exist. It does not require harmony to order its being.

Now imagine a music without rhythm. What would you hear? You would hear no music. While it is possible to conceive of a music without harmony, it is impossible to conceive of a music without rhythm. Rhythm is music's fundamental condition. There may be one exception: under extreme theoretical conditions, where abstract numbers reduce music to timeless and silent equations, rhythm is robbed of its condition for existence. This is why Pythagoras threw out the fifth hammer in his calculations: noise belongs to rhythm. It did not fit his timeless definition of harmony. But even this calculated move to banish rhythm cannot silence it. The numbers, after all, have to be verified; the empirical manifestation of harmonic ratios, whether theorized from a hammer, a pipe, or a string, is rhythm. For as long as something sounds in time, there is always a vibration—a rhythmic pulse.

Repetition

What is rhythm? Rhythm is basically repetition. At minimum, it is to count to two. But the moment something repeats, it can cycle endlessly and undergo infinite permutations. Two might be rhythm's minimum, but there is no maximum count; it can continue to infinity. Conversely, repetition cannot count to one. It cannot be "the One" because, like joy, it only exists as a relation.

In music, everything is rhythm. *Everything.* It may not appear that way: pitch, melody, harmony, counterpoint—these elements can hardly count as rhythm. But they only seem different because we fail to recognize rhythm as a matter of scale. Our ears tend to limit rhythm to discrete units of repetition we can count, but this is to narrow its definition. Repetition is everywhere. It is often beyond our ears. It can be subatomic or intergalactic. Even what our ears define as something other than rhythm in music is essentially rhythm. This includes harmony, rhythm's ancient nemesis. Harmony is the micro- and macroeconomics of rhythm. On the micro scale, its basic component—pitch—is simply repetition at a speed that our ears process as a tone. Take the clickety-clack of an abacus, for example, and gradually ramp up the rate of repetition; the clicks would become a glissando, rising in pitch like a siren starting up. If we isolate the acceleration when it reaches 440 cycles per second (440 Hz), we would hear the pitch "A" used for tuning up an orchestra. The oscillations are so fast we can no longer count the clickety-clacks as discrete units. They merge like a continuous wave.

Had we stopped the process just below twenty cycles per second, our ears would perceive the repeated units as rapid rhythmic pulsations, sounding something like a muffled rumble. Now imagine that we decelerated the rhythmic units further down to a click every twenty seconds. We would no longer hear a clickety-clack but seemingly isolated clicks or clacks. Our brains will no longer be able to connect the dots, and the elongated clickety-clack would appear to snap and fizzle into incoherence. However, if we combine pulsation and pitch to connect these audible dots into melodic cycles or chord progressions, our ears would process these twenty-second units as rotations in a formal structure. Musical form is just big rhythm connecting distant dots. Harmony as formal cycles is the macroeconomics of rhythm. It makes possible a rhythmic coherence on a temporal scale that is beyond what we can normally perceive. In the same way that pitch makes a short piece of time coherent as a continuous tone (a frequency), musical structure makes a long piece of time coherent as a series of rotating sections (a form).

In music, everything is rhythm because music is fundamentally repetition: it repeats itself as cycles within cycles. It is like a weave or a texture of loops that threads different parameters together to shape the fabric of time. These rotations are not silent numbers clocking time. The fabric is a bristling algorithm; like a Chinese abacus, music counts repetition *aloud* for us to make sense of time, even lengths of time that we cannot otherwise measure because they are too big, too small, or too complex for us to count. This is why the philosopher and mathematician Gottfried Leibniz (1646–1716) speaks of music as the "hidden arithmetic exercise of the soul, which does not know that it is counting."[1] Music is infinite computational variety. It is a complex, interwoven series of rhythms that instantly count for us what we cannot immediately compute.

Leibniz calls this system "harmony" which, admittedly, is rather confusing. Leibniz is not referring to ancient tuning but to the *movement* of harmony in the baroque music of his time. It is "harmony" because the change from one chord to another creates rhythmic motion—what music theorists call "harmonic rhythm." This series of chord changes produces a relatively slow rhythmic undercurrent compared to the patterns dancing on the melodic surface: the harmonic rhythm forms an underlying structure for the play of what Leibniz calls "similarity in variety."[2] For example, Leibniz was fond of the chaconne from the opera *Cadmus and Hermione* (1673) by Jean-Baptiste Lully. Written for the French aristocracy, this was highly refined music, with harmonic repetitions that rotate in well-measured cycles; this underlying formality allows for the ornamental splendor of baroque counterpoint to proliferate in complex patterns above.[3] Think of Lully's chaconne as a rhythmic kaleidoscope, with the music's bassline measuring the rate of harmonic rotation. It moves at a rate of one note per measure, descending by step C, B, A, G. Each step marks a change of chord (see figure 18). The four-bar unit consisting of these descending steps continuously repeats; it is analogous to rotating the barrel of the kaleidoscope time and again. Above the bassline, the remaining instrumental parts weave a pattern of melodies that undergo constant variation. This melodic texture is equivalent to the ever-changing pattern of glittering shapes inside the barrel. Counting the bass rotation is simple, but to account for the kaleidoscopic sparkle would require the "hidden arithmetic exercise of the soul."

In modern terms, harmony, in Leibniz's definition, is akin to a complex adaptive system such as the flocking of birds: their flocking patterns are unpredictable, nonlinear forms, and yet they move and morph in fluid blocks across the sky as coherent shapes. A slight change of course in any one of the birds can cause the entire system to ripple. But this highly complex system is generated by a small set of simple rules. In this case, there are three rules: birds must (1) fly in the same direc-

Repeated unit:

Bassline notes: **C | B | A | G | C | B | A | G | C | B | A | G |** *etc.*

Figure 18. A diagram illustrating a typical falling bassline of a chaconne rotating in four-bar rhythmic units.

tion, (2) at the same velocity, and (3) with the same distance between their neighbors.[4] The result is a system where patterns emerge from the interaction of the parts but do not derive from them. Leibniz's "hidden arithmetic exercise of the soul" is the tacit engine the counts the rules of repetition behind the complex system of music: the rhythmic cycles "flock" in "harmony," creating extraordinary patterns. Our ears are basically counting machines, and music delights our ears by amplifying and extending our ability to process time as coherent yet complex cycles.

Rhythm and Blues

These theoretical musings are probably beginning to sound a bit arcane. So let's ground these concepts by way of demonstration in a genre that is synonymous with rhythm: rhythm and blues. In listening to the blues, our ears are processing the rhythmic cycles of a complex system. These are like fractals circulating in time; they spiral inward from

vast harmonic rhythms
to metrical patterns
to pulses and beats
to frequencies and
tiny transient
noises.

Analyzing these elements may make the theoretical discussion more concrete, but it will involve considerable mental labor that may tax your patience. But don't be blue! As we analyze the music, *feel* the joy of its rhythms instead. Rhythm and blues is one of the most tactile vehicles today for disclosing the power of repetition in music and the persistence of joy.

To keep the example concrete, imagine a rotating circle composed of human beings shuffling in an anti-clockwise direction. This circle is a "prototype" of the blues called a ring shout. Originating in West Africa, this religious ritual was transformed in the slave culture of the Deep South as an ecstatic form of Christian worship (see figure 19). The ring of the ring shout is rhythm, a human rhythm. It is not a dance (which would have been regarded as sacrilegious within the church) but a measurement of time embodied both individually—in the swaying body and shuffling feet of each shouter—and collectively—in the shifting motion of the wider circle. These are slowly turning, "well-tempered" repetitions. Within the ring, the bodies of the shouters function as polyrhythmic instruments, each with their own style, measuring different time spans as they turn and twist over a click-track of hand-clapping, stick-tapping, and feet-stomping emanating from stationary group of musicians and singers sitting to one side. The ring shout does not literally shout, although there can be the occasional holler; the shout refers to the incessant rotation of

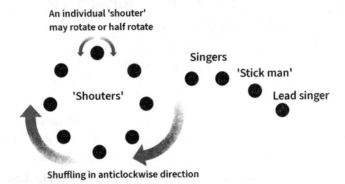

Figure 19. Generalized layout of a ring shout.

rhythm over which laconic melodies shuttle back and forth between the lead singer and the shouters in the form of a call and response. Together, the worshippers weave a complex texture of linear patterns (a rhythmic line) and recursive patterns (cycles nested within cycles). They exemplify, in somatic form, Augustine's "science of measuring well."

Everything about the ring shout is *embodied* repetition. Rhythm is inescapably "made flesh" as a felt presence. More important for our central question—"Is music joy?"—this bodily rhythm is spiritual: it is felt as a defiant, ecstatic joy realized "on earth as it is in heaven." The ring shout, then, is a system of repetition physically inscribed in the black bodies of an enslaved community stamping a pattern of freedom in the white noise of the plantations. In the words of one of its last custodians, Lawrence McKiver, it has been passed down the generations "as a rejoice."[5] In this sense, the rhythm in rhythm and blues should also be understood "as a rejoice" since the origin of the blues is indebted to the ring shout. As a rejoice, rhythm is not blue but operates as an antidote against the blues. So rhythm is to blues as yin is to yang—a complementary pairing of joy and sorrow. The blues, as the philosopher Cornel West writes, is "the black American interpretation of tragicomic hope in the face of dehumanizing hate."[6] It insists on joy in the face of tragedy.

With the ring shout in mind, we can now analyze the rhythm of the blues as a principle of repetition in music. Big Mama Thornton's "Ball 'n' Chain Blues" is a slow-burning twelve-bar blues. The category "twelve-bar blues" has rhythm in its name: twelve bars is its rotational unit. Picture this as the ring of the ring shout turning one cycle. Big Mama (or, to use her actual name) Billie Mae Thornton's 1968 recording stretches our ears to register a rhythmic rotation of one cycle per minute. This is rhythm as form. It is a big circle.

Formal rhythm: Clocking in at approximately sixty seconds, the massively slow timing of the first twelve-bar unit resonates with the lyrics of the opening verse: Big Mama is waiting, staring out into the vacant drizzle of time. It's a long, hard stare in long, hard times.

> Sitting by my window,
> Big Mama was sitting down looking at the rain.
> Hey, hey! Sitting by my window, babe,
> Oh! I was looking out at the rain.
>
> You know something struck me, honey,
> Clamped onto me like a ball and chain.

This is not an empty wait. As she sings, the weight of time hangs heavily over the music. The twelve-bar cycle sets up a rhythm that will rotate four times like the unrelenting swing of a pendulum. Its rhythm is literally a ball and chain. This slow swing is the *formal rhythm* of the blues. At this level, repetition is structure.

Structure—formal rhythm: 12 bars + 12 bars + 12 bars + 12 bars

Repetition by definition has no end; the ring can just keep rotating. Indeed, ring shouts can last all night long. So, theoretically, this formal rhythm can structure time in one-minute cycles that could continue to infinity. The blues can go on and on as long as Big Mama Thornton keeps going, improvising her lines over the rotations.

There is, however, a kink in the rotation. The four twelve-bar cycles in this song are interrupted in the middle by an instrumental interlude. It partitions "Ball 'n' Chain Blues" into two large sections. In a ring shout, sometimes the shouters abruptly stop to mark larger rhythmic structures. Such an interruption does not shut down the cycle; it intensifies the cycle at a higher level of oscillation with the recurrence of each "stop." In "Ball 'n' Chain Blues," the interruption creates a higher level comprised of two twenty-four-bar rotations, as if articulating a giant upbeat and downbeat, each of 120 seconds.

Higher-level rhythm:	24 bars	(interlude)	24 bars
Structure—formal rhythm:	12 bars + 12 bars		12 bars + 12 bars

Theoretically, this too can be repeated ad infinitum since the blues is an additive structure of repetition. The fact that "Ball 'n' Chain Blues" ends after four minutes and thirty-one seconds is somewhat arbitrary. The rhythm wants to continue with its unrelenting swing. After all, this song is about a cycle of love and abuse that clamps the relation like a ball and chain. Or, as Big Mama Thornton sings in the final line: it's "gonna last, oh good God Almighty, for eternity." There is no end to this rhythmic rotation except to break it by force, which is precisely what happens—a screeching silence breaks the momentum just before the closing cadence.

Harmonic rhythm: Humans cannot process repetition on this vast scale without an internal mechanism driving the formal rotations. If you were to click your fingers once every minute, the clicks will not connect. There is too much vacant time. Time needs to be continuously felt. To make such a cycle audible, each verse of the blues has to be supported by smaller internal rotations, analogous to the movement of the polyrhythmic bodies that keep the ring shout in motion. These rotations come in different time spans. The shouters, as they shuffle, often rotate or semi-rotate their bodies like slowly turning cogs. In the blues, these cogs are chord changes. This is harmony as rhythm; each change of harmony

articulates an interval of time. In "Ball 'n' Chain Blues," the
formal rotation of sixty seconds is divided into three twenty-
second cycles, each comprising four bars. Each four-bar unit
begins with a different harmonic function as markers of difference (in music theoretical shorthand: chords I, IV, and V;
or tonic, subdominant, and dominant). As fundamental
chord changes, these three subunits articulate the *harmonic
rhythm* of the blues. At this level, the repetitive unit is a phrase.
Phrases nest within the form as rhythms within a greater
rhythm.

Higher-level rhythm:		24 bars	
Structure—formal rhythm:	12 bars	+	12 bars
Phrase—harmonic rhythm:	4 bars + 4 bars + 4 bars		4 bars + 4 bars + 4 bars
	chord I IV V		I IV V

It is easy to hear the rhythm of the three harmonic
phrases in the blues because they parallel the three sentences
of the verse. The semantic content and rhythmic cycle support
each other. In fact, language, with its own rhyme and rhythm,
adds to the chemistry of repetition. Although there are three
sentences, in terms of content there are only two because the
second sentence, as is customary in the blues, is a varied repeat of the first. It is an AAB form.

A Sitting by my window,
  Big Mama was sitting down looking at the rain.

A Hey, hey! Sitting by my window, babe,
  Oh! I was looking out at the rain.

B You know something struck me, honey,
  Clamped onto me like a ball and chain.

The harmonic rhythm is also in AAB form. At first, it may appear that the three harmonic units are all different: they articulate three different ways to arrive at the tonic (chord I), with the first phrase starting on chord I, the second chord IV, and the final phrase on chord V:

			Arrival of tonic chord
Phrase 1 begins on tonic:	I	IV	I—
Phrase 2 begins on subdominant:	IV	—	I—
Phrase 3 begins on dominant:	V	IV	I—

But the first two phrases—the two A sentences—are closely related harmonically: they share the same chords (I and IV), and these two chords share a common note (the tonic) so that the shift from one harmony to another is contiguous. Placed side by side, the two units mirror each other: I—IV—I—IV—I.

The final phrase—the equivalent of the B sentence—is completely different. Its opening harmony (chord V) is new, and contains notes that are foreign to the previous A sections. Known as the dominant function, this chord is radically different, and creates a surge of energy that speeds up the harmonic rhythm toward the tonic (chord I). This drive toward the cadence makes the tonic chord feel as if it is the final destination, but the sense of finality is merely a foil for disruption as the music suddenly flips back to the dominant at the very last moment to restart the twelve-bar cycle again. Hence the final phrase is called the turnaround: V IV I— (turnaround) V. It closes in order to reopen, repeating the whole cycle in the form of the second verse. The third phrase, in terms of its harmonic rhythm, is an accent. It is a loud clatter of activity that sets the rhythmic abacus back to zero to count the process all over again.

Phrase—harmonic rhythm:	4 bars	+	4 bars	+	4 bars
Meter—chord changes:	2 chords (I IV—I)		2 chords (IV—I-)		4 chords (V IV I—V)
Sections:	A		A		B turnaround

Meter: Since these chord changes operate at roughly five- or ten-second cycles within each phrase, they can be perceived as elongated pulsations. In fact, the tenor saxophone underlines this rhythm in long notes, as if it were stretching the rhythm to hold time in tension within each phrase. The rhythmic cycles at this level begin to articulate repetition as meter. We are hearing each bar of the twelve-bar blues as a slow pulse.

Beat: Meter in music is inherited from poetry (as is evident in Augustine's *De musica*); it groups syllabic patterns over strong and weak accents that you can recite. Similarly, the lyrics of the blues are recited over the meter as rhythmic lines, dividing each bar into smaller units. These units create an insistent, regular beat, equivalent to the shuffling steps or stick-tapping of the ring shout. In a blues, this shuffle is often entrusted to the rhythm section which, in the case of "Ball 'n' Chain Blues," is mostly bass and drums, dividing each bar into four beats. And just as the shouters divide the interval of their steps with clapping, so these beats are subdivided on the cymbals in a pattern that splits each unit into three; these components form a microcosm of the AAB structure of the blues, resulting in a rhythmic lilt or swing. The insistent beat, with its swing moving within the larger rotations of the blues, digs a groove so deep that it traps you in its tracks. Without a conscious effort to resist its lure, your body will automatically sway and shuffle, and move with the groove.

Frequency: So rhythm as form, harmony, meter, and beat rotate in intersecting orbits of different sizes to create a complex texture of linear and recursive loops. This complex system

generates a continuous fabric of time. All the while, the melodic lines—both vocal and instrumental—are weaving a
rhythm of their own in the form of a call and response, based
on recurring pitches that puncture the rhythmic texture like
an embroidered pattern of spirals. The inescapable groove of
the rhythm section releases Big Mama Thornton and the in-
strumentalists to improvise nonlinear patterns above the
rhythmic mesh. The mesh operates like a safety net for their
high-flying acrobatics.

However, the main component of these nonlinear
patterns—pitch—is composed of frequencies that are highly
regular, repetitive pulsations. They are sine waves. Their internal coherence enables these pitch patterns to zigzag freely
across the underlying weave, binding the rhythms into a tighter
and more complex state. They reinforce the network. You could
even scream in an attempt to rip the fabric apart; but, as in the
occasional holler in a ring shout, the rhythmic mesh is so elastic that it can absorb these sonic punches and keep time coherent. So, despite Big Mama Thornton's expressive breakdown
in "Ball 'n' Chain Blues," the rhythm holds her desperate cries
together. You can scream all you want in the blues because its
rhythm will ensure you keep your composure.

Timbre: In fact, even an anomalous scream is rhythm: it
is composed of miniscule irregular repetitions. And Big Mama
Thornton loves to scream in "Ball 'n' Chain Blues." She is not
singing pure sine waves. Her pitches holler and wail. In fact, a
perfect sine wave defines time badly. It is too clean, too pure
to be blue. It lacks rhythmic grit. Its endlessly regular undula-
tions promise to go on for infinity. A "dirty" frequency, on the
other hand, makes time articulate and finite. It turns out that
the noise of Pythagoras's fifth hammer is a necessary condition of music. It is the disturbance of these transient, noisy frequencies that give each pitch its edge and character. You can

hear this in the guttural and viscous quality of Big Mama Thornton's voice, which seems to intensify time by resisting its motion with these sticky edges. These tiny vibrations are as powerful as the vast rotational structures in articulating the timing of the blues. Without the grind of these gritty frequencies in cogs of the blues, the music just wouldn't have enough rhythm to be blue.

Summary: In a complex adaptive system, "one and one may well make two," but it is understanding "the nature of 'one' and the meaning of 'and'" that really counts in the hidden arithmetic exercise of music.[7] Counting to two is not so simple because in the blues everything from its transient fluctuations to its total form is interconnected as rhythm. Its complexity is not some algorithmic abstraction. You can feel it. It is embodied rhythm. You participate in its ring shout, as it were. Big Mama Thornton's "Ball 'n' Chain Blues" is a complex structure of repetition that makes rhythm its mode of perception, and so demonstrates the fundamental process of music. In this sense, all music is kind of blue, because the blues is fundamentally rhythm. It illustrates how our ears operate on a sliding scale of repetition: but this is not a slippery and continuous process but a gritty, sticky, bluesy one. Human ears crease the sliding scale to give a certain "edginess" to our music. Our brains fold the rhythmic sheet into three dimensions—pitch, rhythm, and form. A drone on a sitar (pitch), a funky bassline (rhythm), a movement from a symphony (form) are all coherent repetitive structures operating on markedly different scales. Each dimension has its own speed and mode of hearing, but their interaction along the sliding scale is a relation of "similarity in variety," enabling music to connect across the various jurisdictions in multilayered cycles that are highly differentiated yet integrated.

Repetition, then, makes music. Making rhythm foundational, however, does not undermine the role of harmony or cancel its operations. It is not a matter of rhythm *versus* harmony. It is a question of what is fundamental in music theory. Rhythm as the foundation of music is not opposed to harmony but generates and invigorates it. In fact, defining harmony rhythmically makes it more dynamic. What is called into question is not harmony but the claim that harmony is music's fundamental condition with laws that dictate music's ultimate coherence.

Everything Counts

What happens to music theory if music is fundamentally defined as repetition rather than harmony? For a start, theory changes shape: it ends up with a strip instead of a sphere—a sliding scale of repetition. The harmony of the spheres can no longer enclose theory. It has been spaghettified and stretched into a long interlocking chain of differently sized rhythms that are simultaneously discrete and continuous. This strip stretches to infinity at both ends like an unending glissando of repetition from slow to fast. It is the clickety-clack of the Chinese abacus calibrated to the nth degree. This graduated rhythmic ruler is the new measure for music. Instead of a monochord with just one vibration, music moves in flocking patterns along this strip. This is no longer the simple tuning of two phoenixes in a bamboo forest but a twittering forest of birds migrating in swirling cascades across the sky. The results of the linear scale are nonlinear, but this rhythmic ruler is where the basic rules of the complex system reside. Music can happen anywhere on this strip.

And by "anywhere" I mean *anywhere* . . . including anywhere in the universe, which is everywhere. After all, the music of the spheres was the original theory of everything. Our rhythmic theory simply modernizes it for a space-time universe in order to regain music for modern science. Music can happen anywhere in the universe because everything in the universe repeats, from the looping membranes of string theory to the massive shudder of gravitational waves. Space-time is not silent; it is vibrating energy. Matter is not inert; it oscillates. Life is not a flat line; it pulsates as rhythm and learns by rote. Music vibrates in subatomic particles as "harmonious ensembles"; it circulates in life's biochemical mechanisms; it inhabits the feedback loops of cognitive systems and the ritual forms of social systems.[8] Repetition is everywhere and in everything.[9] As soon as there is repetition there is rhythm. And where there is rhythm there is music. And where there is music there is order. The oscillations, vibrations, and rotations of the universe function as a universal—a kind of background hum that is a fundamental condition for existence.

Humans are just a speck in the oscillations of the universe, scaled by evolutionary necessity to a niche sector of the rhythmic bandwidth. This is our little *Umwelt*. It is in this sense that humans do not make music: music makes humans. It positions us on the cosmic glissando and coordinates our time in the universe. The fact that we feel this music as embodied rhythm testifies to the homeostatic vibrations that shape our sentient existence on this planet. As rhythm, Uexküll's musical metaphor is no longer a silent idea. The biospheres vibrate.

Our little bandwidth in the universe, however, does not demote human music as a shadow of a higher reality: it is an integral part of the spectrum and can be scaled to fit the myriad of receptors that may be out there in the universe. It just depends on the filtering mechanism of the receptors that encounter the repetition. An elephant, if it could process music like humans, would not hear "Ball 'n' Chain Blues" in the same way as we do. Its big, floppy ears would be positioned at a different bandwidth and fold the spectrum differently. Whereas humans perceive 15 Hz as discrete units of repetition, for example, an elephant would hear some kind of a continuous sensation. It is still the same music, just not as we know it.

If music to our ears is different for the floppy ears of a closely related species, then what about the rest of the universe? There may be life-forms out there with vastly different sensors. In 1977, NASA strapped a gold-plated record in an aluminum sheath to the Voyager spacecrafts and rocketed a sample of earth's music into space, ranging from J. S. Bach to Chuck Berry and from Mexican mariachi music to Indian raga (see figure 20). If an alien were to get its tentacles on this golden disc and somehow construct a makeshift gramophone to play it, it would experience human music designed for our narrow bandwidth of the spectrum with alien receptors constructed for its narrow bandwidth of the spectrum. The connection will

Figure 20. Music for alien listening: Voyager's Golden Record and its protective cover with nonverbal instruction for playback.

be a disconnection. Maybe the alien has a brain the size of a planet and can perceive fifteen-minute cycles as a funky tentacle-tapping groove; humans would need to structure this rotation as a Mahler symphony in order to hear such a cycle. Conversely, for the alien, each little track of the Golden Record would be a transient blip. To get Chuck Berry's "Johnny B. Goode" to rock 'n' roll, it would have to play the Golden Record at about 1 rpm—which is really lugubrious for us but truly groovy for the alien. It is all a matter of scale.

If repetition forms the fabric of space-time in which everything is woven, then the universe can be defined musically. Although the big bang was not a bang but an entirely silent affair since there was neither time nor space in the beginning, as soon as the quantum universe leaped into being, its oscillations already tingled the upper frequencies of the cosmic glissando. Some 380,000 years later, when the distribution of matter across the universe started to clump, the cosmos clocked in at the other end of the spectrum; the compression and expansion caused by radiation and gravitational forces generated a wavelength of one-trillionth of a hertz.[10] Measured in light years, this low frequency was a music that no one heard. But just because no one heard it does not mean that music does not exist as a condition of the universe. Music simply *is*. It exists prior to humanity. In fact, it exists prior to any life-form that might sense its vibrations.

Music does not require listeners to exist. Instead, we should imagine that music hears us. Music as a measure of time embeds us in the universe. As mere humans, we can never grasp its infinite rhythms. We may exist in time, but time itself is beyond our conception. We can only know time by responding to a music that is already out there, like Ling Lun in the bamboo forest or Pythagoras in the smithy. So

when we make music, we are *making time* in response to what
is already given. We often imagine that music is something
that happens in time, as if it were an object in a container of
empty homogeneous time. But music does not so much exist
in time as disclose it as a piece of timing.[11] It literally *makes*
time. The music we play on earth enables us to hear how we
inhabit the infinite fabric of space-time. It is as if human
music scales time's immeasurable vastness into an ear-sized
gravitational field.

Take the curvature of space-time in Einstein's theory of
relativity; this is of a dimension that is inaccessible to human
experience. However, a piece of music can shape the density
of time and its gravitational warp on a scale that enables us to
follow its curve and even enact its timing within our being. We
can feel it. In fact, Einstein claims that music was "the driving
force behind [his] intuition" of the theory of relativity.[12] In this
sense, Big Mama Thornton's performance of "Ball 'n' Chain
Blues" in 1968 is a space-time event. There is an infinite series
of possible rhythmic permutations woven in the fabric of time.
Her performance pulls together certain rhythmic strands from
this infinite universe of repetition and weaves them into a particular knot of time for our ears to unravel. These recursive
cycles shape our audition of time. The rhythms regulate its
flow. The blue-notes bend space. Time seems to contract and
expand, its materials coagulate and thin, warp and wane. The
music generates the flocking patterns of time. This is not a
music *in* time, as if it is trapped in some premeasured container, but a music that *makes* time. Music makes time happen as it passes. It discloses time as a beautiful order. And when
we listen to it, the muscles in our limbs and the neural oscillations in our brain begin to align with its rotations. Music enables us *to be* in time with the universe.

If the music we make discloses the cosmic rhythm of space-time as something we feel, then this creates the possibility of a homeostatic relation of universal proportions. To be in time with music is to be in time with the cosmos. And if joy is the virtue of homeostasis, then rhythm might just restore to the universe a joy that rotates as a ring shout rather than a ratio.

13
A Rhythmic Universe

We have just completed step 3: *Connect joy and music to modern science and reposition them in the cosmos.* This was one step back for harmony but one giant leap for rhythm.

In the previous chapters we asked two questions:

1. "Is music harmony?" The answer to this question is no. Music is not fundamentally harmony. It is rhythm. What is more, it is a cosmic rhythm that could potentially be as universal today as the harmony of the spheres was in the past.
2. "Is harmony joy?" The answer to this question is yes and no: joy can be harmony, but its harmony is unstable and inherently dangerous since its virtue can suddenly flip into its opposite and rule by fear.

However, since music is fundamentally rhythm rather than harmony, can joy be more appropriately described as rhythm? Or, at least, can joy be more stable than harmony if it were rhythm?

Music Analysis

In this chapter, we will compare and contrast harmony (tuning) and rhythm (repetition) as possible universes for joy. The quality of joy should be different. In the harmonic system, joy is a ratio. In the analysis of "Ball 'n' Chain Blues," ratio is replaced by repetition. This is a recursive and scalable process along a graded rhythmic spectrum. Everything in music repeats like a rhythmic shuttle weaving a fabric of space-time. So what are the consequences for joy if it is transferred from a harmonic universe to a rhythmic one? Would a joy based on repetition be monotonous when compared to the tuneful variety of harmony? In order to grasp the ramifications, we need to understand their operations. How does tuning work? How does rhythm function? What orders harmony? What makes repetition coherent?

These are music theoretical questions. For the uninitiated, this might seem a forbidding and tedious prospect. Is it really necessary to fiddle with such technical details? If music is fundamentally joy and not some vague analogy, then it is vital to analyze the mechanisms behind harmony and rhythm. We need to understand exactly what it is about rhythm as opposed to harmony that makes it a lesson on the good life. But don't worry. You are not expected to have a rudimentary knowledge of music theory in the following pages: you will survive if you take things slowly and just keep going. For the musically literate, there will be some familiar notation to flatter your knowledge, but beware: my analysis of rhythm is not textbook fare, and notation is always culturally specific and limits the possibilities of music in the process of writing it down. Being uninitiated in the ways of music theory may, in fact, be an advantage.

For illustrative purposes, we will analyze the melody of a Chinese folk song—"On Running Horse Mountain"

Figure 21. The melody of "On Running Horse Mountain"
(or "Kangding Love Song").

(跑馬溜溜的山上)—from both perspectives: first harmony, then
rhythm. The song, first published in 1946 in a collection of folk
songs, is endearingly known as the "Kangding Love Song."

However, before we begin, a word of caution: music examples are particular demonstrations of a general theory. Their
particularity should not then be generalized as a model for how
all music goes. An analysis of a different piece may illustrate
the same principles in a completely different way. This folk
song is deployed as a teaching *moment* and not as a timeless
exemplar for how to apply the theory. It is chosen for what it
can show, not all we can know.

So, with this proviso in mind, here is the melody of "On
Running Horse Mountain" (see figure 21). First, observe the
contours of the melody. You don't need to be able to read music
to track the notation: just follow the shape and spacing of the
dots to get a vague sense of its direction and rhythm.[1]

A Harmonic Universe

What would define this folk song within a harmonic universe?
Imagine Ling Lun foraging in a bamboo forest. He cuts a
bamboo pipe and designates it as the "yellow bell," the frequency from which the remaining pitches of the scale will be

generated. In this particular case, the melody will be held in proportion by the five notes of the pentatonic scale (F, G, A, C, D). If we use the music notation in figure 21 as an analogy, the vertical spacing between the "dots" of the melody have to be precisely measured in order to keep this harmonic universe intact. The "dots" need to stay in their orbit, ordained by the horizontal lines in the notation. These lines represent a scale that has to be perfectly tuned.

To construct the scale, Ling Lun uses the length of the bamboo pipe to measure the interval of a fifth at the ratio 3:2. To do so, he literally cuts another bamboo tube at two-thirds of the original length. He repeats the same measurement with the new pipe until there are five pipes. Before him are an ascending order of bamboo flutes spaced at intervals of a fifth (F, C, G, D, and A) ranging over several octaves. He could bind these flutes together into a panpipe, but the instrument would be unusable since the pitches are too widely spaced and would scatter the melodic line of the folk song as distant dots.

These frequencies need to be rearranged within one octave to construct the contiguous steps of a pentatonic scale. So Ling Lun scales the pipes to the correct octave either by halving or doubling their length (the ration 1:2 or 2:1) and proceeds to assemble his panpipe.[2] He then duets with a passing phoenix to corroborate his tuning as if by magic. The series of pipes in his hands are perfect. Their well-measured tuning is similar to the horizontal lines in our notated example: they form an immovable grid on which the dots are locked in place and held in proportion.

Now imagine this notation as a harmonious universe: the horizontal lines disappear into the blackness of space and the notes glisten as stars. If Ling Lun were to play "On Running Horse Mountain," each tone would be suspended like a constellation in the night sky. The constellation is fixed: the notes may twinkle in time, but the intervals between the twinkling stars cannot change. It is an invariable universe. A mandate from heaven.

In this universe, everything is perfect, and everything is simple. Joy in a harmonic universe is simply perfect and perfectly simple.

A Rhythmic Universe

This cannot be said of a rhythmic universe. It is a complex system. In a rhythmic universe, the measure is not fixed at either end of a tube or string and neatly divided into ratios: rather, rhythm is an infinite series, a repetitive structure, an additive process, an endless rotation. It is not "perfected" by the limitation of a fixed length or constrained by its proportions; rather, its perfection is infinite, which is to say that its perfection is never complete. It just goes on and on and on.

For this reason, there is no original length in a rhythmic universe that can hold the totality in balance. Repetition, by definition, cannot be reduced to one measure, so there is nothing equivalent to Ling Lun's "yellow bell" to calibrate all things. Rhythm is not going to burst into being from a single event. There is no original beat, for a beat on its own has no relation. It is meaningless, without pattern, devoid of coherence, lacking a past to project the future. Rhythm has to be a relation. So the shortest conceivable rhythmic unit consists of two elements. Something must repeat. And once there are two elements in a single relation, a vast universe can suddenly open up, swirling with infinite combinatorial possibilities: two is the possibility of many.

If music discloses the oscillations of time, what makes these repetitions coherent? A harmonious universe is held in balance by the elegance of simple integer relationships. Ratio is its coherence. Rhythm, given its infinite combinations, is potentially a mess. Its universe might at first sight resemble a looping tangle of spaghettified squiggles, which does not tally with the well-tempered order of joy. So, to disentangle rhythm, let's imagine a simple, if not the simplest, case—two beats—and see if it can elucidate the basic principles behind a complex system. The beats can be of any length and in any time. We can label the two beats:

$$A + A$$

It is natural to assume that the similarity between "A" and "A" results in an identity. Coherence, in this reckoning, is a twin, like a game of Snap. But just because something repeats does not mean that the elements will not fall apart. It is not so much the similarity between "A" and "A" as the "+" that clips the two elements together that results in a coherent piece of time. This "+" is the *relation* between the two elements. Even at the simplest level—just two beats—repetition consists not of two elements but of three. This third element makes all the difference: quite literally, because it is the *point of difference* (PoD). Difference is integral to repetition. The dissimilarity at the center operates as a fold or a crease that simultaneously defines and connects the elements (A) on either side of its position. We can describe the fold as a line between A and A:

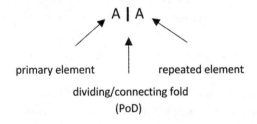

primary element   repeated element

dividing/connecting fold
(PoD)

This articulation (|) is like the partition between yin and yang that divides and interpenetrates both sides. It could be a gap, a noise, or some contrasting material; it doesn't matter too much because, unlike the A elements, the point of difference does not have to be the same with each subsequent recurrence. It can, paradoxically, repeat difference. Thus, the fold can be of varying "thickness" as the A units repeat. For example, it could look something like this:

A ■ A|A▮A|A ▬▬▬ A|A▮ A

The point of difference ensures that unpredictability is integral to repetition: the future in a rhythmic universe is always open and contingent.

Moreover, the fold functions as a filter through which the repeated A is transformed. In crossing the fold, the repeated A element is always less stable, as if it has been marked with difference. There is entropy. Typologically, the repeated A could be misshapen, like this: A|𝐴. Or, perhaps, inverted, like this: A|∀. Or truncated, like this: A|a. Or expanded, like this: A|**A**. Or decorated, like this: A | 𝒜 .

All kinds of things can happen. The point is: what is the same in the process of repetition is never exactly the same. The second A in a rhythmic unit can never be a clone of the primary A. It is always a variant. The difference in the equation means that the second unit is more unstable than the first. Hence, in musical terms, this beat is called the "upbeat" or "off beat" or "back beat." Something has switched "direction." What was "on" is now "off." What was "down" is "up." What was in "front" turns "back." The process between the two A sections could be described like this, where ∀ stands for a varied repeat:

A｜∀

Repetition, then, is not merely about identity or equivalence; it is also about difference and disruption. Musical repetition is fundamentally difference-in-relation. Or to put the matter the other way around, rhythmic coherence is nonidentical repetition. As Leibniz says, music is "similarity in variety." As such, repetition—to borrow Søren Kierkegaard's pithy phrase—"is recollected forwards": it binds the past and present to the future because what is recollected is different.[3] So repetition at the simplest level of just two beats contains everything it needs for infinite generation.[4]

This process can be illustrated in the melodic contours of the Chinese folk song. Of course, as in our analysis of "Ball 'n' Chain Blues," the rhythm of "On Running Horse Mountain" operates on multiple levels: there are metrical pulsations, thematic cycles, formal rotations, harmonic rhythms, frequency modulations; even the harmonic proportions finely tuned by the bamboo pipes are rhythmic relations between frequencies. However, for illustrative purposes, the process of nonidentical repetition will focus on the phrase structure of the melody.

On a melodic level, "On Running Horse Mountain" folds and unfolds in a series of nonidentical repetitions. The opening phrase of "On Running Horse Mountain" actually looks like a horse on a mountain. It consists of a rising slope, a little horse, and a downward slope (see figure 22).

In this opening phrase, the two sloping A sections face each other in a mirror relationship (they literally resemble A｜∀). It is like folding a piece of paper to make an origami mountain—/\. The PoD is the equestrian twiddle prancing on the summit: it is a pirouette that spins the melody around before the horse gallops down the incline. The point of difference

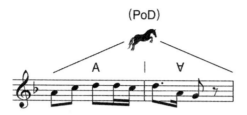

Figure 22. "On Running Horse Mountain"—
galloping up and down the opening phrase.

divides, defines, connects, and transforms the second ∀ as a variant of the first A, turning it upside down and inverting the order of intervals within the pentatonic scale.

The whole unit (A|∀) is then repeated, creating a recursive reflection at a higher temporal level consisting of (A|∀) + (A|∀). The origami mountain becomes a mountain range, separated by another point of difference, this time in the form of a gap (see figure 23). Imagine this gap as a glistening brook intersecting the valley for our little horse to sip some water before bounding up the slope again for another pirouette then cavorting down the other side. This time, the "other side" is much steeper. As with the opening phrase, at this

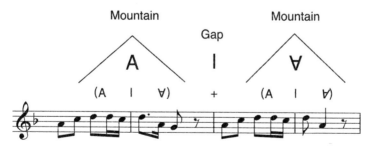

Figure 23. "On Running Horse Mountain"—melodic
mountain range.

Figure 24. "On Running Horse Mountain"—melodic recursions.

higher recursive level, the repeated section is varied: it is a variation of the variation. What was V is truncated and re-shaped as *V*.

Then this whole four-bar section is repeated at the next level of recursion, with the variation (*V*) of the variation (V) undergoing further variation (see figure 24 and compare measures 3–4 and measures 7–8).

The melody is potentially an endless spiral of change. And sure enough, this undulating structure recurs at another elevated level. However, instead of a symmetrical and balanced repeat, the fold results in a fragmentary replication of the earlier materials, consisting of all the variants (see figure 25). The second half of the melody is a variation of variants, as if it were a summary of the chain of changes made up of all the upside-down As (measures 8–14).

The variation of variants rounds off the folk melody as an unstable and irregular balancing section (eight bars | five bars). It is the uneven "balance" that signals the closure of the melody. As a summary of difference, it can also double as a massive fold if the entire melody is repeated, dividing the first verse from the second verse. And why stop there? We could keep going with verse after verse, imagining new vocal inflections, tempo fluctuations, improvised flourishes, and changes in the accompaniment, the texture, the volume, and so on.

Figure 25. "On Running Horse Mountain"—variation of variants.

And this is just the melodic component on our rhythmic glissando of repetitive parameters. An exhaustive analysis of this folk song will require A|Ɐ processes to operate on multiple levels, weaving a complex fabric of rhythmic strands that fold and unfurl like flocking patterns across time.

Similarity in Variety

The rhythmic analysis of "On Running Horse Mountain" demonstrates three core components for a music theory of repetition: identity, difference, and variation. Their interrelation forms the conditions of temporal coherence.

- Identity allows for continuity in time. This is represented by the A in A|Ɐ.
- Difference enables something new to break in as a discrete interruption of time. This articulation is represented by |.
- Variation negotiates the two by generating consistency and contingency at the same time. This flow of anticipation and surprise is represented by Ɐ.

In biochemical terms, these are the principles for rhythmic homeostasis—the components adjust to each other's
differences to create coherent, emergent, generative relationships. Or, to return to Leibniz's phrase, they constitute the computational "harmony" of "similarity in variety." In their most
basic form, they can be summed up as A|V. This axiom is not a
reductive definition but a catalyst for generative possibilities. It
is infinitely scalable and is both linear and recursive, weaving an
intersecting, multilayered space-time network. Far from induc-
ing the monotony of sameness, such repetitive interactions lead
to complex unpredictable outcomes that are constantly moving
onward in the search for a greater equilibrium.

The purpose of the analysis is to demonstrate the properties or qualities of repetition that define rhythm in order to
reconfigure how music operates on both a micro and macro
scale as the medium we inhabit. In the ancient world, equilibrium was defined by joy. It was a *harmonic* equilibrium. So
what happens if joy is transferred from a harmonic system of
equilibrium to a rhythmic one? What if rhythm defines joy
instead?

For a start, joy is no longer a cosmic resonance for our
lives to amplify as sympathetic vibrations. Compared to such
a closed harmonic universe, rhythm is an infinitely open form
that is simultaneously ordered and contingent, generative and
generous. This is why, unlike the harmonic cosmos, you can't
put a number on rhythm to limit its possibilities. There is no
ratio to stunt its growth, no hierarchy to hold it all together.
Rhythm can't stop repeating itself, as if it has a compulsive addiction to addition. It just keeps counting aloud, playing with
new combinations to generate even more numbers to compute.
Given its infinite capacity for recalculation, rhythm cannot be
knocked off balance—whatever you throw at it. An avant-garde
composer might appropriate "On Running Horse Mountain,"

cut it to bits and redistribute its pieces, then mash it up with snippets of Iron Maiden and Hildegard of Bingen, then randomly inject a jackhammer to punctuate the melodic structure in bizarre places; and the outcome could still be a modern masterpiece. In fact, if we are truly listening, 4′33″ of random sounds in an auditorium would be a coherent experience simply because, as *chance* would have it, repetition is a condition of all environments. We would hear a coherent piece of time that brackets for our attention a tacit dimension of life that holds temporality intact.

There is a parallel with these avant-garde gestures in ancient Chinese thought. According to Laozi, the Dao appears as a "square with no corners"—it is beyond our peripheral vision. It also resonates as a "great tone" beyond our peripheral audition.[5] Finding the yellow bell to order our lives within the rarefied resonance of the Dao is a very Confucian thing to do; it fixes the coordinates—the rites—for human conduct. If we were to imagine the running horses of the "Kangding Love Song" as Confucianists, they would canter in formation from point to point. Music is joy because it keeps us in tune with the Mandate of Heaven. But Daoist thought embraces the same homograph that conjoins music and joy and confounds the Confucian order with rhythmic complexity. The Daoist sage Zhuangzi calls it the "piping of heaven" (*tiānlài* 天籟). This sonic energy emanates from the same source as the Mandate of Heaven, but the order of music is no longer fixated on a single pitch pipe: instead, it is a whirlwind of noise, engulfing everything in its vicinity with its whistling vortices. The force would spur our Kangding horses to gallop wildly across the mountain. Zhuangzi writes:

> The Great Clod [the Earth] belches out breath and its name is wind. So long as it doesn't come forth,

nothing happens. But when it does, then ten thousand hollows begin crying wildly. Can't you hear
them, long drawn out? In the mountain forest that
lash and sway, there are huge trees a hundred span
around with hollows and openings like noses, like
mouths, like ears, like jugs, like cups, like mortars,
like rifts, like ruts. They roar like waves, whistle like
arrows, screech, gasp, cry, wail, moan, and howl,
those in the lead calling out yeee!, those behind
calling out yuuu! In a gentle breeze they answer
faintly, but in a full gale the chorus is gigantic. And
when the fierce wind has passed on, then all the
hollows are empty again. Have you never seen the
tossing and trembling that goes on?[6]

Instead of Confucian propriety, rhythm is a giant burp.
It erupts as a symphony of wind instruments. When the heavens play music, the crevices of our planet become a panoply of
pipes, breathing in and out at different rates, huffing and puff-
ing with transient noises, sometimes at gale force, at other
times a mere breeze, to emphasize the rhythmic articulation
and formal cycles of a great celestial music. The wind improvises. In this soundscape, the trees holler, their orifices wailing with the same guttural force as Big Mama Thornton; the
horses of the "Kangding Love Song" would be the rhythm section, pounding the earth with their hooves as if it were a
drum. This is an indiscriminate music that trembles and tosses
with a vibrating order beyond our peripheral audition—a yellow bell beyond human measure. We are simply caught up in
its rotations. We are lost in music.
    If joy is rhythm, then it is an indestructible condition of
time, whether it's a breeze or a gale. Joy is no longer a fitting

measure, predetermined by a perfectly tuned scale; it is a non-hierarchical, flexible, elastic, and emergent measure of infinite variety. The question "Is music joy?" has a completely different answer: as rhythm—as the "piping of heaven"—joy dances to a different beat.

14

Verbal Abuse

Not everyone welcomes rhythm's invitation to a dance. The opposition between harmony and rhythm is complicated by a third component, language. In the history of music, language is aligned with harmony to stop rhythm from dancing to its own beat. Its disciplinary function is based not on a numerical rationality but on a semantic one. The economy of words, with its accuracy in naming things, prevents music from repetitive hyperinflation. As the psychiatrist Iain McGilchrist suggests, language evolved in humans not so much to communicate as to map and manipulate the world. To name something is to gain power over it with precision and fixity.[1] And true to its evolutionary function, language was employed to keep a tight rein on music's rhythmic effusions. Syllables patrolled rhythm, keeping it in step with their metrical feet. Similarly, words controlled melodies by demanding a clarity of meaning and the redundancy of repetition. Language and harmony are rhythmic suppressants. Their alliance, with its numerical elegance and semantic logic, is both cosmic (harmony) and human (language), leaving rhythm with no significance other than to serve its two masters.

Tonal Language

In many cultures, language is the primary conveyor of content in music, subordinating the melody as its affective dimension. Words come first—quite literally in some cases. Before the mid-nineteenth century, opera composers would write melodies for preexistent texts by librettists. The celebrated librettist Pietro Metastasio (1698–1782), for example, would produce an operatic text, such as *La clemenza di Tito* or *Adriano in Siria*, that many composers would set to music. Rhyme and meter provided a musical undercurrent in these texts, but these devices were attributed to poetry rather than to the fundamentals of music. In language, they intensify meaning, securing a verbal ascendancy over music's inarticulate tones.

Chinese is a tonal language: the meaning of its syllables is dependent on relative pitch. In contrast to Western traditions where poetry is set to music, to make sense of a song in Chinese, often the music must come first: words are added later so that their pitch structure follows the contours of the melody. This is particularly true of the Cantonese dialect spoken in Hong Kong, where the same sound can have nine different tones to distinguish its meaning. In Cantopop, for example, the melody inspires the lyricist; it cannot be the other way around without destroying the flow of words as tone and meaning.[2] So, although the Cantonese dialect is musical (it sings as you speak), any form that requires melodic repetition or rotation cannot be generated by the words; the tones would be randomly distributed by the syllables and cannot comply to a fixed tune. This is why translations of English hymns in Chinese hymnals are a jarring experience for native speakers; the translation may make semantic sense but not musical sense. They look right but sound wrong. For example, the character "Lord" (主) may be forced by the melody to sound exactly like the word for "pig" (豬) in Cantonese—which isn't very kosher.

The philosopher Jean-Jacques Rousseau imagined the origin of music the other way around: language comes first, not music. Or rather, *tonal* language gives rise to music. Rousseau proposed an anthropology in which language and music were joined at birth in Neolithic times, but split off into separate domains to their detriment, mutually impoverishing each other. Their bifurcation divorced sense (words) from feeling (tones), leading to the moral decline of modern civilization.[3] Melody, for Rousseau, is the affective dimension of language; rhythm, in this narrative, is inconsequential. What counts is the ability of tones to instill moral sentiments in words. This tale is a common "origin" narrative. Rousseau's theory of the origins of language is basically an eighteenth-century recycling of the seventeenth-century justification for opera—language and music must be reunited again to empower the agency of words. The same argument would be upcycled in the nineteenth century by Wagner to justify his music dramas.[4] The argument goes like this: In the beginning, human society was operatic. People sang to each other and communicated their feelings in tones. Words were both affective and effective. In the modern world, music and language are divided. Humanity has fallen. So, let us return to opera to reconcile words and tone, and save our civilization from moral decline. In the case of Rousseau, his theory was designed to champion Italian opera as the savior of humanity's moral morass. With its mellifluous melodies, Italian opera infused the text with moral feeling. Such artifice seemed so natural and affective that Rousseau could imagine Neolithic peoples speaking to each other in such Edenic tones. They were noble savages. The wild is naturally tamed by tonal language.

But wait! Italian is not a tonal language. If it were, Italian opera would sound weirdly unnatural, with words pulling in one tonal direction and music another. And besides, Cantonese, with its sing-song phrasing, is not more affective than, say, Italian: the tones in Cantonese are bearers of meaning, not feeling. Had Rousseau sung the Cantonese translations of English hymns he would have arrived at a very different theory: tonal language and music do not necessarily mix.

There is no reason why music should branch off from language except as an ideological claim to identify music as uniquely human: music is from *our* voice. The primacy of melody as speech is simply another attempt to control music by reason and bury rhythm in the name of meaning. But music could just as well have evolved rhythmically from flint-knapping among pre-sapiens hominids, as the musicologist Gary Tomlinson suggests.[5] The prehistorical environment would share the same soundscape as the abacus—the clickety-clack of rocks. "Rock" music, in this case, predates language as rhythmic repetition. Flint-knapping could have taught us how to get into the groove as music's original move. If this is so, then human language is not music's native tongue. This is obvious, given the strenuous attempts by various institutions to control music by language. Whether it is liturgical or operatic reforms, the task is to reduce rhythmic cycles to an economy of nonrepetition: the standard injunction, at least in theory, is to limit one syllable to one tone for one meaning. Verbal clarity in such reforms is the sole function of music; its tones should hug the contours of speech to represent its meaning. Ironically, this binary opposition not only limits music, it also robs language of its affective power, reducing it to a disembedded, functional agency aligned solely with the mind to define the world.

Redundant and Abundant

So humanity, in its hubris as a self-defined species "endowed with language," teaches music to be intelligible. But the results are laughable. Music as rhythm cannot be controlled by language. In fact, rhythmic repetition constantly makes fun of attempts to conceptualize music as representation. If music were a language, its rhythmic coherence would be meaningless; its interminable reiterations would be denounced as incoherent stuttering and its repetitions as redundancy. Music is not language precisely for this reason. If anything, music trains language to jump through its hoops, turning its meaning into nonsense that makes perfect sense as rhythmic phenomena.

For example, you might conceivably say to me, "I really, really like you" to emphasize that you really like me. But to say, "I really, really, really, really, really, really like you," as Carly Rae Jepsen sings in the chorus of her 2015 hit song "I Really Like You," is to be really redundant as far as the use of language is concerned: it feels like you are stalking me with an adverb. A linguistic restraining order is required to save me from your adverbial obsession. However, as music, there is nothing redundant in this "senseless" repetition. It is its very logic and the only reason why, if you were singing, I might listen to your obsession.[6]

Or take the Bay City Rollers' rendition of the 1965 hit "Bye Bye Baby" written by Bob Crew and Bob Gaudio. This is the first song I can remember on the television show *Top of the Pops* when I was growing up in London in the 1970s. There is a reason why this song has stuck in my head since I was nine. The chorus is a nifty feat of melodic engineering (see figure 26). If you follow the contours of the melody in figure 26, you'll see it consists of a permutation of only four notes arranged in a

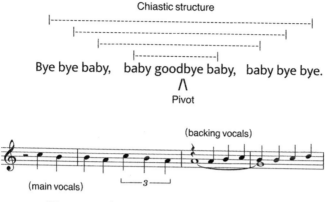

Figure 26. The symmetry of "Bye Bye Baby."

symmetrical order—the first half moves downward and the second half reverses direction. Similarly, if you look at the text, you'll notice it is composed of a concise range of alliterative and rhyming syllables ("bye," "ba," and "be") rotating in various permutations. It is a mini complex system arranged in a chiastic order, pivoting on the nonalliterative word of difference ("goodbye") to mirror the symmetrical contour of the melody.

The words have become music. They form a perfect A|V rhythmic structure. No wonder it was number one on the UK singles charts for six weeks, selling over 1 million copies as the top-selling single of 1975.

This pattern of play is what the anthropologist Alfred Gell would call a "mind trap"; it hooks your attention with its dazzling display of repetition.[7] The chorus is "catchy" because it is a trap. After all, the departing "baby" in "Bye Bye Baby" needs to be caught in the rhythmic web of farewells sung by the lead singer of the Bay City Rollers so that she can't leave her fandom. This is why if you want to hammer home a message

like "I like you," "I hate you," "I miss you," or "I can't stand losing you," it's best to sing it. Language is efficient for evolutionary survival, but sexual attraction, as Darwin points out, is a
risky repetitive business. Just saying "Bye baby" won't do the
trick as far as sexual selection is concerned. She won't come
back. But singing "Bye bye baby baby goodbye baby baby bye
bye" will wriggle in her mind like an earworm and string her
along in a loop that will return her to the arms of the lover to
perpetuate the species.[8]

The mechanism behind this mind trap was illuminated
by the psychologist Diana Deutsch. In a famous experiment,
she looped a recording of her voice saying the phrase "sometimes behave so strangely." At first, the phrase made semantic
sense; the words behaved quite normally. But as the phrase
continued to repeat, she noticed something strange: the repetitive process eventually blurred the semantic focus and turned
her speech into song.[9] The rhythm of the loop created music
out of her words. Repetition makes language musical. So you
don't need tonal language to extract music from speech. Any
language will do! As long as someone repeats a short phrase
enough times it will begin to sing.[10] It becomes music. A song
such as "Bye Bye Baby" simply short-circuits the process and
gets immediately to the hypnotic web of tones to trap the listener with its meaningless patterns.

Unfortunately for Rousseau, this is also the case for Italian opera. Music and language operate on different planes. This
is most evident in the "patter songs" often found in comic operas, where tongue-twisting syllables are rattled off at speed.
They patter because they are primarily rhythmic. The most
famous example is probably the aria "Largo al factotum"
from Rossini's *Barber of Seville*. This aria is a highly evolved
version of the clickety-clack of flint-knapping hominids. The
brilliance of the syllables spouting forth from the tenor's lips

is subordinate to the rhythmic mind trap underlying the aria. The audience are bedazzled and caught in its web. This is not a web of meaning. No one really cares what is being sung. Not even the text of the aria seems to care since it often degenerates into a general "lalalalala." In fact, the only word you clearly remember is when the pattering suddenly stops to announce a term with no meaning, a name made up by the playwright Pierre Beaumarchais for the main character: "Figaro." In this moment, it is as if Rossini wanted to demonstrate the rhythmic process behind the music as a recursive earworm that spirals in on itself in ever-diminishing rhythmic circles. In typological form, it would look something like this:

Figaro Figaro Figaro Figaro Figaro Figaro Figaro Figaro Figaro

The name Figaro in this instance is music, not language, since it is a made-up name with no intrinsic meaning or heritage. Aptly, the kind of music where a short melodic unit is spun out in repetitive form is called figural music. Music is not language. It is essentially figural. Like this.

Figural Figural Figural Figural Figural Figural Figural Figural Figural

The figural in "Figaro" is precisely what music means: it means nothing but repetition.

Sing for Joy

What, then, is the relation between music and language? Language and music are separate and autonomous systems, but they share something of each other's qualities, enabling a certain chemistry between them. Song (including spoken forms such as rap), in combining both systems, attests to this elective affinity. However, neither language nor music should be prioritized as the source of the other. They neither authenticate nor complete each other, as if their fusion supplies what is lacking or reunites what is lost. Rather, when they intersect something *new* is released: a *universal particular.* The particularly human in language is made universally vibrant in music.

As we explored in the previous chapter, if figural music is nothing more than repetition, then it has the potential to be "everything" because everything in the universe repeats. So, imagine dropping a word in "everything." The "figural" in music engulfs the "literal" in language. When we sing a word, we sing for joy, because the verbal sign is made to vibrate with a rhythm that ripples outward. It becomes ecstatic. Song is always a prayer of some kind. Whether it's an operatic diva in full blast or a mother cooing softly to her baby, singing is the full-*bodied* amplification of meaning that resonates beyond what can be said, as if to connect the humanly circumscribed sign with the wider patterns of the *logos*.[11] In song, the shared meaning of language becomes the shared rhythm of music, embodied and embedded in a generative and generous ecology, connecting humans to each other and to their surroundings in ever-widening circles. Under such conditions, language no longer just makes sense: it makes sense of being—of a human being in time.

Song as a universal particular is not some philosophical paradox for you to think about. It is something you do. Song is environmentally embodied grooviness made articulate. It is the counterpoint of a social rhythm dancing in time with the universe. It is a way of participating. So we should stop thinking for a moment. Sing and boogie!

15
Best Possible World

Bodily Rhythm

Wait! Your moves have been censored! If you recall, before we got into the groove, we were discussing music as a discipline. Harmony, with its ascetic deployment of numbers, and language, with its puritanical economy of syllables, are the disciplinary forces that have traditionally kept rhythm bounded in music. They tie its repetitive cycles down with words and pitch, tightening the melodic knot with a harmonic grip. It's all about propriety. So all that boogying needs to come under strict control.

Of course, this has never worked. Despite the elaborate attempts to control rhythm, neither numbers nor words can master its generative processes. In fact, rhythm seems to master you! It's a trap, after all. And this is precisely its problem. Instead of propriety, rhythm is inappropriate, because it appropriates the human body, causing involuntary movements to tic with its cycles. This improper reflex—known as entrainment—makes you want to dance. First you tap your toes, then you wiggle your body, and the next thing you know, you are gyrating like Elvis. This is why in some cultures music

and dance are inseparable: music moves you. The last thing
music-theoretical control freaks want are involuntary movements operating the system. As far as they are concerned, reason is no longer in charge of the body. With rhythm taking
control, words become meaningless; the mind is empty; an
external pulse has taken possession of the will; and self-
governance is overthrown.

So rhythm is precisely what is dangerous in a word-
bound and harmonically controlled universe: it is infectious,
bodily, generative, uncontrollable, uncontainable, and can
knock an ascetic order off balance in a beat. If rhythm were
joy, it would be the "wrong" type of joy; it would be too playful, too effusive, too brainless for that killjoy kind of joy that
keeps things perfectly in order. Rhythm just doesn't fit. It is
without form. It doesn't want to align itself to the smooth crystalline finish of a harmonic cosmos. Rhythm is unruly.

But this is only because rhythm's fittingness is of another
order altogether. Its formlessness is not a lack of order. Its impropriety is not a negation of rules. Rather, its form and fit belong to an alternative universe invisible to both harmonic and
linguistic paradigms. It is not so much that rhythm plunges
you into some formless abyss of interminable repetition where
you are merely a puppet of entrainment: rather, its formlessness is a *form* of freedom. Its unruliness has a rule. In fact, its
unfittingness fits perfectly with the equilibrium of joy.

Joy, if you recall, is a general, open form. It is the underlying relational framework in which all positive emotions operate. Rhythmic joy is also open, but it is paradoxically a
formless structure in that its fit exceeds its size, being always
"more than" rather than "just right." Its abstraction is a relation of generosity—it is not just the right measure but a good
measure. It is an unforced rhythm rather than a perfect tuning. In this sense, joy is the capacious and flexible structure

that Roberts describes, but its relational properties is not simply the perception of a situation that "satisfies a concern," that is, a harmonious fit; joy is a *disproportional fit* that far exceeds the exact proportions of the beautiful.[1] The surprise of joy, then, is not just in its serendipitous fit but in its effusive surplus that is both generative and generous. For the virtuous ascetic, this would be an act of impropriety, an offense against a well-tempered life in which all things in moderation should keep joy sober.

But what makes sobriety possible as a joyful order? In the Confucian tradition, entrainment is kept in line with courtly comportment by ensuring that a strictly measured music choreographs the rites. The movements are highly formalized. Similarly, in *De musica,* Augustine deploys metrical feet to keeps human feet in step with godly propriety. But for both the sage and the saint, the harmonious order is only joyful because a counter-rhythm stirs beneath its formal propriety. Beneath that placid surface, there is a suppressed undercurrent, or what the philosopher Jacques Derrida would call a supplement that, far from being a secondary effect, is an original point that bubbles to the surface and ripples outward. The calm surface is actually dynamic. The supplement turns out to be the source of joy that the harmonic surface conceals.[2] Hence, despite their attempts to harness music with strict measures, both Confucius and Augustine were often overwhelmed by its joy. Music affected them to such an extent that the sage could not recognize the taste of meat for three months because he was overcome by joy, and the saint was reduced to uncontrollable weeping while singing and swaying in church.[3] Their joy was bodily. It was involuntary, a matter of appetite and unbridled emotion. From this perspective of excess, the musical order they imposed on ceremony and ritual was never designed to be an external formality to expunge a rogue element. It was

always a form of desire. A life well lived is not the outer shell
of harmony. Its rituals are not simply a rigid order. The good
life requires a disruptive overflow to authenticate and animate
the form from within. The "piping of heaven," as Zhuangzi calls
it, secretly breathes its immeasurable force within Confucian
conduct; the unspeakable joy of the Holy Spirit blusters loudly
within Augustinian propriety. The name of this abundance is
rhythm. Without this inner dance animating the body and
cultivating its desires, joy's affect would merely be a stoic resolve.
The body registers joy's real presence.

Hairline Fracture

This sense of continual abundance points to the key difference
between a harmonic cosmos and a rhythmic cosmos. A rhythmic order is indestructible, whereas a harmonic order is
highly precarious. Rhythm *gives*—in both senses of the word.
It "gives" as an act of donation, giving more than enough; and
it has "give" as a condition of flexibility, giving way to difference. This is because rhythm, as repetition, is both infinite and
cohesive; the additive units stick together whatever is thrown
at them to disrupt the process. It is open to intervention. The
disruptive slash (|) between A | V is not an option but a condi-
tion of its identity. Disruption is neither absorbed nor rejected.
Rather, disruption strengthens music's cohesive powers and
generates new structures of rhythmic integration, as any composer who has worked with a drone, an ostinato, or drum
track would know. Rhythm is elastic and capacious in its tolerance for the dissonant "other"—in fact, it thrives on it. The
"other," however massive or divergent, cannot throw it off balance, because there is always time to recalculate the pattern
and riff on the difference. As with joy's ability to remain stead-

fast under miserable circumstances, rhythm has a high pain threshold. It suffers gladly.

A harmonic universe, on the other hand, is dangerously fragile precisely because it has to be perfectly proportioned. The slightest imprecision and the whole thing caves in. Tuning this universe is always a task on the verge of breakdown since the crystalline spheres can crack at any moment. In many ways, the history of Western music theory is the elaborate attempt to paper over the cracks, leading to an inevitable crisis. The history is complex and highly technical, but the culprit is a hairline fracture known as the Pythagorean comma (a ratio of 531,441:524,288) that spoiled what would otherwise have been a beautiful relationship between simple integers.

To understand this harmonic crisis, let's return briefly to the tuning system in the bamboo forest. For "On Running Horse Mountain," we only needed to cut fives pipes to tune the scale required by the pentatonic melody. If we continued spiraling upward at intervals of a fifth by cutting more pipes, we would eventually return to the first frequency—the yellow bell—but many octaves higher. Theoretically, we would have closed the system and tuned all twelve notes of the chromatic scale. The first and last notes should be perfectly in tune with each other. Empirically, however, they would be out of tune—the circle does not quite connect. It is misaligned by a ratio of 531,441:524,288—the Pythagorean comma. Nature, it seems, is not in tune with its own equation.[4] It will keep spiraling in on itself because its tuning is always slightly "off key."

Who would have imagined that this hairline imperfection would put the entire cosmos in peril? But this crack came increasingly under stress as composers demanded more complex harmonic structures. And once there was insufficient empirical support for the mathematical speculations, the

Pythagorean comma was prized open and the entire edifice collapsed. It is hard to put an exact date on this harmonic slippage. The cosmos went out of tune unevenly over the course of two centuries, but by the end of the eighteenth century, harmony no longer upheld the universe.[5]

Changing Temperament

For the sociologist Max Weber this moment marked the beginning of musical modernity and the end of an enchanted world. Once the Pythagorean cosmos was detuned, the ancient magic was gone, and modern humans simply divvied up the octave into twelve equal intervals, disregarding perfect integer relations for a totally rationalized system of measurement known as equal temperament. Equal temperament is not a state of equilibrium: it is an equal division of the octave, with a bureaucratic formula ($12\sqrt{2}$) devised by human reason and imposed over the ratios of nature. Weber describes it as a form of imprisonment. Modern music is shackled in "dragging chains," as if its equal division of the octave resembles the bars of an "iron cage," the image that Weber famously uses to describe the bureaucratic structure of Western society. Modern tuning, then, is an efficient machine—a monotonous equality with a "dulling effect."[6] It is joyless. It works, but means nothing. It is a mathematical fact without value in the world. It is a forced fit.[7]

Equal temperament reflects a modern world in which humans are no longer the instruments through which joy operates but an instrumental force that rationalizes the cosmos. But this holds true only if music is fundamentally harmony. If tuning is not the basis for music, then the detuning of the cosmos does not undermine its joy. The magic may be gone from the Pythagorean numbers, but this was a system too perfect for its own good anyway. Its self-destruction under the pressure of modern rationality does not threaten the foundation of music but reveals a more fundamental order that our fixation with harmony has prevented us from perceiving.

The rationalization of tuning does not clamp music in "dragging chains." In fact, this makes no sense, since the "dulling effect" of equal temperament has resulted in one of the most vibrant systems of music making—tonality. Without this system, there is no Bach or Beyoncé. If joy is fundamentally rhythm, then the arrival of equal temperament, however functional and mechanistic, cannot rob modernity of cosmic joy. Rhythm does not promise a perfect world. Perfection merely keeps you in tune, but rhythm keeps you in time. Harmony predetermines your position in the cosmos, but rhythm constantly repositions you in a kaleidoscopic environment. To keep time with rhythm is to engage in a co-creative process, a homeostasis of contingent possibilities that resonates across the universe. This is not a perfect world but what Leibniz would call "a best possible world": *rhythm makes the best of what is possible in any given state.*

Leibniz was ridiculed, most famously by Voltaire in his satire *Candide* (1759), for proposing such a Panglossian world; such optimism was naïve, to say the least, especially in the aftermath of the Great Lisbon earthquake of 1755 that brought the goodness of creation—if not of God himself—into question. Leibniz did not live in the aftermath of the Lisbon earthquake, but he did live in the aftermath of the Thirty Years' War (1616–48), which left Europe decimated and divided: he was no bespectacled academic seeing the world through rose-tinted lenses. Leibniz did not propose a perfect world, which, as with the Pythagorean cosmos, would collapse with the slightest fracture. The best possible world for Leibniz remains joyful in all circumstances, however earth-shattering the situation. Such joy, for Leibniz, is only harmonic in a rhythmic sense. And ironically, the very rhythms he refers to are only made possible by the very tuning that Weber attributed to the disenchantment of the cosmos: equal temperament. Leibniz's ears were attuned to the tonal system of baroque music, which relied increasingly on the equal semitones to structure complex rhythmic cycles. He did not worry about the perfect intervals of ancient tuning. Instead of hearing the grid of an iron cage, he heard a complex system latent with infinite combinatorial possibilities. The tonal system created a new sense of linear motion, driven by harmonic forces that resolved its rhythmic waves ineluctably toward cadences. These rhythmic structures are shaped by common harmonic progressions—or what Leibniz would call preestablished harmonies.[8] They are "progressions" because they progress in time, rotating ineluctably to their destination in a process akin to the chord changes in "Ball 'n' Chain Blues." Their motion regulates "similarity in variety," enabling the musical elements to constantly count, recount, and recalculate their patterns in ever-new ways. As rhythm, music discloses what Leibniz defines as a best possible world: the balance between the maximum variety and the simplest laws.[9] To progress harmoniously in this order is to relate to a dynamic, infinitely complex universe.

Leibniz defined this cosmic rhythm as joy. "Similarity in diversity," he states, is the harmony of joy. It is a result of "taking delight in the happiness of another," that is, an inward-out movement that attunes itself to the order of the world: "All happiness is harmonious."[10] But there is nothing perfect about this joy. It is a relation of opposites bristling with "dirty" frequencies and gritty processes. At its "best," harmony is already differentiated and riddled with dissonances. After all, the new sound of baroque music—what Claudio Monteverdi defined as the "second practice" at the beginning of the seventeenth century—loosened the law of dissonance for the sake of expressive freedom. The delight of baroque harmony is founded on its friction. Aptly, "baroque" means "irregularly shaped," so baroque harmony is not going to be a smooth ride. Similarly, joy, for Leibniz, is the rhythm of friction; it is riddled with affliction, suspended by suffering, and marred by evil. Its harmonious order included the "joy of martyrdom," which is not possible in a perfect world but is perfectly possible in a best possible world, particularly one in which the suffering of God forms the crux of its harmonic progression.[11] Joy, then, is no momentary feeling for Leibniz; it is a preestablished disposition that generates a boundless optimism. Joy's gritty rhythms will result in a pearl of harmonious radiance.[12] For Leibniz, music is joy because it discloses a complex and irregular timing that ultimately reflects the divine providence of the universe.

The philosopher Gilles Deleuze (1925–95) realized that for Leibniz a new musical system in the seventeenth century occasioned a new way to reimagine the harmony of the universe. Cosmic harmony was not merely a remnant of a former order, remaining in orbit as a quaint formality at the very moment of its collapse: rather, Leibniz's musical analogies upcycled a vestigial tradition, retrofitting a Pythagorean relic into the new engine of baroque music. Deleuze intuitively describes this music as simultaneously vertical (harmonic) and horizontal (rhythmic); to compose baroque music is to operate diagonally across the grid, he says, not as a series of coordinates but as a line of difference doodling outside the points. Baroque harmony is not fixed. And neither is the universe it describes. Its rhythms ripple freely across the cosmos. Deleuze pictures the Leibnizian universe as a fabric of cascading folds that curve, curl, crinkle, and crease in a constant flux of becoming. In this universe, we are rhythmic strands woven in the billowing fabric of time.

Inspired by Leibniz, Deleuze and his coauthor, the psychoanalyst Félix Guattari, would assemble their own cosmic machinery with the new music of the twentieth century, reframing the concept of "similarity in variety" as "repetition and difference." For Deleuze and Guattari, as for Leibniz, everything is rhythm. But the avant-garde music of their day was not governed by the pulsations of the tonal system: Deleuze and Guattari heard a new rhythm encoded by cycles that constantly came into being without preordained closures or metrical constraints. This was an off-grid music composed of floating sound blocks, akin to the living stones of a dispersed self-organizing temple, except there is no God for Deleuze but the unanchored system itself.

These blocks are machines emancipated from meter. They are oscillations that calibrate time at a molecular and modular level, knotting the divergent forces of chaos into a spontaneous, emergent, dynamic order. Their rhythms flutter across the entire spectrum of cosmic time, causing the chain of being to fluctuate. Deleuze and Guattari call these rhythms *ritournelles* (translated in English as "refrains"). As the name implies, these are rhythms that turn. But their cycles are not a regular clocking of time; they are asymmetrical, indefinite, incommensurable, nonidentically repetitive fluctuations that operate as creative, relational forces. They literally make time and fabricate space, opening new possibilities and assembling order on the go. Given such ecstatic, open-ended fecundity in the making of time, Deleuze and Guattari declare: "Music is never tragic, music is joy."[13]

The End of Time

Twenty-five hundred years after the Confucian *Book of Rites* declared, "Music is Joy," Deleuze and Guattari released the same statement, seemingly with no prior knowledge of their ancient predecessor. But the path from the first to the second statement is divergent. The joy of the *ritournelle* is not a ruler that keeps difference in proportion like the unbending notes of Confucian rituals. To hear the joy of the *ritournelle*, you have to attend to the music of Olivier Messiaen. Deleuze, as with his affinity with Leibniz, was drawn to Messiaen's music; and the composer's treatise on his own compositional processes, *Technique de mon langage musical* (1944), influenced the philosopher's conceptions of rhythm.

Messiaen's reformulation of time in music is ironically inscribed in a work that declares the end of time. The *Quartet for the End of Time* consists of eight movements inspired by a passage in the tenth chapter of the Revelation of St. John: "And I saw another mighty angel coming down from heaven, wrapped in a cloud, with a rainbow on his head . . . saying 'There will be no more Time.'" Its premier in a Nazi prisoner of war camp ranks as one of the most legendary performances of twentieth-century music. As Messiaen recounts:

> Conceived and composed during my captivity, the *Quartet for the End of Time* was premiered in Stalag VIII A, on January 1941. It took place in Görlitz, in Silesia, in dreadful cold. Stalag was buried in snow. We were 30,000 prisoners (French for the most part, with a few Poles and Belgians). [The] cello had only 3 strings; the keys of my upright piano remained lowered when depressed. . . . It's on this piano, with my three musicians, dressed in the

oddest way—I was wearing a bottle-green suit of a
Czech soldier—completely tattered, with wooden
clogs large enough for the blood to circulate despite
the snow underfoot . . . that I played my *Quartet
for the End of Time,* before an audience of 5000
people. The most diverse classes of society were
mingled: farmers, factory works, intellectuals, professional servicemen, doctors, priests. Never before
have I been listened to with such attention and
understanding.[14]

Aptly, Messiaen described himself as a "composer and
rhythmician" who measures the joy of the created order as a
matter of faith: "I am convinced that joy exists," he states. "I
am convinced that the invisible exists *more* than does the visible. Joy is beyond pain, the invisible is beyond the visible and
beauty is beyond horror."[15] The quartet explores time as the
rhythm of joy.

In Stalag VIII A, Messiaen had time to theorize time. The
monotony of time in captivity inspired him to imagine its freedom. The rhythmic freedom described in his treatise and illustrated by his quartet was forged under Leibnizian conditions
of extreme dissonance. Here was a "best possible world" that
was incomprehensible to those held captive within its walls:
and yet at the premier, a music that was by all accounts incomprehensible to the audience in terms of difficulty left its
listeners in stunned silence. Something had happened. Time
happened—a *ritournelle.*

For Messiaen, this floating sound block makes present
the temporality of the Christ-event within the prison block—a
special administrative region within Hitler's regime. In fact,
the music of the fifth and eighth movements on the eternity
and immortality of Jesus is based on the prologue of John's

Gospel. They voice the creative *logos* "in the beginning," both before time and in time within the context of the end of time. Emerging from the chaos of Stalag VIII A, Messiaen's *ritournelle* knotted a microcosm of order into being—a time of creation and new creation.

"I love time," says Messiaen, "because it is the starting point of all creation."[16] One beat is like the big bang: it "is the birth of time," he states. Two beats "is the birth of rhythm."[17] From this minimum condition of repetition, Messiaen generated a cosmic vision in the quartet.

The first movement, "Crystal Liturgy," is akin to one of Deleuze and Guattari's floating blocks of space-time. In fact, the block is literally a flocking pattern, since the materials are held aloft by birdsong in the clarinet and violin lines (imitating the blackbird and nightingale), and motored by independent asynchronous rhythmic cycles in the cello and piano. The movement is a sound vessel fitted with all the baroque complexity of Leibniz and the quirky machinery of Deleuze to free time from meter. This freedom, however, is strictly organized, consisting of what Messiaen calls "non-retrogradable rhythms." These are palindromic structures of duration that are the same forward and backward. They loop time as a kind of moving still point, as if to suspend time as an eternal moment. But these highly balanced durations are internally asymmetrical, consisting of molecular grains of time equivalent to adding a "Pythagorean comma" to rhythmic units to deregulate meter by rendering everything disproportionate: or, more appropriately, this is a system of *disproportionate proportion* that never just fits because it is always "more than enough." There is always something added, "a note, a rest, or a dot," as Messiaen illustrates in the preface of the published score (see figure 27).

For Messiaen, rhythms are indestructible, unlimited, and generative: they rotate at different speeds, on different scales,

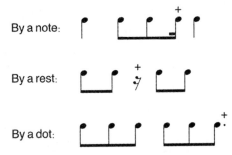

Figure 27. The technique of rhythmic asymmetry
from Messiaen's "Brief Theory of My Rhythmic
Language" in the preface to the score of his
Quartet for the End of Time.

simultaneously subatomic and cosmic. They operate as objective laws in a universe that are only silent because their
rhythms transcend the human ear. For the composer, music
makes this order audible. In "Crystal Liturgy," for example,
Messiaen gives voice to the very plenitude of time itself: the
music, he says, represents the "harmonious silence of heaven."
It is 4′33″ sounding in all its fullness.

A Best Possible Concert

As I write, protest and pandemic have trapped Hong Kong in
an iron cage. The riots in 2019 and the plague of COVID-19
forged a double-edged crisis that unleashed a reactionary force.
Containment is the current state of affairs: we are locked down
by an invisible virus that lays siege to the city and a security
law that polices dissent. The special administrative region of
Hong Kong is not so special; it is merely administrative, regulating its exceptional status in the name of conformity. What
was "special" about Hong Kong has been disenchanted. Of
course, everything looks the same as before. Hong Kong is still

beautiful. Life continues. But "time" has changed. The hustle and bustle of the city with its clickety-clack rhythms squiggling like wild diagonals are now locked with a single click to a grid with no give or grace.

During this time, the *Quartet for the End of Time* was programmed at The University of Hong Kong as a counter-rhythm to the joyless monotony of the region. It was a glimmer in dark times, a flickering rhythm that could easily be snuffed out. But it is precisely this weakness that is its strength. For Deleuze and Guattari, a *ritournelle* is like whistling in the dark or singing under the breath. It is not a heroic act but the feeble song of a child or of a mother sounding a solitary rhythm of comfort and courage in the midst of fear. It is no braver than singing "Twinkle, twinkle little star." "Music is pervaded by every minority," write Deleuze and Guattari, "yet composes an immense power."[18] It can transport "Twinkle, twinkle little star" to the starry heavens, releasing its rhythms beyond the boundaries of fear.

The performance of Messiaen's quartet in Hong Kong was not a heroic intervention but a feeble song. It almost didn't happen. It took place in its own palindromic still point, between two back-to-back typhoons that canceled everything in their wake except the performance. It seemed to be an allegory of our need to compose a nonretrogradable rhythm in the vortex of our times. We needed equilibrium. The performance took place in 2021 to mark the eightieth anniversary of the quartet's premier in the Nazi prison camp; the year also marked the fortieth anniversary of the Music Department at the University of Hong Kong. Of course, at the time it seemed pointless to celebrate either event under such depressing circumstances. If anything, it felt inappropriate—not fitting. In some ways, the performance was a faint echo of its premier, under conditions in which the words "best possible world" would appear naïve if not an insult. And yet something happened. There was a palpable silence in the concert hall as the last note lingered, seemingly forever. It was as if the "harmonious silence of heaven" depicted in the first movement arrived as an experience at the close of the quartet. The plenitude of time hung in the air like the "unalterable peace" that the last movement symbolizes. It wasn't nice. The audience were almost as perplexed by the music as the original crowd of prisoners. It was a difficult experience. This was not something that could be consumed like auditory cheesecake. "My music is not 'nice,'" asserts Messiaen, adding: "I am convinced that joy exists," as if to contradict the word *nice* with its opposite—*joy.* There is nothing nice about joy. Joy is beyond what is visible, continues Messiaen. Or, in musical terms, beyond the audible— not because it is not there, but because it is ineffable.[19]

The silence at the end of the performance is not in the score. It is an extra rhythm, a good measure, that overflows the time bounded by the final bar line. It seems to grasp something incomprehensible, "beyond sorrow," "beyond horror," beyond what we see around us. The silence that evening was not "just right" but promised something "more than enough," "more than fitting," an added value, a donation, something disproportional. Joy.

IV

A Good Measure

Joy is beyond sorrow, beauty is beyond horror.
—OLIVIER MESSIAEN

16

Joyride

Into the Sunset

We had set ourselves the ambitious task of retrofitting ancient music to the engine of the modern world, in the hope of driving into the sunset in a state of joy. To simplify the process, the task was broken down into three steps:

1. Retrofit ancient joy to modern living.
2. Retrofit ancient music theory to modern music.
3. Connect the two retrofitted objects—joy and music—to modern science and reposition them in the cosmos.

With regard to the first step—retrofitting ancient joy to modern living—we plugged cosmic joy into neuropsychology, and synchronized the well-tempered ratios of the former with the biochemical regulations of the latter. Harmony and homeostasis comingled. The top-down joy of ancient science and the bottom-up joy of modern science met in their mutual pursuit for optimal equilibrium. Ancient joy lives on today as a "balanced" lifestyle.

With regard to the second step—retrofitting ancient music theory to modern music—we subsumed ancient harmony under rhythm to modernize its timing. Being in time rather than being in tune reanimated the ancient ratios from their static state to become mobile calculators. Its numbers were no longer silently suspended in parallel but arranged in series, counting its repetitive patterns aloud like an abacus—clickety-clack, clickety-clack, clickety-clack. So harmony is now redefined as a flexible weave of coordinated rhythms. As such, it resembles the music we listen to today. We can get into its groove—whether it's Messiaen or the blues, Bach or Beyoncé.

Finally, the two retrofitted objects were connected to modern science, repositioning joy and music in the cosmos. By reconceiving ancient harmony as rhythm, we returned music to the cosmos because everything in the universe repeats. The cosmos exists musically on a sliding scale of infinitely graded repetition. We may not be able to tap our toes to its cycles, for much of this scale is beyond our hearing range, but we are embedded in its music. We are part of its rhythm. Since the entire universe consists of rhythms-in-relation, joy's well-tempered past can be revived as a rhythmic rather than a harmonic equilibrium. The universe and the order of joy can reconnect again through music. In so doing, rhythmic homeostasis rebooted music theory as an intergalactic music theory of everything.[1] Its jurisdiction is no longer limited to "great works" composed by "great masters." Instead, great music is everywhere. It is the temporal operation of space-time. It forms the background hum of the universe in which human music is but its foreground disclosure.

By connecting these three steps, ancient music has been retrofitted to the modern world. As in the past so it is today: music can be joy again. My succinct question, posed on the opening page of the book, no longer sounds nice and negligible, but connects to the biggest concept of the ancient world and brings it up to speed with the modern world. Music is joy. Mission accomplished. We can head into the sunset for a beautiful ending.

Test Drive

But before we drive off in our retrofitted machine, we should familiarize ourselves with some of the new gadgets on the dashboard. There is a difference in the way music and joy relate; for a start, the new system requires a speedometer. Music is no longer the joy of a beautifully proportioned universe that never changes; it is now a rhythmic cycle that discloses joy as the coherent fabric of space-time. Time is rhythmic computation. It changes on the go. Once in the vehicle, you'll notice the speedometer is not measuring time over distance but seems to be making time as we drive. The space outside appears to adapt to our steering, expanding and contracting with our every move. Clearly, in this retrofitted vehicle, time isn't what Benedict Anderson defines as the "homogeneous, empty" medium we are normally used to in the modern world; we are not driving on some featureless surface, coordinated by timetables to keep us on track.[2] Our retrofitted joyride is an off-road, off-grid, freewheeling spin. So, as we drive in this vehicle and gaze through the windshield, we see the cosmos in a completely different way. At first it seems like a distortion. Things are out of shape. This is a fuzzy, unquantized world with no straight lines. The first reaction would be to check the GPS navigation system, but there isn't one in this new vehicle because it is useless. There are no fixed coordinates. The coherence of this universe is not a map but a well-tempered *temporality* in which all things fluctuate in homeostatic relation. Its beauty is neither an ancient fit too perfect for its own good, nor a modern grid imposed on empty time, but a giving and forgiving fit. The speedometer registers a *good* measure rather than an exact measure—a disproportionate proportion.

It's been a long and winding road to get this far in the book, but we have now arrived at an answer. If you recall, this book began with a question that should not be asked: "Is music joy?" It was seemingly a bad question—irrelevant, outmoded, and obviously flawed. "Music is not joy," we concluded; if anything, it is "miserable" today. But this was only the case because the context of the modern world blinded us from seeing what was obviously true in the ancient world: music is joy. Now that we have retrofitted ancient thought as fuel for the modern engine, the question returns with renewed significance. And the answer? A joyride in a magnificent machine through a disproportionately proportional universe. And *WOW!* It drives beautifully!

Tuning the Engine

But what kind of an answer is this? The idea that the beautiful is a disproportional proportion is an *aesthetic* answer. This might seem inconsequential: isn't aesthetics simply about art appreciation? Or the analysis of beauty? That's "nice." But "nice" only gets us back to square one: "Is music joy?" returns as a question with a "nice" answer.

But aesthetics is anything but "nice." If you recall, Nietzsche, in *The Birth of Tragedy,* justifies life "as an aesthetic phenomenon."[3] For the philosopher Martin Heidegger art discloses truth: it is a way of experiencing the mysterious and hidden forces that ground our existence. This is not a truth we master but one we inhabit. Aesthetics is a kind of knowing that hovers at the fringes, just beyond our reach.[4] It is less a box we open than an opening we fall through. If all this sounds farfetched, let's go to the movies. Aesthetics has a similar function to film music. Often, this music is not something you attend to at the cinema. It is not the star of the show, but seemingly a background murmur, a mood, an unobtrusive sentient experience at the periphery of knowledge. If the eye is reason, collecting, organizing, and analyzing the visual data, then music is the marginal, supplementary knowledge of the ear. It surrounds us like an atmosphere. We are hardly aware of its presence. We feel it rather than know it. But—as is frequently pointed out—if we remove the music from a horror movie, the condition of horror disappears. The suspense is gone. The images are no longer so scary. What was seemingly an ambient murmur turns out to be the very condition of experience: the music orientates the meaning of what is seen and changes how we know things.[5] If you change the music, it changes everything.

We may not be aware of its ambient presence, but aesthetic knowledge conditions the way we experience the world and often grooms our behaviors. So to arrive at an aesthetic answer is to arrive at an orientation that shapes our relation to the cosmos. It changes everything, precisely because music is a background hum. It is everywhere. As the Pythagoreans were wont to say, we are so used to the harmony of the cosmos that we can no longer hear it. We tacitly indwell aesthetic knowledge. In Uexküll's evolutionary terms, we are melodies interwoven in the musical biospheres or *Umwelten* of our planet. Life is aesthetic because we evolve with the music we feel around us.[6] Without a soundtrack for meaningful engagement, there would be no feel for life.

This is why music is a disclosure: in enabling us to keep time with the universe, it reveals something about the world we inhabit. But this is only if we truly listen. If the answer "Music is joy" is merely a propositional statement, it would just be "nice." Nothing would change. Time would remain homogeneous and empty. No disclosure, no big deal. But as an *aesthetic* answer, it should change everything. Music-as-joy modulates the background hum of the modern world.

We've spent many pages tuning the engine to produce a disproportionately proportioned frequency. If this is only learned in theory and not lived in practice, then the ancient fuel in the modern tank has no combustion to move the contemporary world forward. We would be reading the manual and not driving the vehicle. To have any mileage, the answer needs to provide a moral orientation toward the world, repositioning our relation with all that surrounds us. A "forgiving fit" is not just a play on words but has to find the give—the surplus capacity—to forgive. Similarly, a "good measure" has to find the goods to supply the good life. Only in this way would the drive in our retrofitted machine be beautiful.

Speed Trap

So what does it mean for the rhythm of joy to be a disproportionate proportion in the world? How does this retrofitted concept adapt to the current forces that shape our modern condition? Does it make any difference? In the final part of the book, we return to the ancient world for some illumination on these questions. This is partly an exercise in equilibrium. Having just hauled the past into the present to arrive at a new concept of the beautiful, what is new can now learn from the past in order to supplement its application.

But this is also an exercise in humility, because the present offers little illumination on how something disproportionate can be beautiful. It is not that the modern world is deficient in comparison with the ancient order (there are many things *not* to retrofit from the past). Progress is real; but because the modern world breaks with the past for its definition, it forgets that its advances are as much dependent on ancient values and as they from their rupture. In fact, Augustine's notion of inner desire is often considered an explanatory source for the formation of the modern will; similarly, Confucian philosophy was so admired by European intellectuals in the seventeenth and eighteenth centuries for its natural reason and harmonious governance that the sage was virtually the "patron saint" of the Enlightenment.[7] Today, the sleek anonymous sheen of modern efficiency wants to erase the gnarled and knotted conditions of ancient wisdom. But the new engine, for all its sophistication, may lose its grip on reality without ancient friction giving it some traction. So, the test drive in our retrofitted machine will introduce some grit and grime, and probably some ancient traffic offenses as we cruise the modern highway of aesthetic thought.

Here's the problem: living in "homogeneous, empty time," for all its utility, can never be beautiful. It has no proportions. Its "flatness" is efficient but it isn't benign. In fact, it is meaningless. There are no rites or sacred days to mark its cycles.[8] Empty time is a medium of coincidences. There is no inherent order to hold things altogether. It seems that the best way to negotiate this featureless surface is to impose a grid to coordinate space-time and drive as fast as possible. Frictionless speed is the joy of an empty terrain. After all, the emergence of "homogeneous, empty time" came with the invention of trains, planes, and automobiles. Zooming across the globe required careful measurement to coordinate calendars, timetables, time zones, and schedules. Time is the logistics for maximum speed. To paraphrase Augustine, in the modern world, travel is the science of measuring well. Unlike the "Way" of

Confucius, which seeks harmony rather than homogeneity, modern travel masters time to assert dominance over nature. Its "Way" is both a highway and an expressway.

A straight line is the best way to travel as fast and as efficiently as possible. It's exhilarating. In fact, speed captures the joy of modern freedom. The sense of effortless power when you press the accelerator and feel the wind blowing in your hair is the freedom of movement. It is as if you've mastered the terrain, shredding the earth as vast tracks of territory are rolled up under your wheels. But the freedom of movement is also a strategy of war: it is the liberation of speed as pure power and dominance. As the cultural theorist Paul Virilio points out, the freedom of movement leads to "nothing other than the unleashing of violence."[9] And its joy—if you recall the speeding paperweights on Beethoven's desk—is one of advancing victory. From a distance, the machinery of war may look beautiful, like boys' toys, but when a missile screams above your head and plummets to the ground at shattering speed, the disproportional force does not look so proportionate, despite the precision engineering. Forget the beautiful. You need to survive. The fitting and the joyful need to be replaced by the fittest and the fastest just to stay alive in such a world.

So let's slow down and pause before taking our wheels for a modern spin. Our test drive vehicle needs to pull over for a moment to avoid the speed trap.

17

Not So Fast

Taken for a Ride

Retrofitted machines are quirky. By definition, retro*fitted* things don't quite fit modern practices and patterns. They are slightly out of sync, not quite in the right time, a bit "retro." In reorientating the past and present, they fit into neither. Instead, a new relation emerges. This is why the beautiful looks different—quirkily different—through the windshield of our vehicle, requiring a new category to steer a world where things no longer fit the norm.

So, what is the norm? Beauty is traditionally defined as a matter of proportion—a "just rightness" that is always fitting. Any excess verges toward the unnerving or threatening—what Kant would categorize aesthetically as the sublime in distinction to the beautiful. In common usage, we often consider the sublime as a synonym for the beautiful, but philosophically they are diametrically opposed. The sublime is modernity's name for a disproportional aesthetics. Our new definition of music and joy as a disproportional proportion would be a category error in this system: the sublime (the disproportionate)

is "wrongly" defined under the beautiful (the proportionate).
How can this be?

The modern world is obsessed with the sublime as the
aesthetic underpinning of its ecstatic experiences. It is the
modern substitute for joy. The beautiful is too benign for joy
to be of any significance today, especially given the noise and
speed of a complex, interconnected globe. Small is beautiful,
but the sublime is big, formless, and forceful. Its foundation is
chaos. Its objects are too massive to grasp and too powerful to
contain. They can only be comprehended disproportionately.
For Kant, sublime feelings are aroused by vast, irregular objects in the natural world such as icebergs and mountain
ranges: their ugliness is awe-inspiring because the very thought
of scaling their sheer surfaces is dizzying. Like conquering
Everest, the pleasure of the sublime is found in the face of
danger; its joys demand a life lived on the edge. The disproportionate scale between man[1] and mountain induces an excitement based on overwhelming threat—the fear of being
crushed to nothing. To live the sublime is to be swept up in an
adrenalin rush. For Kant, this flight or fight response is not an
either/or dilemma: it is always only a fight response, arousing
the human subject to withstand the object that threatens to
overpower it. In rising to the occasion, something infinitely
greater is discovered inside us. The sublime without awakens
the sublime within. To be fully human is to be truly sublime.

But such heroics are also tragic since a no-surrender policy is ultimately suicidal if the human subject cannot master
the threat. So imagine the scale of the existential crisis if the
universe is no longer beautiful but sublime. This is the logic of
Schopenhauer's philosophy of music, which Nietzsche elaborated in his *Birth of Tragedy*. The universe is no longer harmonious. We inhabit a discordant cosmos. "Musical dissonance,"
writes Nietzsche, is the only pleasure that "can illustrate what

is meant by the justification of the world as an aesthetic phenomenon." Hence, music is tragically sublime for Nietzsche.[2] Its dissonance articulates the wisdom to "die soon" because it is "best not to be" in such a universe. But in affirming this truth, music also weaves its magical illusion, for its dissonances are exquisite. Those complex, unresolved chord structures that the philosopher so admired in Wagner are to die for.[3]

It's all a matter of perspective. From the vantage point of the Primal Unity, our pointless existence is absorbed in its counterpoint, resolving our dissonant lives in the greater artistry of the whole. From our puny perspective, however, it's just a game of chance based on the artistic play of a destructive will: resolution is not for us. So, if you're wise, counsels Nietzsche, play along. Live the game! And do it in style![4]

If the universe is ultimately violent, if chaos is our destiny on earth, then our sublime relation to its greatness is a meaningless relation, however aesthetically invigorating the process might be. Oblivion is our Everest. The cosmos simply swallows us whole. At Alton Towers theme park, there is a rollercoaster ride called "Oblivion": let's rename it "Nietzsche's Joyride." Opened in 1998, it is the world's first vertical drop rollercoaster. What the philosopher describes in the *Birth of Tragedy* as the intoxicated dance of music before the Primal Unity is a rollercoaster ride that loops and undulates like an asymmetrical soundwave screaming across the cosmos. The vertical drop will send you into the womb of oblivion as you plunge into the Primal Unity. To live life is to embrace this inevitable drop and celebrate fate. For Nietzsche, there is no need to steer your individual course. Why struggle? Just get on the track, enjoy the ride, live, scream, and die soon. It's tragic but exhilarating. So, cue the music: and off we go! If you recall, Nietzsche's soundtrack for this ride of oblivion is the ineluctable force and speed that closes Beethoven's Ninth Symphony: it is an acceleration, a vertical drop, that screams wildly as it plunges into the final cadence. You don't literally die listening to the symphony, of course, but "WOW!" that was close. *Phew!*

The tragic sublime conditions modernity's view of the world. We may not be aware of it, but it has taken us for a ride. Life is about overcoming or succumbing to the violent forces around us in a disproportionate play of power relations. Tragedy is premised on a fundamental divide, an opposition that only exists as a contradiction. It is about survival or surrender. It is about the fittest rather than the fitting. The resolution is always a zero-sum game: you are either zero or one, the victim or the victor. Nietzsche famously had it both ways. The young Nietzsche in his first publication is zero; in *The Birth of Tragedy,* the individual is reduced to nothing by the Primal Unity. The later Nietzsche made a volte-face, turning his back on Schopenhauer to proclaim the rule of Overman (*Übermensch*) who, as the name implies, overcomes. He is not zero: he is the one. He unites all, ordering chaos, forging himself out of conflict in a supreme act of self-mastery. The Overman defies not only nature but humanity in becoming more than human. He is sublime in affirming his life in opposition to everything that is beneath him. In both cases, the cosmos is an indifferent, undifferentiated, purposeless force that looms over us; and the sublime is the power, within or without, that seals our destiny. This tragic universe forces the self either to embrace its fate or to rise up in an act of defiant self-determination.

In a tragic universe, music can also be read both ways: it is either sublime nature or sublime self. They are two sides of the same coin; but whether it flips "heads or tails," it is a currency underwritten by death. If you recall, the role of music, from the philosophy of Schopenhauer to his postmodern heirs, is to be the sublime death rattle of our tragic existence.

In Schopenhauer's words, music reveals "the worse of all possible worlds."[5] Its overwhelming force unveils the primordial reality that threatens our very existence. So what distinguishes the disproportional rhythm of the sublime from the excesses of our newly retrofitted joy? Isn't it just the same as Nietzschean joy? Or worse still, a naïve imitation of a deeper joy?

Disproportionate Proportion

Our retrofitted joy incorporates aspects of Augustinian and Clementine thought. Both theologians injected a surplus into the fully fitted cosmos of the Pythagorean order in the form of the Christ-event: they made the proportionate disproportionate. Nietzsche's tragic universe is avowedly anti-Christian. As a corollary, it is almost commonplace to regard the Christ-event as anti-tragic. According to the literary scholar Richard Sewall, the gospel "reverses the tragic view and makes tragedy impossible."[6] Or, to borrow the title of George Steiner's book on the demise of tragedy, the great joy affirmed by the resurrection is the very *Death of Tragedy*. This is tragic for tragedy, of course, but otherwise it is good news all round. The Christ-event puts an end to tragedy.

It's a nice idea—at least, in literary studies—but clearly, if modern history is anything to go by, tragedy has not gone away. Such naïve joy overstates its case and underplays the tragic. It is not that the Christ-event makes the tragic impossible (in fact, it is very possible and very real); rather, the intervention of joy changes the condition in which tragedy lays claim to permanence. Joy neutralizes its sting and swallows its gaping abyss because joy's excess exceeds everything that tragedy can throw at it. Any vertical drop into oblivion bounces back out because joy is elastic. The tragic moment cannot undo its rhythm.

After all, the Christ-event is not merely the great joy announced by the Christmas angels, it also faces tragedy head-on in its embrace of the cross. Without the crucifixion, there is no joy of resurrection. In the Christian tradition, it is precisely by receiving the tragic that the Christ-event derails its course and cuts the ground from under the sublime. Chaos is not the sea from which order emerges and submerges. Beauty is the ground. Creation is good. The tragic is "merely" a passing figure in the excess that is beauty. Small is not beautiful. The beautiful is a disproportionate and outsized proposition.

In the Gospels, the Greek word *kalon* is seldom translated as "beautiful" because the beautiful is synonymous with what is true and good in Greek thought; in most contexts, "good" would be the fitting translation. There is perhaps only one occasion where the "beautiful" is called for as a positive term for an aesthetic act—and it arises in a tragic context. During a conversation at a formal dinner, Jesus speaks of a "beautiful thing" (*kalon ergon*), literally "a work of proportion."[7] But this "work of proportion" was so disproportionate to anything imaginable within the ethical framework of his followers that they were indignant at this thing of beauty. As far as they were concerned, this thing was neither "beautiful" nor "good"; it was improper. A woman—Mary of Bethany in the account in John's Gospel—had broken an alabaster jar of pure nard worth a year's wages, and poured the perfume in its entirety on Jesus's head in front of the dinner guests. She then proceeded to wash Jesus's feet with a mixture of nard and tears, using her disheveled hair. It was an extravagant act of inappropriate abandonment. Her performance was deemed "wasteful" by the offended onlookers.

"Why wasn't this perfume sold and given to the poor?" mutters Judas Iscariot indignantly.[8]

"She has done a beautiful thing to me," says Jesus.[9]

It is a familiar scene. The men around the table had all the authority but no idea what was happening: the one woman in the room understood perfectly the situation but no one listened to her. Mary's wordless act speaks volumes, but Jesus had to interpret her performance to the dim-witted men in the room: "Why are you bothering this woman?" he says. "When she poured this perfume on my body, she did it to prepare me for burial."[10]

The contrast between moral propriety (sell the perfume and donate the money to the poor) and moral impropriety (waste the perfume and make an ugly scene) is telling. Judas spoke beautifully; his suggestion was fitting; he seemingly said the right thing. But the outcome was tragic. He was in tune but out of time since his sense of moral superiority would lead to the betrayal of Jesus and to his suicide.[11] Mary, on the other hand, acted tragically but the outcome was beautiful. She was out of tune, creating a dissonant scene at a dinner party, but ultimately, she was in time: her unfitting act transcended the present to fit the future. The moral question in the Gospel accounts is an aesthetic one: what does it mean to do something beautiful (*kalon ergon*)?

The "beautiful thing" performed by Mary was a mess of entangled hair, dirty feet, broken shards, nard, saliva, and tears. It was an ugly, dissonant assemblage of matter and smell far removed from the balanced ratios of the Pythagorean order implied by the words *kalon ergon*. The choice of words in the Gospels is as shocking as Mary's act of worship. *Kalon* implies something measured, good, and harmonious, which was seemingly everything Mary was not. Her unwarranted piece of performance art was not measured, not good, and not harmonious. But the improper act is more than fitting because its extravagance is woven into a rhythm. It is the downbeat for the upbeat. It is a matter of time. Mary's "downbeat" is "tragic": she has no premonition of an upbeat. This is a lament of utter devastation, an act of adoration anticipating the imminent death of Jesus by anointing him for burial. But its costly profusion, mistaken as wastefulness, is beyond tragedy: it is an unintended investment in the upbeat of joy.

In the Gospels, Mary's wasteful use of perfume acknowledges a debt of love that no act can repay. Nothing is appropriate for the love expressed in the utter destitution and desolation of the crucifixion. The anointing, then, is Mary's response to one whose love compels her by its disproportional nature to respond in proportion: that is, *dis*proportionately.

This disproportionate proportion is the "so much more" that is the structure of joy. Mary's act may be a lament, but tragedy is not the ultimate ground of its meaning. Joy is the open form underlying her lament; its generosity not only makes the act of mourning "a beautiful thing" but creates the space for a divine response beyond anything imaginable within a perfectly proportioned cosmos. Mary initiates a rhythm that, like the fragrance lingering in the room, is uncontainable. It continues long after the act of adoration has shocked the indignant observers. The rhythm weaves unpredictably through the tension of the "now and not-yet," searching for meaning, holding the interval between death and resurrection intact. This is the downbeat of the Easter Vigil that waits in the darkness for resurrection morning; it is this rhythmic expectation that will turn the lament into elation.[12] Rhythm, then, does not erase the tragic. It does not retune a dissonance: rather, it receives the tragic, works with it, and hopes beyond hopelessness. Joy is the unbreakable rhythm that breaks out from the jar, embracing a terrifying contradiction that no harmonic proportion can possibly hold together. What Mary sets in motion with her unseemly act is "a beautiful thing" that is uncontainable (the perfume is out of the jar) and incalculable (any attempt to count the numbers and give the money to the poor is inappropriate). It is sublimely beautiful—a disproportionate proportion.

Modern philosophy segregates the beautiful and the sublime.[13] In so doing it partitions the harmonious and the tragic as opposing universes. But this binary logic is itself tragic: it is based on an opposition, or dialectic, in which one side—the sublime—threatens to take it all. And because one side takes all, a tragic universe, despite the chaos of its sublime violence, is the most tightly fitted entity imaginable: all opposition is ultimately absorbed into itself as the One. Hence, Nietzsche's deity is named the Primal *Unity*. The sublime can appear quite "fitting" because its formless process aims at totality. But it is not a disproportionate proportion because "one" is not a proportion. It relates to nothing, and there is nothing generous in the disproportion of its chaos. Nothing is donated. There is no give, only division. The rhythm simply stops when it counts to one.

Incense

By all accounts, Hong Kong is a tragedy. Its history is one of dispossession. Its existence is one of contradiction. It is a region out of sync with its own identity, always living on borrowed time as a political pawn played by higher powers. Beneath the sublime game of global politics, its local pieces move myopically, trapped in their own petty bureaucracies and ideological divisions, oblivious to the social forces that have now erupted into violence only to be crushed by the counterforce of law and order. Zero and one form the binary structure of its tragic identity. All or nothing seems to be the only deal left on the table.

Thankfully, in this history of brokenness, Hong Kong has yet to lose its rhythm. Maybe its strength is in the fragility of its name: Hong Kong means "fragrant harbor." The jar may be broken, but the fragrance remains.

To define Hong Kong tragically would be ironic. According to the philosopher Yuk Hui, tragedy is unknown in Chinese cosmology because the oppositional elements of its cosmos are not contradictions but continuities: they comingle like incense. Chinese thought, in this sense, is often said to be incapable of tragedy.[14] Yin and yang are not embroiled in some cosmic contradiction that plays out on the human stage as tragic drama. They curve, curling a little into each other, as if to delineate a path for a more flexible rhythm.

Hong Kong's fragrance has its own rhythm, which is often hard to divine. Its patterns are like the smoky prayers spiraling upward from the joss sticks in its temples and shrines. At times the orange embers produce so much smoke it is hard to breath. I vividly remember being enveloped by a cloud of incense at a funeral in Hong Kong. Fake dollar bills were being incinerated for the deceased in one corner of the hall, and Buddhist priests were chanting melodies that seemed to cling to the suffocating fragrance smoldering from thick bundles of joss sticks. The music, like the smoke, hung in the air, its monotonous convolutions gathering into a nebulous cloud of ancestral prayer. It seemed to me that this haze was a microcosm of Hong Kong. As I sat in the funeral hall, my imagination wandered outside: I pictured the city's pollution as an ashen cloud of fragrance hovering over the harbor, a prayer offered to the heavens in the vague hope of a better life beyond.

In ancient China, observing the movement of ashes was music, or at least a way of seeing an inaudible sound. The ritual, which replaced the need to forage in the Xie Valley, involved burying twelve bamboo pitch pipes in the earth, tuned to the harmony of the heavens, with their open ends above ground and filled with the ashes of reeds. Each pipe represented a month in the calendrical cycle. The winds would blow. Nothing would be heard, but the ethers would rise from the pipes in cloudy wisps to indicate the movement of the cosmic breath as it plays the pipes. The patterns were kind of a diagnostic chart, a way for the imperial court to divine the Mandate of Heaven and to adjust the rule of the emperor to the harmony of the cosmos. To see the fragrance of music was to understand the state of joy and to adjust one's tuning accordingly.

What is the state of joy in Hong Kong? It is hard to see the fragrance rise from the bamboo pipes of its skyline. But I imagine that its nebulous rhythms are still curling and coiling above the divisions that have now congealed into an inert substance embalming the population. For many, the fragrance is for a burial. We are at a funeral. Hong Kong is dead; her people are scattered, some are in prison, many have left, a few soldier on. But who knows the rhythms of the future? Or where the winds may blow? Or how the perfume, released from the jar of history, will rise? If there is any fragrance stirring in this harbor, then joy is still an excess that the tragic cannot outplay. Perhaps, this moment in history is merely the interval of a rhythm yet to be determined. Maybe this "dead-time" is Hong Kong's own Easter Vigil.

Interval

We can learn a lesson from Augustine's baptism. If you recall, it took place in Milan on Easter Vigil, 387 CE. Augustine did not live in "an empty, homogeneous time." Time had a rhythm. The timing of his baptism was highly symbolic. To rise with the sun on Easter morning from the waters of baptism is to become a new creation. This is the rhythm of downbeat and upbeat—of dying to self and rising in Christ. Rhythm is the interval of time that connects the two as a single wave. But there is nothing inevitable about this motion. After all, resurrections are unexpected and surprising. Augustine wrote *De musica* during this time, from his baptism in Milan to his ordination in Hippo. The treatise, as we noted earlier, undergoes its own baptism in the sixth volume. It suddenly comes to life. It is a new creation. The rhythm it describes is the unchanging joy of a newfound faith. However, the life that accompanied the writing of the book was anything but unchanging. The event on Easter Vigil set in motion an oscillation that was as tragic as it was joyful. Death took everything away from the young convert except his life. And yet, *De musica* is not a consolation. The joy described in *De musica* is an eternal rhythm that undergirds the tumultuous cycles of loss and hope in Augustine's life, exceeding everything that tragedy can throw at it.

So, if you were to open *De musica*, what would you expect to fall out of its pages? A clatter of stiffly proportioned measuring sticks to be rearranged as a framework for life? There is definitely a strict order for adherence. But something else would appear if you disturbed its pages: a cloud. This is not because it is an ancient, dusty book. These are rhythmic clouds. For all their metrical order, the rhythms of *De musica* are more wispy than crispy. The interval of time between downbeat and upbeat is not a straight line for Augustine, because only fate—the determined outcome of tragedy—is a vertical drop. Rather, it curls. It behaves more like incense following the drift of air currents, offered up as prayers in search of order. "The science of measuring well," as Augustine defined music, is not strictly predetermined, let alone imposed. It flows. The temporality of music is a "free movement," he says.[15] Be-

tween the downbeat and the upbeat is an unpredictable gap—a
mini creation ex nihilo—from which equilibrium emerges.[16] For
Augustine, the flow of time requires the three-fold movement
of past, present, and future corresponding with a beginning,
middle, and end—or A|V. This is why three is the minimal
number for time to hold together in *De musica*.[17] Augustine
calls the middle an "interval" (*intervallum or interuallum*). If we
were to retrofit modern science into *De musica*, this *intervallum*
becomes the interface of homeostasis.

But before plugging neuropsychology into *De musica*, we
need to bring out our souvenir from Hippo—the ladder—to
remind us how to scale these intervals. If you remember, the
ladder is composed of numbers that ascend from the corporeal to the incorporeal realms: they vibrate together. This is
what Augustine calls *consonantia* (sounding together). For the
theologian Graham Ward, these vibrations function as primordial feelers or motion detectors that literally make *sense*
of what is sensed in the world. Their resonance enables an exchange—a homeostasis—through which meaning emerges
co-creatively.[18] Fitted with these sensors, Augustine's ladder
becomes a sentient life-form; its wooden frame morphs into
Damasio's evolutionary tree of emotive growth (see figure 14).
Beginning from the precognitive stirrings of moods, desires,
and affects, the rhythmic feelers climb upward toward the
light, their tendrils searching and probing the environment
to make sense of the world.[19] These resonances are felt at
first rather than understood, but as they loop in regular patterns they begin to weave a rhythm of meaning. Each step
creates new possibilities. So, as we clamber from rung to rung
(or branch to branch) through the metabolic, physiological,
affective, psychological, sociological, and spiritual realms,
nothing is predictable in the ascent. The steps are uneven.
Perhaps a rung is missing. Everything requires a symphony

of relations—a sounding together of rhythmic cycles to divine the equilibrium in which our lives are ordered. In *De musica*, this resonance between heaven and earth is the condition for the meaningful to emerge and the possibility for joy to be understood.

In the same way, Augustine's journey from baptism to ordination "feels" its way through the rhythms of a divine music to make sense of this interval in his life. It is as tentative and contingent as it is certain. Joy does not trump the tragic as a fait accompli: joy emerges from the *consonantia* that constantly measures its motion in the tension between downbeat and upbeat. Music enables him to attend to the world and the cocreative process of making sense of it. The *intervallum*, in its unpredictability, is a caesura as well as a connection that disrupts the routine cycles of life and opens out a renewed relation of co-dependence with the contingency of existence.

Ward points out that Augustine uses the term *consonantia* and never speaks of *harmonia* in his writings for the very reason that the cosmic order is not already decided: that would be fate.[20] Harmony as tuning implies a predetermined order with no wiggle room. But meaning is not some "grand design" out there, even if sublimely ungraspable: it unfolds meaningfully in real time as difference in relation. The meaningful emerges as a homeostatic, rhythmic order.[21]

So what is the lesson for Hong Kong? This fragrant harbor is still unfurling its clouds of incense. Its vigil may have yet to see the light, but the music is not over. The fragrance is still sensing its way unpredictably toward equilibrium in search of the meaningful. *Consonantia*—sounding together—is a symphony of co-creation. It is a desire for a life *together*, a messy but "beautiful thing" (*kalon ergon*) that is dissonant to the politics of the modern world, in which victors and vanquished alike proclaim their antagonistic slogans in a zero-sum game of opposition and oppression. Such sublime defiance looks heroic but lacks all beauty, for it is predicated on a disproportional force rather than a disproportional proportion.

Of course, it is not only Hong Kong that must find a rhythm out of seeming tragedy. So much of modern politics is tragic, conditioned by a sublime soundtrack. Beauty cannot overcome the sublime, for it would itself become sublime in the process of overcoming. But it doesn't have to play along with this zero-sum game, because the sublime is neither permanent nor universal. It merely claims to be so: its eternal reign is the necessary propaganda of all totalizing regimes, a pose to uphold power. But if the tragic cannot even be properly conceived of in the cosmology of Confucius or Augustine, then *it does not have to be*. The contradictions that compose its sublime soundtrack do not have to orientate our actions. If it rears its head now as some terrifying force, it needs to be seen as a tangle that will unravel in the rise and fall of a greater rhythmic weave. Tragic terror can be real, even if its eternal pose is delusional, but there is no need to succumb to the sublime, let alone overcome the sublime, because that will only perpetuate its rule and fulfill its claims to permanence in the act of resistance. The beautiful thing about beauty is that is already greater than the sublime, even in lament: it is more magnanimous than its magnitude, and more integrated than any primal unity. Its *intervallum* is a disproportionate measure because it is latent with generous and generative possibilities: yet its rhythm is a proportionate measure in its homeostatic, co-creative relations. So there is nothing benign, decorative, or insipid about the beautiful: its charm is utterly disarming and can disable the sublime without even a show of strength. And that's truly great.

Two Ways to Move

In case you've forgotten, we are still in a vehicle: the test drive
in our retrofitted machine is not yet over. We need to check
out the sound system! It's beautiful. If joy is the ambient mood
of the universe, then its music changes our relation to everything that surrounds us. To indwell its rhythms is to transcend the tragic and to make the beautiful our soundtrack. So
let's give the sound system a blast. You will see that it gets
things moving.

Music has always been regarded as a vehicle for the self
because it moves us. Somehow, when listening to music, we are
virtually in motion even though we are physically in situ.
Something moves inside us. This internal ride is often amplified as an external ride if blasted from the sound system of a
fast-moving open-top V12 coupé. But that's a dream for another book. In our quirky retrofitted vehicle, the joyride is
reckless only in an internal sense, and the sound system has
an ancient-looking knob that only toggles between two modes
marked A1 and A2. A1 is the Augustine mode. A2 is the Aristotle mode. Both are good. But for the best performance, turn
the knob to A1.

There are two ways for humans to move internally: one
is the will, defined by Aristotle as self-motion. The other is
love, defined by Augustine as a motion toward the good.[22]
Originally, they were both fairly similar—a kind of rational
inclination to do the right thing—but in the subsequent development of the will, Aristotle's concept was put into full throttle, and self-motion spiraled inward, flinging the good from
its orbit. The will assumed the motion of self-determination.
It became autonomous, whereas love remained a motion of
dependency.[23]

Music is often mapped onto these two very different motions; its movements are either volitional or emotional; its moral force is based either on decision or desire. Modern aesthetics prioritizes the will. This is the sublime force that stands against the chaos that rages against us. As we discovered in the analysis of the "Ode to Joy," the composer who usually represents this heroic will in the history of music is Beethoven.[24] His music is unadulterated self-motion.[25] Just listen to his Fifth Symphony. The work is synonymous with victory, and purportedly describes Beethoven seizing fate by the throat in a sublime act of self-determination. This is a vehicle in full throttle. *Da-da-da-daaah!* The symphony bursts into being out of nothing as an autonomous force driving ineluctably across a vast terrain to arrive triumphantly at the final cadence. This decisive act is a straight line of command, an unswerving movement from darkness (C minor in the first movement) to light (C major in the finale).

This joyride is a self-gratifying and self-amplifying circuit. The ancients would categorize this as pleasure rather than joy since its force is directed inward: it fuels self-motion. True joy faces outward as a movement desiring the good. It is love. It is not a straight line of command that seizes the objective by the throat to possess it in a self-absorbed cycle of wanting and taking. Joy is always out of line, slightly improper, a bit curved, and never returns with what it wants to augment the ego. A motion toward the good seeks the other in a transformative journey, with all kinds of ups and downs that are unpredictable and bumpy. Back in Augustine's day, it was like taking a walk, a perambulation of metrical feet. Measuring well, for Augustine, was a plod of long and short steps across the syllabic terrain; it was a poetic form of "wayfaring" in search of a balanced relationship within the divine order.[26]

Now that we have retrofitted music by pumping ancient fuel into the modern machine, our biped has wheels! The key for the good life is not to press the accelerator and drive straight into the sunset. That would be the A2 mode, which is fast and furious and ends with a vertical drop. Toggle the knob to A1. Don't drive straight. Just take music for a spin and wait for the sunrise on Easter Vigil.

18

Feeling Groovy

Another Way

Are you ready? We've turned the knob to A1. We are in "Augustine mode." Our driving manual, *De musica,* is before us. We open its dusty pages. It's all about rhythm. As such, it should connect to our rhythmic definition of joy and illuminate the good life. In fact, we've squeezed considerable mileage from this ancient text in the previous chapter to get the new definition going. The *intervallum* seemed to connect an ancient beat to a modern one. So we insert the key and give music a spin in A1 mode, expecting a joyride. Unfortunately, *De musica* doesn't quite work.

Theoretically, the numbers in *De musica* may vibrate as drives, appetites, and desires toward the good, but the rhythms measured out by the metrical feet in the first five volumes are anything but instinctive. It's a *scientia* of measuring well, after all. The end result of the calculations is not some innate, touchy-feely resonance but a tightly controlled regulation based on the Pythagorean tetractys. We knew from the start that *De musica*'s rhythmic cycles demand an uphill drive, but the gears are not kicking in to get us to the promised summit. Maybe the wheels of the tetractys are just too triangular.

The original upward journey in *De musica* was an ascent by metrical feet. Each step needed careful consideration. Practice should make perfect. But the ladder of *De musica* is a very tall order. And the final step for Augustine is a leap of faith. Having arrived at the top, he expects you to kick the ladder away in an act of deliberate amnesia. The eternal and immutable numbers are supposed to suspend you in the higher realms with such blissful forgetfulness that you no longer react to the temporality of music or its sentient vibrations below. In fact, it would be improper to do so. They should just murmur subconsciously without any titillation or stimulation of the senses.[1] Now, that's all very well for a saint like Augustine; he might be able to fold his metrical feet and levitate without a ladder, but most of us would just be left dangling without a leg to stand on. For the modern world, Augustine's rhythmic theory is too rarefied, requiring so much mental exertion to arrive at a state of joy that it might just give you a headache instead.

Ultimately, there is a disconnect between the mental propriety of *De musica* and the mundane informality of the modern world. In theory, it's lovely: its vision of joy can sustain the good life. But in practice, its ancient rhythms are too tightly buttoned to get the party going. Reason has to labor tirelessly, diverting, rechanneling, and policing the moral boundaries of the self in order to attain the joy of a heavenly music. If *De musica* is the answer for today, then the good life has lost its groove.

But maybe this is not simply a modern problem. The disconnect between theory and practice was already nascent in Augustine himself. In fact, this rift has torn its way through the entire history of sacred music. It is evident from Augustine's *Confessions* that the saint loved music. He was moved by it. Music caused him to sway; it choreographed his body and churned his emotions with such uncontrollable joy that he burst out in tears. In Augustine's account, the singing he experienced in Milan under Bishop Ambrose was anything but rigid and rarefied: "How copiously I wept at our hymns and canticles, how intensely was I moved by the lovely harmonies of your singing Church! Those voices flooded my ears, and the truth was distilled into my heart until it overflowed in loving devotion; my tears ran down and I was better for them."[2]

Yet in theory, Augustine distanced himself from these automatic responses precisely because he loved music too much. It was such a vortex of pleasure for him that it could disorientate his love and suck him in the wrong direction, away from God. Music, the vehicle designed to order his love, would become the cause of a compulsive disorder.

So what's going on in Augustine's head? In terms of neuropsychology, it appears that the reward circuits of liking and wanting in the limbic area of Augustine's brain were highly susceptible to music; when stimulated by rhythm, his hedonistic hotspot would gyrate in self-affirming cycles of liking, wanting, and desiring more of the same, generating a vicious circle of addiction. If he was not careful, music would cause him to forfeit joy for pleasure and lead him astray into all kinds of lewd and idolatrous practices that music was associated with in his day.

Joy, if you recall, is a circuit breaker that disconnects liking from wanting. It is a balancing act that tempers basic instinct with a limbic snip. This act is an aesthetic move because to en-*joy* the beautiful, according to Kant, requires an attention that is "disinterested"; it is to *like* an object without *wanting* it (whereas addiction is to want an object without necessarily liking it).[3] So to preserve the "disinterest" demanded by beauty, joy must seek the object it loves without using, consuming, or possessing it for its own purposes. Joy is, therefore, an aesthetic form that is both affective (liking) and cognitive (not wanting), tempering passion and reason into a harmonious play. It needs to find an equilibrium. But given his overactive pleasure zone for music, Augustine seemingly overcompensates: *De musica*'s calculated moves result in a detachment that alienates rather than complements passion and reason. Joy, the circuit breaker, creates too big a gap between theory and practice. The ascetic controls cancel out the affective response. In Augustine's brain, rhythms are being processed by different and contradictory regions, juggling the numbers to ensure that all the motion and commotion of music balance out as a motionless constant to contain his passions. And that's why it is enough to give anyone a headache.

So how can the good life reconnect with the modern world and find its groove today? Can the aesthetic disposition of joy be less ascetic and feel more spontaneous? Can its "liking" be decoupled from "wanting" in an instinctively upbeat way? Thankfully, Augustine has another path to arrive at joy. This alternative route does not require you to memorize five volumes of metrical patterns for an exam in temperance. Its calculations won't give you a massive Pythagorean migraine. This music is not only defined by human reason. Rather, its joys are instinctive, bodily, and truly groovy. This theory leverages the wiggle room already latent in Augustine's *intervallum* and opens it out to create a generous and generative measure. It is a theory of disproportionate proportion that Augustine himself names joy.

Jubilation

This alternative rhythm is the melisma.[4] It operates in total disregard for syllabic feet. A melisma is composed of notes that spill out from a word; instead of fitting one syllable to a note, the note generates more notes and the syllable extends "word-lessly" as a form of rhythmic propulsion or effusion. An apt example is the aria "Rejoice Greatly" from Handel's *Messiah* (see figure 28). It begins normally enough—"Rejoice, rejoice"— as if the singer were speaking. But then, the music starts to giggle: "Re-joi-oi-oi-oi-oi-oice greatly." And then the last syllable of the word *rejoice* is disproportionately extended, like this: "Re-joi-oi-oi-oi-oi-oi-oi-oi-oi-oi-oi-oice"; then a few measures later the extension is further extended: "Re-joi-oi-oi-oi-oi-oi-oi-oi-oi-oi-oi-oi-oi-oi-oi-oi-oi-oi-oice."[5] The melisma is the *intervallum* in these phrases, the point of difference that generates the possibility of infinite variation. It would make the syllable sound rather silly if it were theorized in *De musica*. It would literally be twittering nonsense—which Augustine hears in birdsong—rather than the science of measuring well.[6]

This syllabic silliness in "Rejoice Greatly" could simply be explained as a bit of baroque word painting, which was a common technique of representing emotions in the seventeenth and eighteenth centuries. The melisma sounds like the joy of laughter with its diaphragmatic convulsions; and its ridiculous length may represent the voluminous command to "rejoice *greatly*." Handel's disproportionate rhythmic extensions are verbal representations.

Figure 28. "Rejoice Greatly" from Handel's *Messiah*— measures 9–14.

But there is nothing bizarre about these musical phrases that requires words to justify their meaning. Melismas are totally normal. This kind of "silly" repetition is precisely what music does *all the time* when it is not artificially constrained by syllabic boundaries or handcuffed by poetic feet. There is more to a melisma than what the words they extend convey. In fact, for Augustine, a melisma means precisely more than what any words can convey. It speaks of the ineffable. There is a joy that cannot be put into words, a joy that is beyond conceptualization and verbalization. Augustine, for all his rhetorical prowess, considered earthly eloquence a clamor compared to the noiseless truth of God: the saint believed heaven to be a silent realm of immutable and ineffable communion.[7] In contrast, human words, claims Augustine, are earth-bound signs separated from the things they represent: they are restless, temporal utterances that "chop and change," flitting about in the mind in search of the privilege to name things as they are.[8] Words get in the way. The melisma, in this sense, can free the mind from this "chopping and changing motion" of words and point to an ineffable condition of rest directly—a joy without end. It is as if the melisma names joy perfectly.[9]

To grasp the joy of music in Augustine, the final book of *De musica* is best read in conjunction with his commentaries on a tradition unrelated to Pythagorean theory: the Jewish psalter. His commentaries on the Psalms reflect the affective dimension of psalm singing that Augustine knew at first hand during his conversion in Milan.

Psalms are not just songs, but often songs about singing. For example, Psalm 32, which begins with the exhortation "Sing to the Lord a new song," is not only a song but a song that commands one to sing.[10] Indeed, if properly enacted, it generates what to sing—"a new song" (preferably, to recall Clement, in duet with Christ, the "New Song"). As a performative speech act, theory and practice merge together as one gapless formula. Singing this psalm, writes Augustine, involves articulating a new song "not only with our tongues but with our lives" because the song is not only about jubilation, it is the act of jubilation itself.[11] To sing it is to be it. Doing and being coincide. For Augustine, it is the very newness of the "new song"—namely, the sense of rhythmic excess that spills out as melismatic improvisation—that is at the heart of jubilation. It is improvised joy.

There is nothing rarefied about the melisma for Augustine. No mental levitation is required. The ladder is firmly planted on the ground for our feet to make a stand if not a stomp. In fact, for Augustine, the melisma is a sweaty, smelly, bodily, and earthy rhythm. It is a kind of grunt, an Augustinian heave-ho that is performed every day by ordinary people going about their normal business.

To describe the melisma, Augustine references the *jubilus,* a repetitive chant (or more precisely a shout) heard from laborers harvesting in the fields as they move rhythmically to the strain of their toil.[12] It is a communal rhythm. Or rather, it is rhythm that enables community, tapping into the human aptitude for entrainment. The *jubilus,* observes Augustine, arises from "any work that goes with a swing."[13] It's got rhythm, punctuating the everyday soundscape under the African sun with whoops, and entraining the community to keep time with the swaying of their bodies. As far as the *jubilus* is concerned, Duke Ellington is right: "It Don't Mean a Thing If It Ain't Got That Swing" (doo-wah, doo-wah, doo-wah, doo-wah, doo-wah)—the important words here being the improvised "doo-wahs" representing the melismatic swing where words mean nothing and rhythm everything.[14]

This music transforms work into play, because the rhythm expresses the joy of abundance—the imminent harvest—and so connects the hardship of the present to the abundance of the future. "Greatly cheered by a plentiful crop," writes Augustine, they "rejoice over the fecundity and bounty of the earth" by interjecting shouts of joy between the words they sing.[15] The spontaneous exchange is a permanent state of joy in the goodness of creation that overrides the momentary toil and struggle of hard labor. In the *jubilus,* what begins with the meager pickings of words proliferates into a bumper crop of tones. Augustine transfers this rhythmic holler to the Psalmist's exhortation "to shout for joy" or "to sing for joy":

> What is it to sing in jubilation? To be unable to understand, to express in words, what is sung in the heart. For they who sing, either in the harvest, in the vineyard, or in some other arduous occupation after beginning to manifest their gladness in words of songs, are filled with such joy that they cannot express it in words, and turn from the syllables of the words and proceed to the sound of jubilation. The *jubilus* is something which signifies that the heart labors with what it cannot utter. And whom does jubilation befit but the ineffable God? For he is ineffable whom you cannot speak. And if you cannot speak, yet ought not be silent, what remains but that you jubilate; so that the heart rejoices without words, and the great expanse of joy has not the limits of syllables? "Sing well unto him in jubilation."[16]

For Augustine, the *jubilus* does not keep us regimentally in time with its swing; rather, its swing releases a surplus of improvised interactions. When Augustine exhorts his readers to let the "heart overflow with a good word" (Psalm 44), this

overflow that gushes forth from the word is a rhythmic effusion of joy.[17] "Anyone who finds words insufficient to do justice to overflowing joy," he writes, "bursts out into noisy
happiness, to make a joyful noise for the God of Jacob" (Psalm
80:3).[18]

The theologian Carol Harrison compares this noisy
practice to "singing in the bath."[19] To refine her definition a
little, this is not just any kind of singing in the bath; it is especially the kind of singing where you forget the words and you
still sing anyway; it is a kind of "doo-be-doo-be-doo-be-doo"
singing in the bath that repeats itself differently each time
precisely because it is made up on the spot. It is in this sense
that "singing in the bath" is the aquatic parallel of "singing to
the Lord a new song." It swaps the North African landscape at
harvest time for the modern plumbing of bath time to arrive
at an everyday image of worship. Of course, for the modern
analogy to truly reflect the *jubilus,* we would need to be in a
communal bath—which may not be so attractive for the more
demure among us.

Melismatic music preempts the joy of heavenly rest,
which for Augustine is "silent" inasmuch as it does not require
spoken language. But clearly, there is nothing remotely placid
or incorporeal about this eternal rest! It is full of bodily desires. It is an instinctive everyday activity that we already do
on the streets, in the fields, or in the bath. Normal and infor-
mal, the *jubilus* of the fourth century resonates with the ca-
sual hum of the modern world.

Arguably, given its everyday informality, the *jubilus* is
akin to some forms of contemporary worship in churches
today: already happy, clappy, and filled with the kind of the
bubbly praise fit for "singing in the bath." There is nothing
wrong with this in the Augustinian playbook! But some may
prefer the sobriety exemplified by *De musica* to keep the order

of worship "proper." Nothing wrong with this either! The *jubilus* is not a matter of style or taste. It is a matter of the heart. In fact, it was a source of inspiration for the liturgy of medieval Europe, which was bound by strict rules of syllabic clarity. When formalized by medieval liturgical practice, the *jubilus* connected with the moment at the end of the Alleluia where the singers would launch off on the last syllable into a melismatic melee of joy.[20] It could even be regarded as a form of glossolalia or singing in tongues. The law of one syllable per note no longer applies when the spirit still insists on singing when there are no syllables left.

An Alleluia, as with many of the Psalms, is a phrase that performs what it sings; it fulfills the command while singing it: "Praise the Lord." There is no gap—no delay—between the command and the action. There is no time for numerical calculation or linguistic conceptualization. There is only the time of music itself as a kind of ineffable and potentially infinite rhythmic extension that issues from an improvising heart rather than from a cogitating mind. But this is not so much a bypassing of the mind as an expansion of the mind that short-circuits the time to think.[21] Rhythm has become such a habit that it is immediate and spontaneous, a portal for what Augustine calls "leaping across" from the earthly dimension to a divine realm.[22] When there is no other time but the very time of music itself, then there is no division between the heart and the song, no "choppy" words to break the flow of praise, no gap between thinking and doing or uttering and living or cognition and affection. There is no restless search for a concept or need for an explanation; there is only the feeling that this time and no-other-time abounds with such a sense of a not-enough-time that you can only burst out in extended improvisation.[23] You literally run out of words. Or, as Augustine describes it, this is a music "filled with too much joy." The ineffable results from not having enough space-time to contain the abundance. It is a disproportionate proportion:

> One who jubilates does not speak with words. It is rather a sort of sound of joy without words, since it is the voice of a soul poured out in joy and express-ing, as best it can, the feeling, though not grasping the sense. A man delighting in his joy, from some words which cannot be spoken or understood, bursts forth in a certain voice of exultation without words, so that it seems he does indeed rejoice with his own voice, but as if, because filled with too much joy, he cannot explain in words what it is in which he delights.[24]

The musicologist Mark Evan Bonds suggests that Augus-tine's *jubilus* foreshadows the early Romantic elevation of in-strumental music to the infinite realm of yearning circa 1800 where music exists as an autonomous form, emancipated from words and the functions of church and court.[25] It is exempli-fied by the Beethoven symphony: it is one giant melismatic complex. "Absolute music," as this aesthetic position came to be known, could be construed as a modern counterpart to the melismatic practices of the distant past.[26] But whereas for the Romantics, the ineffable sign of music gestured to an unknown and unattainable Other, for Augustine it articulates an Other who is known but ungraspable: music's incalculable rhythms that seem to overturn the neatly arranged integers of Pythag-orean theory find their fittingness—their disproportionate proportion—in God. Music's ineffable state is not Romantic yearning but divine rest—albeit a dynamic one of unending

desire toward the good. It is not sublime but sublimely beautiful. It is not the flux of indefinite longing but the animated certainty of joy.[27]

So, for all its spontaneity, the joy expressed as a melisma
is highly stable. It gestures to a permanent condition. As such,
joy is as much a rhythm in times of suffering as it is times of
abundance. Indeed, the *jubilus* has witnessed unimaginable
evil. Its joy, for example, traveled across space and time as part
of the African diaspora to strange lands of desolation and oppression. Augustine would likely acknowledge the ecstatic
hand-clapping, feet-stamping, body-writhing, glory-shouting
worship of the Black American church today as an echo of the
jubilus. In fact, its origins are closer to what Augustine heard
in the fields than the rarefied and privileged forms of the
melisma in medieval chant and Western instrumental music.
But these origins have been transplanted from the harvest
fields of North Africa to the cotton fields of the Deep South.
Instead of resounding in a cathedral or concert hall, the *jubilus* was made manifest as a sacred genre in the American
plantations. Music assembled a mobile temple of displaced,
enslaved people. In the work songs, spirituals, calls, and shouts
of slave culture, the melismatic powers of the *jubilus* were re-
tooled to bring the spiritual realm into the material present and
to prophesy freedom into being. Recall the ecstatic ritual of the
ring shout, where worshipers would shuffle in a circle, stomp-
ing their feet, clapping their hands, and crying out to heaven
in improvised fragments of song and prayer: this was not only
a source for the blues but reflects the African heritage of the
Black gospel tradition. The "belief that musical sound can turn
spiritual power into physical reality" materialized in these
shuffling circles.[28] The divine rhythms, pulsating in the bodies of those reduced to animals by their white oppressors,
articulated the freedom of a new humanity. Here was new

creation in action. Repetition unchained the present with the
certainty of difference. Every shuffle ploughed the earth in anticipation of a harvest of justice. It was joy and not despair
that enabled the slaves to reimagine the strange land as a promised land. Here was a defiant *jubilus* that gestured to the ineffable by refusing to capitulate to or imitate an unspeakable evil.
Joy, then, is a dynamic, disproportional equilibrium in which
the divine melisma co-creates the future together with a broken humanity.

Common Ground

The gospel may not be your ultimate rhythm, but given the
wonder of the universe, the beauty of the earth, the miracle of
being human, and the givenness of music, we can at least begin from what is familiar yet ungraspable around us in order
to achieve a form of melismatic "rest." There are many ways to
navigate ancient wisdom to find a common ground with the
modern world. In a way, this negotiation is itself a kind of balance with the past. Ideally, the still point would be a moment
of doxology, since wonder should consecrate the ground we
stand on. But we need to swing with the *jubilus* in order to be
still. "Rest" is not so much a suspended state of inaction as a
dynamic movement that underpins our everyday engagement
with our environment, weaving past and present in a rhythm
of joy. There is always a generative surplus at work, because
without surplus life is merely survival. But in that surplus,
there is a measure, an order, a rule to keep us in balance in the
complex adaptive system of the modern world. The ancient triangulation of obedience, freedom, and joy is still possible
today as an equilibrium of forces. Indeed, it is desirable in a
world increasingly torn by the politics of sublime division and
dissonant coercion:

- Obedience is to align our melody to the measure of a given world. As in the homonym *nomos* or the homograph 律 (*lǜ*), obedience is both a tune we play and the law we obey.
- Freedom is to improvise harmoniously with what is given. As in the word *consonantia* or the homograph 龢 (*hé*), it is a relation of homeostasis, a creative attunement in the rhythms of an ever-changing environment.
- Joy is the new song achieved in this co-creative relation. It is embodied in the homograph 樂 (*yuè/lè*): to make music is to make joy.

In this way, the melisma of joy is a form of spontaneous propriety; it flourishes in the same way that a musician, trained in the discipline of rhythm, imbues a given melody with a flourish, embellishing, expanding, and amplifying the original form with the rest of the band. Such rhythms resist the process of endless atomization pursued in the name of identity as well as mitigate against the totalities of a zero-sum world. A freedom without measure is as oppressive as an order without melisma. Finding the balance together is the *jubilus* that leads to joy.

The End of Sad Music

With Augustine's *jubilus* in mind, let's return to Handel's *Messiah* and the aria "Rejoice Greatly." The fact that the melisma on "rejoice" is a form of word painting points to joy in both its mimetic and structural sense as an underlying condition of musical expression. The content and form coincide. The melisma is mimetic by painting joy as a giggle of notes, but it is not simply the representation of the emotion itself but its *structure* of excess that is key. Joy is an open form, a music that repeats itself recursively as a perpetual rhythm. You could replace the word *rejoice* with *capybara* or *baba ganoush* and the music would still jubilate. Music does not need to be about joy to be joyful. It is inherently joyful merely by being a melisma, which is to say that music in its purest form, when unconditioned by words or numbers, is already joy. It is a wordless language of the abundant and superfluous. There is always an ineffable component to any song we sing.

What does this say about sad music? Remember, when we explored sad music at the start of this book, it was a far more significant proposition than "Music is joy." Its profound undertones drowned out the seemingly superficial overtones of joy. So now, if the melismatic abundance of joy is the condition of music, does this cancel sad music?

Oddly, the superfluous signs of joy also constitute the language of lament. Joy is linked to pain, writes the psychiatrist George E. Valliant, "because grief is joy inside out."[29] It appears that in music, joy and sadness inhere secretly within each other: the excess that is laughter is also the excess that is weeping; the noise that is joy is also the noise that is sadness. This noise is both the shout of the *jubilus* and the ululations heard during funeral rites.[30] With its sighs and sobs, the lament is also a melisma beyond words. Grief expresses itself in wailing, in half-torn sentences, stammering syllables, agonizing groans, and breathless stutters. Its inability to speak announces itself repeatedly with superfluous and unnecessary signs. It is a "meaningless" rhythm, a form without words, improvised spontaneously. These sounds are what the philosopher Emmanuel Lévinas calls the "sensorial content" of suffering. Their "uselessness" underlines the intrinsic "nothingness" of such affliction: the pain is "for nothing." This "refusal of meaning" is a linguistic dysfunction, as if such suffering were unutterable. Grief is ineffable.[31] And, like joy, it is music.

Joy and sorrow coexist in music because they share the same stylistic tic. This may explain why joy and sorrow can coexist, but it also throws in doubt the very premise of the question "Is music joy?" It is not just that their similarities enable the coexistence of opposite emotions, but that joy and sorrow are interchangeable and reversible. The question "Is music joy?" could equally be "Is music sadness?" and we would arrive at the same answer. Joy would have no exclusive relation to music.

However, joy and sorrow are not musically reversible. The simplest evidence for this is, ironically, the obvious objection posited at the start of the book: sad music exists. Sad music may exist, but the very fact that it is *music* ensures an order that is fundamentally *not* sad. Consider the misery of "Ball 'n' Chain Blues." However much sorrow wants to tear meaning apart, the music keeps making sense of itself, not in words or concepts but in the very cohesiveness of its generative reiterations. As with the ring shout, it is a "rejoice." Similarly, a lament may embody grief and its words may express sorrow, but as music it can never truly despair. If it did, we would not want to listen to it. Even in compositions that deliberately aim for despair, observes Adorno, music cannot but express hope; music insists on continuing. "Ever since music has existed," claims the philosopher, "it has always been a protest, . . . against myth, against fate . . . and even against death. . . . However feeble its guarantee that there is an alternative, music never abjures its promise that one exists."[32] The rollercoaster ride may aim for oblivion, but as far as Adorno is concerned, even if the tracks inevitably end with a vertical drop, somehow, oblivion is impossible: there is always something more—a melisma, another twist of hope.

What Adorno calls hope is the structure of joy: it is a rhythm that continues, a structure that opens out, a melisma that reaches for something more. From this perspective, sad music is inherently contradictory. And this is precisely the reason why sad music is so exquisitely expressive. The tragic content is enveloped by the coherence and generosity of its medium. In fact, the medium is the content inasmuch as music cannot but make good the tragic. The tragic remains—it is neither canceled nor denied—but it has lost its sting. So Nietzsche and his circle of grumpy philosophers are not wrong: they are just half wrong. Music is exquisitely tragic because of joy. As with Mary's act of lament, music is "a beautiful thing" because its measure is one of abundance. Its "perfect fit" is always more than enough because what it seeks is not the survival of the fittest but the flourishing of the fitting. Music is new creation. Music is the unforced rhythm of grace, and as such redeems the sublime with the beautiful.

This is also why critique can never have the last word in music. I promised to redeem Beethoven's Ninth Symphony, having trashed it for its gratuitous violence. It is violent. We should not be blind to the ideological content of music; critique is necessary, but it is never the end. If under the critical gaze, Beethoven's "Ode to Joy" harbors an odious joy with dubious politics, such "content" can never exhaust or define the meaning of the symphony because there is always a musical surplus, a certain grace, a capacious form, that insists on a coherence beyond critique. As music, Beethoven's "Ode to Joy" *is joy*, however doubtful its content. It might put us in an awkward position at times, especially when what is doubtful is amplified by political ideologies that glorify authoritarian terror. But neither Hitler's (nor, for that matter, Nietzsche's) use of the symphony can have the last word. The music's melismatic "meaning" testifies against the crimes we commit in music—whether known or unknown—by refusing to bend to their meaning.

If we make music purely human, defining its meaning in terms of our technological prowess, then it can only be violent because humans weaponize the world to survive: the bow will sound beautifully as it shoots the arrow; the atom bomb will vibrate in splitting subatomic particles; death will haunt the skin of a drum as we beat on those we kill to make its sounds; the sound of victory, at its most transcendent, comes at the cost of those, like the Cossack horsemen raging to their deaths on Beethoven's working desk, who are charged to gain the world by losing their lives. If the violent tales of music, exemplified by Dionysius and Orpheus, are its ultimate source of meaning, then terror and panic will follow and ultimately lead to a hatred of music and a desire for an empty silence rather than the silence of heaven.[33] Our human failing will always be evident in the music we compose, but music's disproportionate proportion invariably points beyond the human to a different fit, a different relation, a different sense that is woven in the fabric of the universe. Music's rhythm of joy is ineradicable and indestructible.

At the start of the book I mentioned that if we lose what we love, we might learn to love it more when we find it again. We lost human music to the vast rhythm of the universe. Its greatest hits disappeared in a greater music, and the selfie we took it to be was effaced. But if we turn our ears to these works again and hear in their rhythms the fabric of space-time, then our greatest hits are no longer tiny packages of human culture to feed our ego; they tap into a greater rhythm. In making music, we experience the universe we inhabit. It is not homogeneous and empty. It is not chaos. It is not random. It is not whatever we want to make of it. It is given as music and it is infinitely vibrant. Our music, however faltering, is a portal, scaled for our enjoyment, to reflect a complex cosmos. That the wonder of human music is possible points to the wonder of time and space. That music imprints itself in our bodies as instruments of joy means that we can weave our song in counterpoint with the rhythmic ecology around us. That it shapes our desires, entrains our communities, and never stops pulsing means that we should be custodians of its rhythms to keep the things entrusted to us in good measure. We humans sing for joy, with and without language, in times of plenty and in times of want, to remind us of something greater.

If the created order is musical, then its joy points to a way of being in the world. But are we listening?[34] Today, we are knowingly destroying our planet; and, in our politicized divisions and delusions of grandeur, we are destroying each other. Our entrepreneurial exploits have created new business opportunities for injustice and inequality. Totalitarian posturing is trumpeted in the interest of self-interest. Nations condemn nations of crimes for which they themselves are equally guilty. A pandemic has exposed the truth that we prefer to live in "immunity" rather than community; we are "iPodic" individuals isolated and protected from the contagion of others.[35] And most catastrophically, our hubris as masters of our environment has even ushered in a new geological age—the Anthropocene—in which our foolishness will be fossilized for a nonhuman future if we fail to listen to music.

Music is not simply a commodity for complacent consumption. We should take 4′33″ of every day to frame the world around us and listen to its music. The environment we inhabit always makes sense even if seemingly uncomposed, because we are embedded in a musical ecology of complex intersecting rhythms. Nihilism is not possible because, as John Cage notes, 4′33″ of nothing does not exist. There is no silence. The world insists on making music, on making sense.

In response to its rhythms, human beings make music in the world; our "works" are pieces of a greater masterpiece. They scale the universe to an ear-size big bang to disclose the coherence of a space-time fabric that is infinitely generous, gracious, and gratuitous. In listening to music, we discover a portal into a flexible, elastic, unfolding fabric, in which we are interwoven as co-creative participants, seeking the good in homeostatic relation with the rhythms around us. This is the rhythm of the Dao, of the singing *logos,* of Augustine's *consonantia,* of Uexküll's symphonic *Unwelt,* of Leibniz's "best possible world," of Kant's reflective concept of the beautiful, of the melisma. It is home.[36]

Music is a cypher of the universe hiding in plain sight. As such, music does not merely indicate a way of being in the world but of believing in the world. Joy is a doxological relation that points to the goodness of creation, and ultimately to the *logos* behind it. Nature is not against us as something to master instrumentally, but an environment to tend and attend to as instruments of a greater song. Its resonance moves us. And since human beings are hardwired to keep in rhythm, we can vibrate as living stones that continually adjust to the environment in order to build and rebuild a peripatetic sanctuary for the sound of joy to reflect the cosmos. Rhythm can keep us together as a complex community that imparts joy to the world with a good and generous measure. Whatever the circumstances, however tragic or violent, as long as music exists, nothing can seal our fate because, in its very ineffability, music articulates a *jubilus* that refuses to end.

· · ·

Afterword
The Making of the Book

I didn't intend to write this book. Accidents happen. I attribute the existence of this book to moral luck; or more appropriately, given my musings on St. Augustine, to providence. Joy is a surprise.

In 2014, I took a sabbatical at Yale. I was there to complete my monograph *Beethoven and Freedom*. It was supposed to be the final book of a tryptic on the composer. But it also turned out to be the first book of an unintended trilogy based on things that you can't write about in musicology. Now, you can say all manner of things in musicology. Breaking taboos is de rigueur these days and, styling myself as an enfant terrible, I happily complied, titillating the musicology community with my thoughts on Beethoven's testicles and gynecological symptoms in the slow movements of Mozart piano sonatas. But there are things you can't really write about. Normal, everyday things that are just too embarrassing: like love. *Beethoven and Freedom* is a book about love. You can't talk about love in musicology. It's too sentimental, too naïve, and totally brainless. Obviously, *Beethoven and Freedom* turned out be none of the above: it was an impenetrably complex book that demanded a level of philosophical concentration that few musicologists could stomach—it was tough love.

In a completely unrelated event, Miroslav Volf, the director of the Yale Center for Faith and Culture, invited me to join his Theology of Joy Project just when I was about to travel to Yale from Hong Kong. How fortuitous! And how could I say no? I had to say yes to such an eminent theologian. But deep inside I could hear my guts rumbling, "*NOOOOO!!!* Don't do this. There is no research question here. Music and joy—that's a really bad idea." Joy, like love, is something no one talks about in musicology. It's sentimental, naïve, and brainless. So, when I agreed to join the project, I had it in mind to keep my engagement relatively superficial. After all, joy seemed like a pretty lightweight subject compared to the seriously critical work in current musicology. The joy project just needed a light touch, I thought. Unfortunately, the project leaders had a different view, and fleshed out the proposal with so many heavy promises to procure their research grant that they were forced to work me to the bone. So I labored hard with unpromising prospects. At the end of five years, I had written all this heavy and heady stuff on music and joy that was virtually unpublishable—it was neither musicological nor theological enough.

But no worries. I simply regarded the work on joy as a serious hobby since my second book in my accidental trilogy was already well underway. This book, coauthored with Alexander Rehding, was designed to be an out-of-the-box and out-of-this-world experience: an intergalactic music theory for aliens. *Alien Listening* is premised on NASA's pacifist mantra most famously repeated by its toy spokesman Buzz Lightyear: "We come in peace." Peace, of course, is also something we are not supposed to talk about in musicology. Like love and joy, it's considered too ditzy. But having toughened love, I sharpened peace's warm fuzzy feelings with some cold, hard science. This came in the form of NASA's Voyager mission, which rocketed a record of earth's greatest hits into space. *Alien Listening* is about the mechanics of music reproduction as cultural diplomacy—a technology of peace.

With the tough love of *Beethoven and Freedom* and the techy peace of *Alien Listening* published, my accidental trilogy on love, joy, and peace was taking shape; but the project on joy seemed destined to reside as a dusty file in the back of my computer waiting to die in an old operating system. Besides, I wasn't sure that musicology in the West was ready for a dose of theology. In Asia, secular purity is not an academic demand: in fact, the Western bias would not make sense except as a postcolonial import. The mildly theological connotations in *Beethoven and Freedom* already made some musicologists who still believed in a purely secular and singular Enlightenment rather grumpy. There is no doubt that religion has profoundly shaped Western modernity and has not gone away, but they needed to erase or debase it to uphold their version of academia. I realized that just a whiff of theology could set off an allergic reaction that said more about their overblown symptoms than my research. Love, joy, and peace are not only too kitsch for musicology but also too religious. With my research on joy explicitly linked to a theological project, I thought it was best to leave joy alone . . . or else all hell might break loose.

But then, as moral luck would have it, disaster struck. Quite out of the blue, the dean of Yale Divinity School invited me to give the 2020 Bartlett Lecture. Avoiding theology was now off the table. Again, my guts rumbled "*NOOOOO!!!*" But my brain said yes. How could I say no? I took a deep breath, gathered my scattered papers on the theology of joy, and worked in a bit of tough love and intergalactic peace in an attempt to sum up my research agenda over the last five years.

Made alone, at home, and on an iPhone, I dispatched a video entitled "Is Music Joy? Retrofitting Ancient Music" to Yale Divinity School (COVID-19 prevented me from delivering the lecture in person). Finally, there was some closure on my joy research. The video lecture wrapped things up nicely. And that, I thought, was the end of that.

However, in a completely unrelated incident, a colleague randomly suggested that we should invite the mathematician Francis Su to give a talk at the University of Hong Kong. "Francis Su?" I thought to myself. "Hmmm, the name rings a bell. Yes, of course, Francis—I haven't seen him for—*whoa!*—over twenty-five years, when we were at Harvard." Francis Su had just written the book *Mathematics for Human Flourishing*. It just so happened that I was scheduled to give a talk in Pasadena where he lived. We arranged to meet. Francis handed me a copy of his book. As I perused its pages, I wondered to myself: "If mathematics can help humans to flourish, why not music?" It struck a nerve. For some years now, I've been pondering whether the decoupling of fact and value in the humanities has rendered it useless for life and brought it into its current crisis. STEM subjects are marketed as useful skills, but musicology and many others of the liberal arts seem to have lost their value, if not their way. "Musicologists make a living by teaching music," I thought to myself, "but has music taught musicologists how to live?" Is anything we do in musicology useful for our being in the world? Or is it just "auditory cheesecake," as Steven Pinker suggests, something to clog our moral arteries with full-fat pleasure rather than keep us fit for the good life? If Francis Su could integrate numerical facts and human values to enable mathematicians to live well, how much more should music, "the hidden arithmetic exercise of the soul" (as Leibniz famously describes music)?

I asked Francis how his book came about. It turned out that someone at Yale University Press had approached him after hearing his lecture on *Mathematics for Human Flourishing*. It was his farewell speech as the president of the Mathematical Association of America. "Wait!" I thought to myself. "I am the president of the International Musicological Society." Not to be outdone, I made a mental note to keep up with the Su's: "If Francis Su can do that as president of his society, so can I. I may not have a speech in hand, but there is a video lecture that I could expand into book." So I made beeline for Yale University Press and . . . the rest is history: the final if somewhat accidental book of my unintended trilogy on love, joy, and peace came to pass.

"The rest is history" is an understatement. I had set myself an almost impossible task. If you recall, my project on joy had fallen in the abyss between musicology and theology. It was neither here nor there. In the worst-case scenario, musicologists would be offended by theology, and theologians would likely see musicology as a sort of interesting but mostly tangential addition to their research. In all likelihood, they would pass each other as ships in the night and my book would sink without a trace. To grab their attention, I decided to ignore them completely and write for the average person in the street instead. Admittedly, surrounded by my stellar team of collaborators (see the acknowledgments), I may have overestimated the average. Still, it was a brilliant solution, since on average, the disciplinary biases would balance out and I wouldn't need to cater to niche issues and local taboos in musicology and theology. No one would need to believe in God and no one would need to be able to read music, and I could include all kinds of other disciplines in the mix. But it was also a stupid solution since I now had to write in a way that the average person in the street would understand.

Plain, simple English is not an academic's native tongue (at least not mine). Plus, I would need to persuade the average person in the street to stop their humdrum activity and listen to me. But why would they be interested? How would I convince the average person with no confessional stance or musical literacy that the relation between musicology, theology, and a host of other disciplines is vital to their self-interest, let alone ponder whether music is joy?

But that was not my only problem. In the streets, the relation between music and joy is of marginal interest at best; there's not much to say about it. But academically it is a huge globe-trotting, time-traveling, mind-boggling concept that demands an engagement with intellectual and cultural history, moral- and neuropsychology, ancient and modern philosophy, and various branches of musicology and theology. Try making that plain and simple to grab the average attention span!

So I was confronted by a dilemma. My self-imposed brief in writing this book was to express my ideas using the simplest language in the shortest number of pages possible without diluting the complexity of the subject. Why was this my brief? It was not just to cater for the average person. It has always been my policy that the content of any book I write should determine the form. The way a book is put together is as much a medium for communicating the message as the ideas in it. *Beethoven and Freedom* is in three movements to reflect Beethoven's compositional technique; *Alien Listening* is an odd assemblage of items as an homage to the makeshift machinery of NASA's sound technology. So what does joy demand of my book? Two things.

First, joy, in Leibniz's definition, equates the simplest laws with the maximum variety. This means that my book has to be both simple and complicated at the same time. It has to be simple enough for the average person in the street and generate sufficient complexity to stimulate the average academic in their ivory tower.

The second demand is play. Anyone familiar with my writings would know that wordplay has always been my "thing." So it is fortuitous that joy, being a playful subject, invites my wit to tickle its interrogation. Puns are a form of logic that are seemingly not very logical. But that is precisely the point. Novalis, in his "Monologue," pointed out that puns are contingent configurations of words that would not normally belong together; their accidental connection opens up new ways of thinking. In fact, this is exactly how the ancient world understood music—through puns. Music is joy (樂) is a pun. Melody is law (*nomos*) is a pun. Homographs and homonyms are a form of logic operating under chance: it is moral luck at work! So my puns are intended, not only as an expression of music and joy but as the very structure of their relation. Indeed, for Novalis, wordplay is the very logic of music—which is to say, music is joy!

But there is a serious side to all this. Ancient wordplay had cosmic implications for how we live and how we govern ourselves. Music as joy is not just something to think about: it is lived knowledge. The good life is not a good life if it just cogitates inside the brain. It seemed incongruous, then, for me to write a book on music and joy without some engagement with the political climate and the climate of the planet that are both threatening our very existence. In particular, in my small corner of the world, my accidental trilogy on love, joy, and peace coincides with the political upheavals in Hong Kong. The first book, written just after the Umbrella Movement of 2014, proved to be prophetic. The dedication page reads: "As I write these words in the University of Hong Kong, I am conscious of the freedom I have because I can no longer take it for granted. The Umbrella Movement and its political backlash has flushed out the demons from the indigent and distorted crevices of this gleaming metropolis. Freedom is on trial, and its ideals distorted as a clash of wills in a zero-sum game where any victory is destined to fail."

I penned these words in 2016 just before rushing the manuscript to the press. Five years later, the zero-sum game has resulted in a glorious failure—even for those who claim victory—that has only exacerbated the divisions. The demons have wreaked havoc. But it is precisely in such circumstances that love, joy, and peace take on an urgency. Contemplating these virtues is not a form of escapism but engagement, without which there is no purpose to politics except the will-to-power. It is a mistake to imagine love, joy, and peace to be too naïve or too religious for rigorous thought: the fact that we cannot talk seriously about them without embarrassment in musicology (and other areas in the arts and sciences) indicates a failure of thought, a failure of culture, and a failure of nerve.

So although I did not intend to write this book, the book took on some agency and urgency of its own: in one sense, it intended me to write it. The timing could not be better to keep me joyful and hopeful in times of difficulty. With serendipity guiding this book, I hope that it is a providential find for you in whatever circumstances you find yourself. There is one circumstance we share for sure: the planet is in critical condition, and this circumstance should bend our ears to the wisdom of an ancient music. Music is not a consolation or opiate in times of trouble, but a joy that is resilient and hopeful; it surrounds us and, alongside love and peace, plants a seed for the future. I would consider myself lucky if in reading this book, you secure your future—and perhaps that of our species—in discovering a rhythm in the Way of joy.

Notes

1
Is Music Joy?

1. Steven Pinker, *How the Mind Works* (New York: Norton, 1997), 534.

2. See Immanuel Kant, *Critique of the Power of Judgment,* ed. Paul Guyer, trans. Paul Guyer and Eric Matthews (Cambridge: Cambridge University Press, 2000), 208–9.

3. John Cage, *Silence: Lectures and Writings* (Middletown, CT: Wesleyan University Press, 1961), 8.

2
A Tragic Turn

1. Eduard Hanslick, *The Beautiful in Music,* trans. G. Cohen (New York: Liberal Arts Press, 1957), 68–69n.

2. In preparing Schiller's text for the Ninth Symphony, Beethoven removed all references to the consumption of alcoholic beverages from the original poem.

3. See measures 208–17.

4. See measures 216 and 237–40.

5. See measures 331–593.

6. See measures 431–525.

7. Richard Wagner, "Zum Vortrag der neunten Symphonie Beethovens," *Gesammelte Schriften und Dichtungen von Richard Wagner,* vol. 9 (Leipzig: Fritzsch, 1873), 241.

8. See measures 543–93.

9. See measures 843–940.

10. The telltale sign of joy's oppression is first found in a seemingly inconsequential line of the ode: "He who cannot rejoice, let him steal weeping away from this group." The exclusionary politics of this line is sung with a sudden hush as if to describe someone "stealing away" from the crowd; but it also sounds like a quiet blush that gives away the lie that the unity the symphony champions is one of discrimination. For more commentary on the speed and violence of the symphony, see Daniel K. L. Chua, *Beethoven and Freedom* (Oxford: Oxford University Press, 2019), 88–99.

11. For example, the symphony is used as a soundtrack for violence in Stanley Kubrick's film adaption of Anthony Burgess's novel *A Clockwork Orange* (1971); in *Sherlock,* season 4, episode 2, "The Lying Detective" (2017), where it accompanies a sports car driving violently through traffic in a police chase; it is also used as a comically violent plot in Peter Segal's film *Get Smart* (2008), in which the villain, Siegfried (Terence Stamp), plants a bomb in the Walt Disney Concert Hall to be triggered by the sound of the Ninth's final chords.

12. See measures 843–50.

13. Theodor W. Adorno, *Quasi una Fantasia: Essays on Modern Music* (1963), trans. R. Livingstone (London: Verso 1992), 34.

14. As Adorno questions concerning Beethoven's heroic music: "Does not music perhaps stand firm against fate precisely in *becoming* fate? Is not imitation the canon of resistance? . . . Does not gaining-power-over-oneself, freedom, lie only in imitation, in making-oneself similar?" Theodor W. Adorno, *Beethoven: The Philosophy of Music,* ed. Rolf Tiedemann, trans. Edmund Jephcott (Cambridge, MA: Polity, 1998), 169.

15. See Carl Dahlhaus, *Nineteenth-Century Music,* trans. J. Bradford Robinson (Berkeley: University of California Press, 1991), 81–83.

16. Martin Heidegger, *Heraclitus. The Inception of Occidental Thinking and Logic: Heraclitus Doctrine of the Logos,* trans. Julia Goesser Assaiante and S. Montgomery Ewegen (London: Bloomsbury, 2018), 114.

17. Arthur Schopenhauer, *The World as Will and Representation,* trans. E. F. J. Payne (New York: Dover, 1969), 2:450.

18. For a summary of the role of Beethoven's Ninth Symphony in the tragic culture of German philosophy during this period, see Lydia Goehr, "The Ode to Joy: Music and Musicality in Tragic Culture," in *4/2006 Ästhetik und Philosophie der Kunst / Aesthetics and Philosophy of Art,* ed. Karl P. Ameriks and John Stolzenberg (Berlin: De Gruyter, 2007), 54–87.

19. I will move to Nietzsche's extension of Schopenhaurian thought to answer this question. Within Schopenhauer's philosophy, the answer is

more complex and seemingly contradictory in places: see Judith Norman, "Music and Pessimism," in *The Palgrave Schopenhauer Handbook*, ed. Sandra Shapshay (London: Palgrave Macmillan, 2017), 197–210.

20. See Friedrich Nietzsche, *The Birth of Tragedy and Other Writings*, ed. Raymond Geuss and Ronald Speirs, trans. Ronald Speirs (Cambridge: Cambridge University Press, 1999), 18 (on the Ninth Symphony), 22–23 (on "to die soon"), and 40 (on nausea or revulsion).

21. Nietzsche, *The Birth of Tragedy*, 114. Section 24 of *The Birth of Tragedy* (111–15) is key to the philosopher's affirmation of life in view of Schopenhauer's pessimism, providing a joyous if fateful conclusion on how to live a dissonant life.

22. Nietzsche, *The Birth of Tragedy*, 17. Ironically, the very death-drive that Nietzsche tries to overcome in Western metaphysics drives his pursuit for vitality—an irony that Nietzsche himself was well aware of. See Jonathan Dollimore, *Death, Desire and Loss in Western Culture* (New York: Routledge, 2001), 231–48.

23. Nietzsche, *The Birth of Tragedy*, 37–38, 111–15.

24. Nietzsche, *The Birth of Tragedy*, 23.

25. For an overarching critique of these grumpy old *men* of philosophy and the "necrophilic" neurosis of the West, see Grace M. Jantzen, *Foundations of Violence: Death and the Displacement of Beauty* (London: Routledge, 2004), 1–46. Jantzen's feminist critique traces the source of Western necrophilia to the very culture that Nietzsche celebrates in the *Birth of Tragedy*: the ancient Greeks.

26. Philippe Lacoue-Labarthe, *Typography: Mimesis, Philosophy and Politics* (Stanford, CA: Stanford University Press, 1989), 193.

27. Jean-François Lyotard, *Postmodern Fables*, trans. Georges van den Abbeele (Minneapolis: University of Minnesota Press, 1997), 226.

28. On this kind of violent ontology or violent habitus see, for example, Jantzen, *Foundations of Violence*, 3–34; John Milbank, *Theology and Social Theory: Beyond Secular Reason* (Oxford: Blackwell, 1990), 278–325: and David Bentley Hart, *The Beauty of the Infinite: The Aesthetics of Christian Truth* (Grand Rapids, MI: Eerdmans, 2003), 1–5.

3
Reorientation

1. In ancient Chinese, *yuè* is sometimes pronounced *yuo* (music), and *lè* is pronounced *luo* (joy), which cements their relation not only with the same character but in rhyme.

2. Following Western convention, I will capitalize "Way" and "Dao"; in Chinese, there is neither the possibility of capitalization nor the use of the definite article "the" before "道." Doing so gives a certain metaphysical and theological dimension to the term. While this might resonate interculturally with Western notions, the term, as we will see, is more down to earth, denoting a harmonizing process in the world and with others.

3. This phrase—"樂者, 樂也."—is twice stated in the "Record of Music" (Yue Ji 樂記) in the Book of Rites (Li Ji 禮記); see Book of Rites, English-Chinese version, trans. James Legge (Beijing: Intercultural, 2013), 178, 183. For a modern English translation of the "Record of Music," see Scott Cook, "'Yue Ji' 樂記 — 'Record of Music': Introduction, Translation, Notes, and Commentary," Asian Music 62, no. 2 (1995): 1–96; quotations at 59 and 67 (Scott translates le as "happiness"). There is considerable debate concerning the "lost" Book of Music. Some scholars have proposed that The Book of Music was never actually a physical text, but rather a musical artefact passed on by aural tradition. Martin Kern suggest that it was a product of the late Western or early Eastern Han Dynasty, several decades after Sima Qian's Records of the Grand Historian (c. 94 BCE) was completed, since the chapter on music is largely identical to "Record of Music" in the Book of Rites (in fact, the latter also dates from the same period). See Martin Kern, "A Note on the Authenticity and Ideology of Shih-Chi 24, 'The Book on Music,'" Journal of the American Oriental Society 119, no. 4 (1999): 673–77.

4. "夫樂者, 樂也." Xunzi: The Complete Text, trans. Eric L Hutton (Princeton, NJ: Princeton University Press, 2014), 218.

5. On the concept of qing (情), see Brian Bruya, "Qing (情) and Emotion in Early Chinese Thought," Ming Qing Yanjiu (2001): 151–76.

6. Book of Rites, "Record of Music," 560.

7. See Erica Fox Brindley, Music Cosmology and the Politics of Harmony in China (Albany: State University of New York Press, 2012), 89–90.

8. "大樂" literally means "big music."

9. The Spring and Autumn Annals (Lüshi chunqiu 呂氏春秋): The Annals of Lü Buwei, trans. John Knoblock and Jeffrey K. Riegel (Stanford, CA: Stanford University Press, 2001), 138, translation modified. On the notion of social harmony and the significance of Confucian and Daoist concepts of music in The Annals, see Scott Cook, "The Lüshi chunqiu and the Resolution of Philosophical Dissonance," Harvard Journal of Asiatic Studies 62, no. 2 (2002): 307–45.

10. On the wisdom of "government by music" in Confucian thought, see Lin Yutang, Between Tears and Laughter (Muriwai Books, 2018), 84–94.

11. The construction of the Forbidden City started in 1420 when the capital moved from Nanjing to Beijing during the Ming Dynasty. The names of the great halls acquired their musical names in the Qing Dynasty in 1644.

12. The first formally recorded story about Ling Lun is in the *Lüshi chunqiu* (chapter 5); see *The Annals of Lü Buwei*, 147.

13. The actual Chinese measure is 3.9 *cun* (寸). Oddly, given that Chinese music theorists were dependent on the dimensions of instruments to determine pitch, this is the only measurement given in the *Lüshi chunqiu* account. To reconstruct the pitch from this object, it would be necessary to know at least the width of the pipe.

14. For a detailed explanation and translation of this passage, see Cook, "The *Lüshi chunqiu*," 324. See also *The Annals of Lü Buwei*, 136.

15. For more details on tuning, see chapter 13 in this book.

16. There are various accounts of this legend. See, for example, Liu Xiang, *Shuo yuan* (Beijing: Zhonghua shuju, 1985), 196; Ban Gu, *Han shu* (Beijing: Zhonghua shuju, 1962), 959; and Ying Shao, *Fengsu tongyi* (Shanghai: Shanghai guji chubanshe, 1990), 44.

17. Given the unlikelihood of corroborating a pitch pipe with a *fenghuang*, subsequent imperial music theorists foraged in their own backyards to determine the standard frequency, using an alternative method known as "Watching for the Ethers" in which bamboo pipes filled with ashes would emit inaudible sounds in the form of ash clouds as the wind blew across the opening of the pipes. The imperial Daoist-cum-music theorist Wei Hanjin in 1102 CE even modeled the standards of pitch, measure, volume, and weight from Emperor Huizong's middle finger—which is a safe bet in the absence of the *fenghuang* in determining the authority of a rule: music and the finger of the emperor became one ring to rule them all.

18. *Xunzi: The Complete Text*, 221 (translation slightly modified).

19. See *Book of Rites*, "Record of Music," 560, 576.

20. Section 8.8 of Confucius's *Analects* combines poetry, rites (choreographed movement), and music: "It is through poetry that one's mind is aroused. It is by rituals that one's character is established. It is from music that one's perfection is achieved (興於詩, 立於禮, 成於樂)." Annping Chin's translation of the passage is more pedestrian, rendering the final line as "Music is the final lesson"; however, the translator explains that a way of understanding the line is to see music as the culmination of a process of ecstatic balance, "drawing together a life that is as fluent as music." See Confucius, *Analects*, trans. Annping Chin (New York: Penguin, 2014), 121.

21. This object, along with the other two trinkets on our tour of ancient China, alludes to both Confucian and Daoist ideas of human order and the natural environment. The intermingling of these traditions in regard to music has a precedent in the *The Annals of Lü Buwei* (that is, the *Lüshi chunqiu*, the earliest text to formally record Ling Lun's musical adventures), and Liu An, King of Huainan, *The Huainanzi: A Guide to the*

Theory and Practice of Government in Early Han China, ed. and trans. John S. Major, Sarah A. Queen, Andrew Seth Meyer, and Harold D. Roth (New York: Columbia University Press, 2010). Intellectuals in the Wei-Jin period (220–420 BCE), such as Lü Buwei, attempted to reconcile Daoism with Confucianism; see Cook, "The *Lüshi chunqiu.*" On its significance in the aesthetics of Chinese *shanshui* ink painting and Chinese philosophy more generally, see Yuk Hui, *Art and Cosmotechnics* (Minneapolis: University of Minnesota Press and E-Flux, 2021), 126–70.

22. See Jakob von Uexküll, *A Foray into the Worlds of Animals and Humans: With a Theory of Meaning,* trans. Joseph D. O'Neil (Minneapolis: University of Minnesota Press, 2010).

23. "The great square has no corners. . . . The great note is rarefied in sound." Lao Tzu, *Tao Te Ching,* trans. D. C. Lau (London: Penguin Books, 1963), 2.41.91, 48.

24. See, for example, Tim Ingold, *Being Alive: Essays on Movement, Knowledge and Description* (London: Routledge, 2021), 145–64.

25. See Immanuel Kant, *Critique of the Power of Judgment,* ed. Paul Guyer, trans. Paul Guyer and Eric Matthews (Cambridge: Cambridge University Press, 2000), 63–80; note that Paul Guyer uses the term "reflecting power of judgment" in this translation. Although Kant's third *Critique* is not particularly musical—especially given his "intestinal view" of musical benefits mentioned in my opening chapter—it was nonetheless a generative book, inspiring the Romantic philosophers and artists in the early nineteenth century to wax lyrical about music. The idea of the "reflective judgement" as a harmonious play in the mind contributed greatly to the elevation of music, with all its nonrepresentational patterns, as the quintessential Romantic art form. See Daniel K. L. Chua, *Absolute Music and the Construction of Meaning* (Cambridge: Cambridge University Press, 1999), 167–217; and "Beethoven Going Blank," *Journal of Musicology* 31, no. 3 (2014): 307–12.

26. Igor Stravinsky, *Poetics of Music in the Form of Six Lessons,* trans. Arthur Knodel and Ingolf Dahl (London: Oxford University Press, 1947), 55–56.

4
Music by Numbers

1. The best-known and most influential retelling of this myth is in Boethius, *De musica* 1.10. See Anicius Manlius Severinus Boethius, *Fundamentals of Music,* ed. Claude V. Palisca, trans. Calvin M. Bower (New Haven, CT: Yale University Press, 1989). The earliest surviving record of

the myth is in Nicomachus of Gerasa, *Enchiridion harmonices;* see *The Manual of Harmonics of Nicomachus the Pythagorean,* ed. and trans. Flora R. Levin (Grand Rapids, MI: Phanes, 1994), 83. For a modern account, see Daniel Heller-Roazen, *The Fifth Hammer: Pythagoras and the Disharmony of the World* (New York: Zone Books, 2011).

2. See Mike Goldsmith, *Acoustics, Astronomy, Mathematics, Science Writing: History of Noise,* https://mikegoldsmith.weebly.com/history-of -noise.html (accessed November 13, 2023).

3. On the influence of the tetractys, see Leo Spitzer, *Classical and Christian Ideas of World Harmony: Prolegomena to an Interpretation of the Word Stimmung,* ed. Anna Granville Hatcher (New York: Angelico, 2021), 5–79.

4. In Greek, the Latin term ratio is *logoi* (the plural of *logos*). In this sense, ancient music is both *rational* and *logical*.

5. As I am writing (May 10, 2022), Apple has just announced the iPod's obsolescence. But the iPod is not really dead. Rather it has transcended its own material form. As Apple's senior vice president of worldwide marketing, Greg Joswiak, puts it: The iPod no longer requires its own existence because "today, the spirit of iPod lives on . . . integrated across all of our products, from the iPhone to the Apple Watch to HomePod mini, and across Mac, iPad, and Apple TV." The iPod is now a prosthetic extension of the way we live with music. See "The Music Lives On: iPod Touch Will Be Available While Supplies Last," *Newsroom,* May 10, 2022, https://www .apple.com/hk/en/newsroom/2022/05/the-music-lives-on/.

6. I borrow the term "expressive individualism" from the analysis of modern American identity by Robert N. Bellah, Richard Madsen, William M. Sullivan, and Steven M. Tipton in *Habits of the Heart: Individualism and Commitment in American Life* (Berkeley: University of California Press, 1985).

7. Pertinent to this discussion is Hartmut Rosa's concept of resonance as the mutual relation between things, persons, and transcendent ideas: resonance is precisely what is missing in a hyper-productive, narcissistic consumer society. Music should naturally resonate; today, however, its vibrations are contained in a soundproofed pod. See Hartmut Rosa, *Resonances: A Sociology of Our Relationship to the World,* trans. James Wagner (Cambridge, MA: Polity, 2019).

8. See Iamblichus, *On the Pythagorean Way of Life: Text, Translation, and Notes,* ed. and trans. John Dillon and Jackson Hershbell (Atlanta: Scholars, 1991), 88–90, 135–37.

9. See Plato, *The Republic,* ed. G. R. F. Ferrari, trans. Tom Griffith (Cambridge: Cambridge University Press, 2000), 3:398d–399d.

10. See Plato, *The Republic* 4:430d–432b, citation at 432b (in this instance, I prefer to use Benjamin Jowett's translation, which is more musical).

11. See Plato, *The Republic* 3:413e.

12. Plato, *Timaeus and Critias,* trans. Robin Waterfield (Oxford: Clarendon, 2008); see *Timaeus* 90a, 41d, and 43e.

13. See Plato, *The Republic* 3:411E–412A, 7:522–34.

14. Plato, *The Republic* 7:522a, 530–532b.

15. Plato, *The Republic* 2:370d, 51, 3:413e.

16. This discriminatory practice has a parallel with the Confucian "Record of Music" in the *Book of Rites,* which begins by making a three-fold hierarchical distinction: *shēng* 聲 (the sound of animals), *yīn* 音 music (the music of common people), and *yuè* 樂 (the superior music of the cultivated person). Although in practice this distinction is not evident in other Confucian texts and is sometimes indirectly critiqued in Daoist texts, the elevation of ritual music in the *Book of Rites* as a joyful state of governance comes at the expense of removing the "dissonance" of common and non-human sounds. However, the distinction is inherently blurred, particularly with regard to the tuning of the yellow bell, which is directed by the Mandate of Heaven and revealed in nature. See So Jeong Park, "Musical Thought in the *Zhuangzi*: A Criticism of the Confucian Discourse on Ritual and Music," *Dao* 12, no. 3 (2013): 331–50.

5
Event Organizer

1. Luke 2:10. All citations from the Bible are taken from the New International Version.

2. On the event and the supernumerary in general, see Alain Badiou, *Being and Event,* trans. Oliver Feltham (London: Continuum, 2006). On their application to the resurrection, see Alain Badiou, *Saint Paul: The Foundations of Universalism,* trans. Ray Brassier (Stanford, CA: Stanford University Press, 2003).

3. See Genesis 1:3, and John 1:9 and 14.

4. Hildegard of Bingen, *Scivias* (1151), trans. Columba Hart and Jane Bishop (New York: Paulist, 1990), 152.

5. It is uncertain if Hildegard is the actual painter of the images in the *Scivias;* the illuminations were more likely to have been painted under her personal supervision.

6. The vision alludes to Hebrews 12:2, which states that Jesus, "for the joy set before him," endured the cross to usher in a new beginning through his resurrection. Also see John 16:22.

7. Hildegard of Bingen, *Scivias,* 59.

8. Hildegard of Bingen, *Scivias*, 150.

9. Hildegard of Bingen, *Scivias*, 155.

10. Unfortunately, there is no musical notation in the *Scivias*, but Hildegard collected seventy-seven of her songs, including those in the *Scivias*, in her *Symphonia armoniae celestium revelationum* (Symphony of the Harmony of Heavenly Revelations).

11. Hildegard of Bingen, *Scivias*, 532–33.

12. I mention here the translation in the Greek Septuagint (the Hebrew word is *tob*) since, as we saw earlier in Plato, the word *kalon* means both "good" and "beautiful."

13. Proverbs 8:22–31 (slightly modified).

14. See Colossians 1:16–17.

15. Job 38:4–7.

16. Revelations 22:16.

17. On the singing Jesus, see Michael O'Connor, "The Singing of Jesus," in *Resonant Witness: Conversations between Music and Theology*, ed. Jeremy S. Begbie and Steven R. Guthrie (Grand Rapids, MI: Eerdmans, 2013), 434–53.

6
New Song

1. Clement of Alexandria, *Protrepticus*. The translation is from *Clement of Alexandria: The Exhortation to the Greeks*, trans. G. W. Butterworth, Loeb Classical Library (Cambridge, MA: Harvard University Press, 1960), 11, 15.

2. Clement, *Exhortation*, 15 (translation slightly modified).

3. See Clement, *Exhortation*, 2–9, where Clement plays on the name of the minstrel Eunomus (Eu-*nomos*) and his song (*nomos*), as well as the independent music (auto-*nomos*) of chirping grasshoppers; similarly, Christ is described as the "law and Word" (*nomos/logos*), and as the new song of Moses (representing the law).

4. Clement, *Exhortation*, 4–5. The term *autonomos* is used to describe the music of grasshoppers, particularly of one who hopped onto the lyre of the minstrel Eunomos when one of the strings on his instrument snapped. According to Clement, as a substitute for the missing string, the grasshopper played a more godly song than the human music sung in praise of an idol. Musical "autonomy" is a familiar concept in modern times, but in the ancient texts, this is the first and only use of the political term for music. Clement's use of "auto-nomos" probably refers to the music of creation as

a sound independent from the music of human cults. Autonomous music freely celebrates the goodness of creation. This is the true music of creation. See Miguel Herrero de Jáuregui, *The Protrepticus of Clement of Alexandria: A Commentary* (PhD diss., University of Bologna, 2008), 111.

5. Plato, *Timaeus and Critias,* trans. Robin Waterfield (Oxford: Clarendon, 2008), 90d.

6. Clement, *Exhortation, 7.*

7. See Clement, *Exhortation, 9.*

8. As Clement writes in his *Stromata* 6.11.89.4: "The study of music [should serve] the proper arrangement and restraint of manners" rather than cultic revelry or bawdy dinner entertainment. See *Stromata Buch I—VI,* ed. Ludwig Früchtel (Berlin: Akademie-Verlag, 1960), 5:476; the translation is from Charles H. Cosgrove, "Clement of Alexandria and Early Christian Music," *Journal of Early Christian Studies* 14, no. 3 (2006): 258.

9. Clement, *Paedagogus* 2.5.46.2–3, in *Protrepticus und Paedagogus,* ed. Ursula Treu (Berlin: Akademie-Verlag, 1972), 12:185–86. The translation is from Cosgrove, "Clement of Alexandria and Early Christian Music," 259.

10. Clement also discusses the manly and effeminate ethos of these different modes in his *Paedagogus.* Cosgrove, "Clement of Alexandria and Early Christian Music," 270–276.

11. See Clement, *Exhortation, 13.*

12. *Xunzi: The Complete Text,* trans. Eric L. Hutton (Princeton, NJ: Princeton University Press, 2014), 221.

13. See Plato, *The Republic,* ed. G. R. F. Ferrari, trans. Tom Griffith (Cambridge: Cambridge University Press, 2000), 4:424b.

14. This explanation of sin as a dissonance within the tuning system will continue for many centuries. Even as late as the early eighteenth century, sin (in the guise of its tempter Lucifer) is described by the music theorist Andreas Werckmeister as an irrational number detuning the perfect ratios of the harmonic order, requiring Christ to adjust the intonation. See Andreas Werckmeister, *Musicalische Paradoxal-Discourse: A Well-Tempered Universe* [1707], trans. Dietrich Bartel (Lanham, MD: Lexington Books, 2018), 137–40.

15. See Ezekiel 11:19 and 36:26, and 2 Corinthians 3:3.

16. See Clement, *Exhortation, 9–10.*

17. Clement, *Exhortation, 11* (translation slightly modified).

18. Clement, *Exhortation, 14–15.*

19. Clement, *Exhortation, 13* (translation slightly modified).

20. See Werckmeister, *Musicalische Paradoxal-Discourse, 26.*

7

Baptism

1. Romans 13:13–14.

2. See Augustine, *The Confessions*, ed. John E. Rotelle, trans. Maria Boulding (New York: New City, 1997), 8.12.28–29, 246–48.

3. See Augustine, *The Confessions* 9.6.14, 264–65.

4. Augustine, *De musica*, ed. Martin Jacobsson with an introduction by Martin Jacobsson and Lukas J. Dorfbauer (Berlin: De Gruyter, 2017). English citations will mostly be from Augustine, *On Music*, trans. Robert Catesby Taliaferro, in *The Fathers of the Church*, vol. 4 (Washington, DC: Catholic University of America Press, 1947), 153–379.

5. See Augustine, *De musica* 1.12.20–26.

6. See Carol Harrison, "Augustine and the Art of Music," in *Resonant Witness: Conversations between Music and Theology*, ed. Jeremy S. Begbie and Steven R. Guthrie (Grand Rapids, MI: Eerdmans, 2013), 31.

7. In *De libero arbitrio* 2.16.47, Augustine declares that all things in creation "have forms because they have numbers: to take away their numbers would mean that nothing would remain." On Christ as number, see Carol Harrison, "Measure, Number and Weight in Saint Augustine's Aesthetics," *Augustinianum* 28, no. 3 (1988): 599. On Augustine's application of Pythagorean numbers, see Junxiao Bai, "Numbers: Harmonic Ratios and Beauty in Augustinian Musical Cosmology," *Cosmos and History: The Journal of Natural and Social Philosophy* 13, no. 2 (2017).

8. Augustine, *De musica* 6.11.29.

9. Augustine, *Epistola 101, ad Memorio, 3*. The translation is in Bai, "Numbers: Harmonic Ratios and Beauty," 196. The comment in this letter is in reference to *De musica*.

10. See Augustine, *De musica* 6.9.23

11. See Augustine, *De musica* 6.14.43.

12. See Martin Jacobsson and Lukas J. Dorfbauer, "The Time-Frame and Circumstances of the Composition of *De musica*," introduction to Augustine, *De musica*, 1–10.

13. The physical travel was also a mental journey; Augustine describes the first five books as a necessary form of wayfaring (*itinerandi*), to arrive at book 6. See *De musica* 6.1.1.

14. On the effect of the fall in *De musica*, see Carol Harrison, *On Music, Sense, Affect and Voice* (London: Bloomsbury Academic, 1919), 44–54.

15. See Hans Urs von Balthasar, *The Glory of the Lord: A Theological Aesthetics II* (Edinburgh: Ignatius, 1984), 117. See Augustine, *De musica* 6.4.7, 6.5.9.

16. See Augustine, *De musica* 6.17.57, 6.4.7.

17. See Augustine, *De musica* 6.11.29, 6.14.46.

18. See Augustine, *De musica* 6.11.30.

19. See Augustine, *De musica* 6.17.57, 6.13.40. On pride and the knowledge of beauty, see Augustine, *Confessions* 4.13.20–4.15.27, 133–38.

20. See Augustine, *De musica* 6.4.7.

21. See Augustine, *De musica* 6.1.1, 6.4.7.

22. Augustine, *De ordine* 2.11.34. On this critical distinction and the relation between *De ordine* and *De musica*, see Harrison, *On Music*, 54–60.

23. It might be instructive to compare Augustine's concept of beauty and harmony expressed in *De musica* with the description in his *Confessions* of his book *On the Beautiful and Harmonious*, written before his conversion at the age of twenty-six or twenty-seven. The book, which Augustine himself had lost, was regarded by the saint as a misguided and erroneous attempt at contemplating the question of beauty: it focused on material objects as internally beautiful and externally fitting based solely on human reason. In other words, Augustine himself was guilty of fixating on one decontextualized syllable that merely made "a din in his heart" instead of catching the "inner melody" of God's truth, and so lost the "joy" that would have come from hearing "the perfect sound" of the call of Christ. Presumably, he found that joy by the end of *De musica*. See his *Confessions* 4.13.20–4.15.27, 133–38; citation at 4.15.27, 138.

24. See Augustine, *Letters*, vol. 2, ed. Boniface Ramsey, trans. Roland Teske (New York: New York City Press, 2003), letter 138.1.5, 228.

25. See Augustine, *De musica* 6.17.58. The opening chapter of his *Confessions* famously states: "You [God] have made us for yourself, and our hearts are restless until they rest in you (cor nostrum *inquietum* est donec *requiescat* in Te)."

26. Incidentally, there is an apt but totally apocryphal account claiming that the Te Deum was composed antiphonally by Ambrose and Augustine during Augustine's baptism. If there was an exchange, perhaps Ambrose and Augustine sang alternate lines or verses of *Deus creator omnium*.

27. The translation is by Toomas Karmo, February 12, 2018: http://toomaskarmo.blogspot.com/2018/02/toomas-karmo-literal-translation-with.html. The entire hymn is structured around night-day imagery.

God, creator of all things,
And governor of the world, clothing
The day in decorous light
And the night in gift of sleep:

May repose restore relaxed limbs
To purposes of labor,
And may repose relieve the burden of tired minds,
Bringing resolution to anxious cares.

Our thanksgiving prayers
In our now-completed day and in our night's upwelling:
We, consecrated, deliver to You, singing, our hymn,
That You might give sinners your support.

May our hearts' depths sing You in harmony,
May the sonorous voice proclaim You,
May chaste affection love You,
May sober minds adore You,

So that when deep nocturnal gloom
Shuts in the day,
May faith know nothing of shadows,
But night shine back in faith.

May You not permit the mind to slumber,
But may Guilt know slumber;
And may Faith, refreshing the upright,
Temper Sleep's steamy breath.

With the treacherous garment of Sense now cast off,
May the heart's heights dream of you,
And let not Fear, through the jealous Enemy's trick,
Rouse those who rest.

Let us beg Christ and the Father,
And the Spirit of both Christ and Father,
One full-powerful through all things:
Protect and cherish, O Trinity, these who pray.

---

28. Augustine, *Confessions* 9.12.29–33. The recollection of *Deus creator omnium* may have also reminded him of what was likely his first encounter with the hymn, when his mother, "full of joy," sang a line from the final verse in answer to the question "What is the happy life?" The memory of the hymn may have also been a confirmation of his mother's "happy life" in this world and the next. See Augustine, *De beata uita* 4.35; and also Harrison, *On Music,* 102–3.

29. Augustine, *De musica* 6.1.1.

30. See Graham Ward, "Aesthetics, Music and Meaning-Making," *Religions* 10, no. 3 (2019): 215.

9

Retrofitting Ancient Music

1. See Rujing Huang, "'A Theory of Our Own': Reconstructing National Scales in the Chinese *Yayue* Revival," *Naxos Musicology International* (July 2020); and Rujing Huang, "Sounds of Heaven: Reconciling History, Ethnicity, and Nationhood in the Divine Music of the Qing Empire," presentation at the 63rd Annual Meeting of the Society for Ethnomusicology, Albuquerque, November 15–18, 2018.

2. Pythagoras and Niels Bohr used the same process of spectroscopy to arrive at their theories—one by examining the frequency of musical notes on a monochord, and the other by analyzing the frequency of the colors of light produced by a hydrogen lamp. Both found simple integer relationships between frequencies. The notes of a scale are ratios formed by integers such as 1:2 (n/m), whereas the ratios for hydrogen are square numbers (n^2/m^2).

3. Benedict Anderson, *Imagined Communities: Reflections on the Origin and Spread of Nationalism,* rev. ed. (London: Verso, 1991), 24–36; in his first use of the phrase (24), Anderson is quoting from Walter Benjamin's *Illuminations,* but with its subsequent use, the phrase gathers new impetus as the framework for time in modernity—a time of transverse, temporal coincidences among anonymous individuals organized by clock and calendar. In contrast, the calendar in ancient China was marked by the stars and the notes of the twelve pitch pipes. See, for example, *The Huainanzi* 3.28–3.30, 133–34.

4. Theodor W. Adorno, *Minima Moralia: Reflections from Damaged Life,* trans. E. F. N. Jephcott (London: Verso, 2002), 35–37.

10

Facial Recognition

1. See Paul Ekman, "Universal Facial Expressions of Emotion," *California Mental Health Research Digest* 8, no. 4 (Autumn 1970); and Paul Ekman, "Universal and Cultural Differences in Facial Expressions of Emotion," *Nebraska Symposium on Motivation* 19 (1972). The number of primary emotions varies from four to eight in current literature, although joy (used interchangeably and inconsistently with happiness, even in Ekman's research) is in each list, along with fear, anger, and sadness. In his more recent work, Ekman tends to use the term *enjoyment* as a more complex category that encompasses a host of joyful feelings from peace to ecstasy.

2. *Book of Rites,* English-Chinese version, trans. James Legge (Beijing: Intercultural, 2013), 104, states: "What are the feelings of men? They are joy, anger, sadness, fear, love, disliking, and liking. These seven feelings belong to men without their learning them." As with the current literature on the basic emotions, in the Confucian texts there are four, six, or seven basic emotions, in which anger, sorrow, joy, and pleasure are always included.

3. *The Book of Rites,* 171. Also see Scott Cook's translation in "'Yue Ji' 樂記—'Record of Music': Introduction, Translation, Notes, and Commentary," *Asian Music* 62, no. 2 (1995): 27–287.

4. See Antonio Damasio, *Looking for Spinoza: Joy, Sorrow, and the Feeling Brain* (Orlando: Harcourt, 2003), 164; and George E. Valliant, *Spiritual Evolution: A Scientific Defence of Faith* (New York: Broadway Books, 2008), 124.

5. Sylvan S. Tomkins, *Affect Imagery Consciousness,* vol. 1: *The Positive Affects* (New York: Springer, 1962), 356.

6. Miroslav Volf, "The Crown of the Good Life: Joy, Happiness and the Life Well Lived—A Hypothesis," Australian Broadcasting Corporation, August 20, 2025, https://www.abc.net.au/religion/the-crown-of-the-good-life-joy-happiness-and-the-life-well-lived/10097970.

7. Robert C. Roberts, *Spiritual Emotions: A Psychology of Christian Virtues* (Grand Rapids, MI: Eerdmans, 2007), 116.

8. On happiness as circumstantial and metaphysical attunement, see Robert C. Roberts, *Emotions in the Moral Life* (Cambridge: Cambridge University Press, 2013), 157–87.

9. Robert C. Roberts, "A Brief Geography of Joy," 2. The paper is available at http://www.robertcroberts.net.

10. Damasio, *Looking for Spinoza,* 38.

11. On the central role of homeostasis in the evolution of the cultural and moral life of our species, see Antonio Damasio, *The Strange Order of Things: Life, Feeling, and the Making of Cultures* (New York: Pantheon Books, 2018).

12. Damasio, *Looking for Spinoza,* 30–56.

13. Damasio, *Looking for Spinoza,* 137. Matthew. E. Sachs—with the contribution of Damasio—assigns music (even sad music, in this case) a homeostatic function in balancing our emotional well-being. See M. E. Sachs, M. A. Damasio, and A. Habibi, "The Pleasures of Sad Music: A Systematic Review," *Frontiers in Human Neuroscience* 9, no. 404 (2015): 7–9.

14. Damasio, *Looking for Spinoza,* 137.

15. Roberts, "A Brief Geography of Joy," 2. In this respect, Roberts's definition of joy resonates with Paul Ekman's current use of "enjoyment," which covers a range of pleasurable states including peace, pride, amusement,

schadenfreude, compassion (which Ekman equates with joy), and excitement; see Paul Ekman Group, "Enjoyment," September 17, 2019, https://www.paulekman.com/universal-emotions/what-is-enjoyment/.

16. For Roberts, the open form would need to operate within the right kind of construal to guide the concern. On emotions as concern-based construals, see Robert C. Roberts, *Emotions in the Moral Life,* 38–67. Roberts and Damasio use the term *emotion* very differently: for Roberts, emotions are a way of seeing a situation independent of how one feels; for Damasio, emotions are embodied, whereas feelings are mental states.

17. For a clear statement of such a view, see Robert J. Zatorre and Valorie N. Salimpoor, "From Perception to Pleasure: Music and Its Neural Substrates," *Proceedings of the National Academy of Sciences* 110, no. 2 (2013): 10430–37; and David Huron, "The Plural Pleasures of Music," in *Proceedings of the 2004 Music and Music Science Conference,* ed. Johan Sundberg and William Brunson (Stockholm: Kungliga Musikhögskolan and the Royal Institute of Technology, 2005), 1–13.

18. David Huron, *Sweet Anticipation: Music and the Psychology of Expectation* (Cambridge, MA: MIT Press, 2006), 29.

19. Huron, *Sweet Anticipation,* 55.

20. Huron, *Sweet Anticipation,* 67. I have substituted, rather inadequately, "surprise" for what Huron calls "laughter": the connection between flight and laughter requires a rather convoluted and speculative explanation; see Huron, *Sweet Anticipation,* 60–61.

21. Charles Darwin, *The Descent of Man, and Selection in Relation to Sex* (Princeton, NJ: Princeton University Press, 1981), 2:336–37. In fact, for Darwin music was something of a mystery, and he was uncertain why it should exist at all in terms of evolution; see Charles Darwin, *The Life and Letters of Charles Darwin,* ed. Francis Darwin (London: John Murray, 1887), 100–102.

22. In his recent work with Jonna Vuoskoski, Huron has explored more complex relational emotions in music in terms of compassion, although it seems that this can only be conceived through sad music: feelings of empathetic concern evoked by sad music make for an enjoyable listening experience. Compassion feels good as a reaction to pain. So it appears that only a tragic order commands love—which is aptly Schopenhauer's response to his own philosophical pessimism. In this respect, Huron remains consistent with his biological pessimism. See David Huron and Jonna K. Vuoskoski, "On the Enjoyment of Sad Music: Pleasurable Compassion Theory and the Role of Trait Empathy," *Frontiers in Psychology* 11, no. 1060 (2020): 1–16.

23. Music neuropsychology is often too reductive: it is *only* human, focusing on transient experiences, locking music in the brain, with one single

evolutionary narrative. See Huron, for example, "The Plural Pleasures of Music," 1. For a critique of the current state of music psychology and a constructive and broader way forward, see W. F. Thompson, N. J. Bullot, and E. H. Margulis, "The Psychological Basis of Music Appreciation: Structure, Self, Source," *Psychological Review* 130, no. 1 (2023): 260–84.

24. Jakob von Uexküll, *A Foray into the Worlds of Animals and Humans: With a Theory of Meaning,* trans. Joseph D. O'Neil (Minneapolis: University of Minnesota Press, 2010), 48, 171, 202–3.

25. See Dorian Sagan's introduction to Uexküll's *A Foray into the Worlds of Animals and Humans,* 18.

26. See Uexküll, *A Foray into the Worlds of Animals and Humans,* 171, 188, 189, 208.

27. We can take our cue here from Elaine Scarry who, in her book *On Beauty and Being Just* (London: Duckworth, 2000), discusses the ethical implications of beauty as an aesthetic experience today.

28. See Immanuel Kant, *Critique of the Power of Judgment,* ed. Paul Guyer, trans. Paul Guyer and Eric Matthews (Cambridge: Cambridge University Press, 2000), 25, 47, 63–80.

29. Kant, *Critique of the Power of Judgment,* 95–96. Note that we are adapting Kant's *Third Critique* for our purposes here since, for the philosopher, beauty is in the eye of the beholder and not in the object itself.

30. See Anjan Chatterjee, *The Aesthetic Brain: How We Evolved to Desire Beauty and Enjoy Art* (Oxford: Oxford University Press, 2014), 118; and Anjan Chatterjee and Oshin Vartanian, "Neuroscience of Aesthetics," *Annals of the New York Academy of Sciences* 1369, no. 1 (2016): 184.

31. This process is akin to the neuro-aesthetic description of aesthetic experience as a dual perspective or sequential process in the brain, involving a bottom-up, stimulus-driven sense of pleasure and a top-down evaluative judgment. See Helmut Leder et al., "A Model of Aesthetic Appreciation and Aesthetic Judgments," *British Journal of Psychology* 95, no. 4 (2004): 489–508; C. J. Cela-Conde, J. García-Prieto, J. J. Ramasco, C. R. Mirasso, R. Bajo, E. Munar, A. Flexas, F. del-Pozo, and F. Maestú, "Dynamics of Brain Networks in the Aesthetic Appreciation," *Proceedings of the National Academy of Sciences of the United States of America* 110, supplement 2 (2013): 10454–61; and L. K. Graf and J. R. Landwehr, "A Dual-Process Perspective on Fluency-Based Aesthetics: The Pleasure-Interest Model of Aesthetic Liking," *Personality and Social Psychology Review: An Official Journal of the Society for Personality and Social Psychology* 19, no. 4 (2015): 395–410.

32. The prospect of earning money also stimulates the hedonistic hotspots in the brain. See B. Knutson, C. M. Adams, G. W. Fong, and D. Hommer, "Anticipation of Increasing Monetary Reward Selectively Recruits

Nucleus Accumbens," *Journal of Neuroscience: The Official Journal of the Society for Neuroscience* 21, no. 16 (2001): 1–5.

33. On such expertise, see Chatterjee and Vartanian, "Neuroscience of Aesthetics," 182. We should also remember that beauty can have a dark side: to discriminate in matters of taste can also mean to discriminate and violently eliminate what we regard as elements that mar beauty, especially if the criterion for beauty is purity. For this reason, it is vital to pair Kant's reflective judgement with Cage's *4′33″*. A reflective judgment should always let go and let be in seeking the beauty of an object. On the violence of beauty as form, see Daniel K. L. Chua, "Beethoven's Other Humanism," *Journal of the American Musicological Society* 62, no. 3 (2009): 577–80.

34. See Darwin, *The Life and Letters of Charles Darwin*, 100–102, quotation at 102. Ironically, in raising the question of character and emotional intelligence in music, Darwin points to a more ancient path not taken by current neuropsychologists of music in their commitment to Darwin.

35. Jeremy Bentham, *An Introduction to the Principles of Morals and Legislation* (1780), ed. J. H. Burns and H. L. A. Hart (Oxford: Clarendon, 1996). See chapter 4, "Value of a Lot of Pleasure or Pain, How to Be Measured," 38–41.

36. See Roberts, *Emotions in the Moral Life*, 183–85. The quotation is from Hebrews 12:2; also see James 1:2.

11
Counting to One

1. I am indebted to my colleague Youn Kim for carrying out this experiment in her classes on music and the mind. Students in the context of Hong Kong are invariably confused by which raga is happy and which is angry. I am equally unsure, despite my cosmopolitan background and musical training! This outcome runs against some studies that claim that there is a correlation between certain types of music with certain emotions not only in ragas but in music in general. See, for example, Laura-Lee Balkwill and William Forde Thompson, "A Cross-Cultural Investigation of the Perception of Emotion in Music: Psychophysical and Cultural Cues," *Music Perception* 17, no. 1 (1999). However, it is too reductive to conclude from these studies if the emotional properties are universally expressed in the music, since it is difficult to bracket culturally nurtured categories in a globalized world from natural responses. Other studies show that listening to the same music in different geographical location can have radically different meanings; see, for example, E. H. Margulis, P. Wong, C. Turnbull,

B. M. Kubit, and J. D. McAuley, "Narratives Imagined in Response to Instrumental Music Reveal Culture-Bounded Intersubjectivity," *Proceedings of the National Academy of Sciences of the United States of America* 119, no. 4 (2022). For a summary of the issues in music psychology, see John A. Sloboda and Patrik N. Juslin, "At the Interface between the Inner and Outer World: Psychological Perspectives," in *Handbook of Music and Emotion: Theory, Research, Applications,* ed. John A. Sloboda and Patrik N. Juslin (Oxford: Oxford University Press, 2010), 73–96.

2. This definition of harmony does not mean that the ancient Greeks were not capable of perceiving and theorizing consonances as the blending of two pitches simultaneously. See Andrew Barker, "Greek Acoustic Theory: Simple and Complex Sounds," in *Sound and the Ancient Senses,* ed. Shane Butler and Sarah Nooter (London: Routledge, 2019), 92–104.

3. Lao Tzu, *Tao Te Ching,* trans. D. C. Lau (London: Penguin Books, 1963), 2:41.91, 48.

4. In *Philosophy of New Music,* this flip between joy and fear is described by Adorno as the "dialectic of Enlightenment" exemplified in the harmonic totality of Schoenberg's twelve-tone compositional system. What sets out to be a liberating order ends up as a repressive regime that dominates the very rationale for emancipation. See Theodor W Adorno, *Philosophy of New Music,* trans. Robert Hullot-Kentor (Minneapolis: University of Minnesota Press, 2006); and "Drifting: The Dialectics of Adorno's *Philosophy of New Music,*" in *Apparitions: New Perspectives on Adorno and Twentieth-Century Music,* ed. Berthold Hoeckner (New York: Routledge, 2006), 1–17.

5. The actual term used during the 2019 unrest was more succinct: 攬炒 (lam chow). The term literally means "hug frying." A translation would be something like "We die together—if I'm fried in the fire, you're fried with me. Everybody goes down together."

12

Counting to Two

1. Gottfried Leibniz, Letter to Christian Goldbach, April 17, 1712, original in Gottfried Wilhelm Leibniz, *Opera omnia,* ed. Ludovic Dutens, 6 vols. (1768; Hildesheim: G. Olms, 1989), vol. 3, *Opera mathematica,* 437–38.

2. Gottfried Wilhelm Leibniz, *Confessio philosophi: Papers concerning the Problem of Evil, 1671–1679,* trans. R. C. Sleigh Jr. (New Haven, CT: Yale University Press, 2005), 28–29.

3. This *tragédie lyrique* (Lully's first experiment in this operatic genre) is music fit for a king—for the Sun King, Louis XIV, no less. "Always to sing the airs from the opera of *Cadmus and Hermione*," writes Leibniz, would be too much of good thing; it would be like "eating nothing but partridges." For Leibniz, one piece, however good, is a merely a microcosm that points to a greater music of infinite variety that encompasses all things in their ever-changing interaction. High and low, far and wide, great and small are counted in its cosmic rhythm. See Gottfried Wilhelm Leibniz, *Theodicy: Essays on the Goodness of God, the Freedom of Man, and the Origin of Evil*, trans. E. M. Huggard (New Haven, CT: Yale University Press, 1952), 198 (§124), translation slightly modified. Incidentally, the chaconne—a dance that originated from Aztec and African practices in the New World—accompanies a ballet depicting a group of Africans, two of whom would later be eaten by a giant serpent. Perhaps this dance foreshadows Lully's own demise. In 1687, rhythm killed Lully. During a performance, while beating time by tapping the floor with a stick, he accidentally stabbed his foot; claiming he would rather die than lose his ability to dance, he refused to have his foot amputated, and consequently died of gangrene.

4. Craig W. Reynolds, "Flocks, Herds, and Schools: A Distributed Behavioural Model," in *ACM SIGGRAPH Computer Graphics* 21, no. 4 (1987): 25–34. For an overview of complex adaptive systems, see John H. Miller and Scott E. Page, *Complex Adaptive Systems: An Introduction to the Computational Models of Social Life* (Princeton, NJ: Princeton University Press, 2007); and Melanie Mitchell, *Complexity: A Guided Tour* (Oxford: Oxford University Press, 2009).

5. See Art Rosenbaum, *Shout Because You're Free: The African American Ring Shout Tradition in Coastal Georgia* (Athens: University of Georgia Press, 1998), 102.

6. Cornel West, *Democracy Matters* (New York: Penguin Books, 2004), 20.

7. Miller and Page, *Complex Adaptive Systems*, 3.

8. For "harmonious ensembles," see Frank Wilczek, *A Beautiful Question: Finding Nature's Deep Design* (New York: Penguin, 2015), 225.

9. See Catherine Pickstock, *Repetition and Identity* (Oxford: Oxford University Press, 2013).

10. See Mike Goldsmith, *Discord: The Story of Noise* (Oxford: Oxford University Press, 2012), 13.

11. On music as making time, see Daniel K. L. Chua and Alexander Rehding, *Alien Listening: Voyager's Golden Record and Music from Earth* (New York: Zone Books, 2021), 190–96.

12. Einstein described how he arrived at the theory of relativity in a conversation with the musical educator Shinichi Suzuki: "The theory of

relativity occurred to me by intuition, and music is the driving force behind this intuition. My parents had me study the violin from the time I was six. My new discovery is the result of musical perception." Shinichi Suzuki, *Nurtured by Love: A New Approach to Education*, trans. Waltruad Suzuki (New York: Exposition, 1969), 90.

13
A Rhythmic Universe

1. A performance of the melody is available at https://youtu.be /rogbefl_QQI. The performance on the *dizi* is by Daniel Tsz-shing Lei, a Hong Kong University music student during the time of protest who was exemplary as a person of propriety and harmony in his engagement with political change.

2. The earliest account of this story in the *Lüshi chunqiu* (*The Annals of Lü Buwei*) does not explain how Ling Lun arrives at the twelve pitch pipes. However, there is an efficient way of tuning the pipes that was well known in ancient China: instead of spiraling up the circle of fifths then readjusting some pipe lengths to group the pitches in the same octave, the pitches can be measured from the yellow bell by alternating pipes two-thirds (2:3) and four-thirds (4:3) of the length of the previous pipe. (The 4:3 proportion equates to cutting a third to arrive at a perfect fifth, then doubling the length to bring the pitch down an octave.) The technique, known as "a third removing and extending" method, was first recorded in the *Guanzi,* a treatise that dates from the seventh century BCE (although the dating of the treatise is highly disputed; it could even postdate the *Lüshi chunqiu*). See Joseph C. Y. Chen, *Early Chinese Work in Natural Science* (Hong Kong: Hong Kong University Press, 1996), 49–51. For a clear demonstration of how this up-and-down tuning works to produce a pentatonic scale, see Guangmin Li, "Chromatic Scale Construction in Ancient China," *History of Music Theory* (blog), April 12, 2017, https://his-toryofmusictheory .wordpress.com/2017/04/12/chromatic-scale-construction-in-ancient -china/. For a more detailed commentary on Chinese tuning, see the chapter "The Cycle of Fifths: The Musical Theory of the Chinese" in Alain Daniélou, *Music and the Power of Sound: The Influence of Tuning and Interval on Consciousness* (Rochester, VT: Inner Traditions, 1995).

3. Søren Kierkegaard, *Repetition and Philosophical Crumbs*, trans. M. G. Piety (Oxford: Oxford University Press, 2009), 3.

4. For a more detailed exposition of this theory of repetition, see Daniel K. L. Chua and Alexander Rehding, *Alien Listening: Voyager's Golden Record and Music from Earth* (New York: Zone Books, 2021), 65–98.

5. Lao Tzu, *Tao Te Ching*, trans. D. C. Lau (London: Penguin Books, 1963), 2:41.91, 48.

6. Zhuangzi, *The Complete Works of Chuang Tzu*, trans. Burton Watson (New York: Columbia University Press, 1968), 36–37.

14

Verbal Abuse

1. Iain McGilchrist, *The Master and His Emissary: The Divided Brain and the Making of the Western World* (New Haven, CT: Yale University Press, 2010), 113–15.

2. This is also the case in older genres: in classical Chinese *ci* (詞), for example, the writer composes a poem according to the pattern of a particular tune. Indeed, many of these poems are identified by the name of the melody. There are also cases where words seem to come first: the melody and the tonal rise of fall of the words do not align. In fact, this is the case for the "Kangding Love Song." However, with the standardization of Chinese to Mandarin, this song is known only in Mandarin today. In general, matching the melodic tones to Mandarin (a dialect with only four tones) is less of an issue: the misalignment of words and music is less jarring. Since the song is from Kangding, it is probably the case that it was originally composed in another dialect with a different tonal character from Mandarin. On the relationship between different Chinese dialects and music, see Xi Zhang and Ian Cross, "Analysing the Relationship between Tone and Melody in Chaozhou Songs," *Journal of New Music Research* 15, no. 4 (2021): 299–311. For a summary and further ruminations on the complex relation between music and speech in Cantopop, see Edwin K. C. Li, "Cantopop and Speech-Melody Complex," *Music Theory Online* 27, no. 1 (2021).

3. See Jean-Jacques Rousseau, *Essai sur l'origine des langues* (1764), in *The First and Second Discourses Together with the Replies to Critics and Essay on the Origin of Languages,* ed. and trans. V. Gourevitch (New York: Harper & Row, 1986).

4. The narrative still persists: see Steven Mithen, *The Singing Neanderthals: The Origins and Music, Language, Mind and Body* (London: Weidenfeld & Nicolson, 2005). Also see the discussion in McGilchrist, *The Master and His Emissary,* 102–5.

5. Gary Tomlinson, *One Million Years of Music: The Emergence of Human Modernity* (New York: Zone Books, 2015), 74.

6. See Jeremy Begbie, "The Word Refreshed: Music and God-Talk," in *Theology, Music and Modernity: Struggles for Freedom,* ed. Jeremy Begbie,

Daniel K. L. Chua, and Markus Rathey (Oxford: Oxford University Press, 2021), 358–74.

7. Alfred Gell, *Art and Agency: An Anthropological Theory* (Oxford: Oxford University Press, 1998), 80.

8. See Charles Darwin, *The Descent of Man, and Selection in Relation to Sex* (Princeton, NJ: Princeton University Press, 1981), 2:336–37.

9. Diana Deutsch, Trevor Henthorn, and Rachael Lapidis, "Illusory Transformation from Speech to Song," *Journal of the Acoustical Society of America* 129, no. 4 (2011): 2245–52. Even noise or a sound fragment association with a source or referent, as the composer Pierre Schaeffer points out, loses its "narrative" component and becomes music when repeated: "Repeat the same sound-fragment twice: There is no longer event, but music." See Pierre Schaeffer, *In Search of a Concrete Music,* trans. Christine North and John Dack (Berkeley: University of California Press, 2012), 13.

10. Ironically, this speech-to-song illusion is reduced in speakers of tonal languages. See Kankamol Jaisin, Rapeepong Suphanchaimat, Candia Mauricio A. Figueroa, and Jason D. Warren, "The Speech-to-Song Illusion Is Reduced in Speakers of Tonal (vs. Non-Tonal) Languages," *Frontiers in Psychology* 7 (May 2016): 662.

11. Such cooing as a mother articulates to her baby, known as "parentese," is speech as a form of song, and is apparently similar across all human culture. See C. B. Hilton, C. J. Moser, M. Bertolo, et al., "Acoustic Regularities in Infant-Directed Speech and Song across Cultures," *Nature Human Behaviour* 6, no. 11 (2022): 1545–56. Humans also speak in a similar way to their pets and sometimes to their plants. Since the language spoken is only putative at best in the brain of the baby (or pet), the musical component of repetition with its patterns of pitch and beats seems to communicate as a kind of universal code, sending good vibrations to their recipients.

15
Best Possible World

1. Robert C. Roberts, "A Brief Geography of Joy," 2, http://www.robertcroberts.net 2; also see a similar definition in Robert C. Roberts, *Spiritual Emotions: A Psychology of Christian Virtues* (Grand Rapids, MI: Eerdmans, 2007), 116.

2. Derrida discusses supplementary logic most famously in his commentary on texts by Rousseau that pit speech against writing, melody against harmony, masturbation against sexual relations, and so on. See

Jacques Derrida, *Of Grammatology*, rev. ed., trans. Gayatri Chakravorty Spivak (Baltimore: Johns Hopkins University Press, 1998), 95–316.

3. See Confucius, *Analects*, trans. Annping Chin (New York: Penguin, 2014), 7.14, 102; and Augustine, *The Confessions*, trans. Maria Boulding, ed. John E. Rotelle (New York: New City, 1997), 9.6.14, 9.3.6. In Annping Chin's translation, the passage concludes: [Confucius] said, "I never imagined that music could be this beautiful." A better and more accurate translation in this context would be: "I never imagined that music (樂) could provide such perfect joy (樂)." On Augustine's singing and his tears of joy, see Carol Harrison, *On Music, Sense, Affect and Voice* (London: Bloomsbury Academic, 1919), 79–86.

4. This problem was particularly acute in Chinese music theory and cosmology where there was an exact correlation between the calendrical cycle and the tuning of the twelve tones. See Joseph S. C. Lam, *State Sacrifices and Music in Ming China: Orthodoxy, Creativity, and Expressiveness* (Albany: State University of New York Press, 1998), 85. As with the West, this led to the development of equal temperament in order to close the tuning system. But the reasons for this new tuning were divergent: in China, equal temperament was an attempt to align tuning with the cosmos, whereas in the West it resulted in a detuning of the cosmos (as explained later in the chapter).

5. See Daniel K. L. Chua, *Absolute Music and the Construction of Meaning* (Cambridge: Cambridge University Press, 1999), 3–72.

6. Max Weber, *The Rational and Social Foundations of Music*, trans. D. Martindale, J. Riedel, and G. Neuwirth (Carbondale: Southern Illinois University Press, 1958), 102–3. See also Chua, *Absolute Music*, 12–15.

7. There is a certain irony in this detuning narrative of modernity. Recently, a heated debate has erupted within musicological circles on the question of who discovered equal temperament first—the West or China? Arguably, China pipped the West to the post. But as Alexander Rehding points out, this is hardly a significant "win" since these are divergent histories, with different cultural meanings. The critical point here is that the formulation of equal temperament in China did not result in a "disenchantment narrative" or China's entry into modernity. The twist is that China—including its tuning system—was regarded in the West as an equal during the seventeenth and eighteenth centuries, and was championed as a model to emulate. Ancient China was not a foil for the development of Western modernity but a catalyst: it was modern *avant la lettre*. See Alexander Rehding, "Fine-tuning a Global History of Music Theory: Divergences, Zhu Zaiyu, and Music-Theoretical Instruments," *Music Theory Spectrum* 44, no. 2 (2022): 1–16. On the Confucian influence on the European Enlighten-

ment, see Christopher Hancock, *Christianity and Confucianism: Culture, Faith and Politics* (London: T&T Clark, 2021), 140–54.

8. For examples of such patterns and how musicians elaborated upon them, see Robert O. Gjerdingen, *Music in the Galant Style* (Oxford: Oxford University Press, 2007).

9. See, for example, Gottfried Wilhelm Leibniz, *Discourse on Metaphysics and Other Essays*, ed. and trans. Daniel Garber and Roger Ariew (Indianapolis: Hackett, 1991), chapter 5, "What the Rules of the Perfection of Divine Conduct Consists in, and That the Simplicity of the Ways Is in Balance with the Richness of the Effects,"4–5.

10. See Gottfried Wilhelm Leibniz, *Confessio Philosophi: Papers concerning the Problem of Evil, 1671–1679*, trans. R. C. Sleigh Jr. (New Haven, CT: Yale University Press, 2005), 28–29.

11. See Gilles Deleuze, *The Fold: Leibniz and the Baroque*, trans. Tom Conley (Minneapolis: University of Minnesota Press, 1993), 131.

12. In this regard, it is apt that the term *baroque* may have originated from the Portuguese word *barroco,* meaning "a flawed pearl."

13. Gilles Deleuze and Félix Guattari, *A Thousand Plateaus: Capitalism and Schizophrenia*, trans. Brian Massumi (Minneapolis: University of Minnesota Press, 1987), 299.

14. Antoine Goléa, *Rencontres avec Olivier Messiaen* (Paris: René Juillard, 1960), 63, translation from Rebecca Rischin, *For the End of Time: The Story of the Messiaen Quartet* (Ithaca, NY: Cornell University Press, 2003), 5.

15. *Olivier Messiaen: A Music of Faith,* London Weekend Television, April 5, 1985.

16. Olivier Messiaen, "Address Delivered at the Conferring of the *Praemium Erasmianum* on 25 June 1971, in Amsterdam," in Almut Rössler, *Contributions to the Spiritual World of Olivier Messiaen*, trans. Barbara Dagg et al. (Duisberg: Gilles & Francke, 1986), 40.

17. "Conférence de Bruxelles" (1958), cited in Robert Sherlaw Johnson, *Messiaen* (Berkeley: University of California Press, 1975), 32.

18. Deleuze and Guattari, *A Thousand Plateaus,* 299–300.

19. In his novel *Doctor Faustus,* Thomas Mann describes a similar concert that expresses "a hope beyond hopelessness." The novel explores the rise and fall of Nazi Germany through the allegory of German music and its development in the first half of the twentieth century. The work performed at the concert—*The Lamentation of Dr Faustus*—is the final composition of Adrian Leverkühn before syphilitic madness reduces him to an infantile state. The composition is a masterpiece of unrelenting despair; it permits "no consolation, appeasement, transfiguration." But the silence at

the end of this cantata enables a meager sense of hope to rise like a spectral vision; the last fading note, even as it disappears into nothing, repeats as a rhythm in the memory. The silence "abides as a light in the night." In contrast, Messiaen's actual concert in a World War II prisoner of war camp offers a plenitude of joy in its silence. In this sense, the *Quartet for the End of Time* is stranger than fiction in its articulation of hope. But both concerts—real and imagined—demonstrate the refusal of rhythm, even in silence, to end without hope. Joy cannot be erased. It is in this sense that rhythm is indestructible. See *Doctor Faustus: The Life of the German Composer Adrian Leverkühn as Told by a Friend,* trans. Helen Tracy Lowe-Porter (London: Secker & Warburg, 1949), 491.

16

Joyride

1. Affectionately known as IMTE, this theory is expounded in Daniel K. L. Chua and Alexander Rehding, *Alien Listening: Voyager's Golden Record and Music from Earth* (New York: Zone Books, 2021).

2. Benedict Anderson, *Imagined Communities: Reflections on the Origin and Spread of Nationalism,* rev. ed. (London: Verso, 1991), 24. For a short and intensive history and critique of modern temporality and musical temporality see Martin Scherzinger, "Temporalities," in *The Oxford Handbook of Critical Concepts in Music Theory,* ed. Alexander Rehding and Steven Rings (Oxford: Oxford University Press, 2015), 234–70.

3. Friedrich Nietzsche, *The Birth of Tragedy and Other Writings,* ed. Raymond Geuss and Ronald Speirs, trans. Ronald Speirs (Cambridge: Cambridge University Press, 1999), 114.

4. See Martin Heidegger, *The Question concerning Technology and Other Essays,* trans. William Lovitt (New York: Garland 1977), 3–35.

5. See Giorgio Biancorosso, *Situated Listening: The Sound of Absorption in Classical Cinema* (Oxford: Oxford University Press, 2016).

6. In fact, according to Antonio Damasio, if the universe were merely neutral matter and empty time, then "feeling-driven homeostasis" would have neither the joy nor anguish to shape evolution and arrive at any moral sense. See *The Strange Order of Things: Life, Feeling, and the Making of Cultures* (New York: Pantheon Books, 2018), 193–205.

7. On Augustine and modernity, see, for example, Charles Taylor, *Sources of the Self* (Cambridge, MA: Harvard University Press, 1989), 127–42; the link between Augustine and the modern self is a highly contested narrative; see note 23 in chapter 17 below. On Confucius and the Enlighten-

ment, See see Christopher Hancock, *Christianity and Confucianism: Culture, Faith and Politics* (London: T&T Clark, 2021), 90–182. On Confucius as the patron saint of the eighteenth-century Enlightenment, see Yongjin Zhang, "Worldling China, 1500–1800," in *The Globalization of International Society,* ed. Tim Dunne and Christian Reus-Smit (Oxford: Oxford University Press, 2017), 204–26, citation at 209.

8. For a critique of empty time and the need for a ritualized space-time today, see Byung-Chul Han, *The Disappearance of Rituals: A Topology of the Present,* trans. Daniel Steuer (Cambridge: Polity, 2020), 1–15. Aptly, repetition is the basis of ritual.

9. Paul Virilio, *Negative Horizon: An Essay in Dromoscopy,* trans. Michael Degener (London: Continuum, 2008), 42. Virilio writes: "If the *freedom of movement* (*habeas corpus*) would seem to be one of the first freedoms, the liberation of speed, the *freedom of speed,* seems to be the fulfillment of all freedoms. . . . The progress of speed is nothing other than the unleashing of violence." On speed as freedom and violence in Beethoven's Ninth Symphony, see Daniel K. L. Chua, *Beethoven and Freedom* (Oxford: Oxford University Press, 2019), 88–99.

17
Not So Fast

1. For Kant, only men are sublime.

2. Friedrich Nietzsche, *The Birth of Tragedy and Other Writings,* ed. Raymond Geuss and Ronald Speirs, trans. Ronald Speirs (Cambridge: Cambridge University Press, 1999), 114. On the prevalence of the sublime in Nietzsche's early philosophy, see Keith Ansell-Pearson, "'Holding on to the Sublime': On Nietzsche's Early 'Unfashionable' Project," in *The Oxford Handbook of Nietzsche,* ed. Ken Grime and John Richardson (Oxford: Oxford University Press, 2013), 226–51.

3. See Nietzsche, *Birth of Tragedy,* 100–101.

4. For a critique of Nietzsche's position of affirming life in the face of the tragic as a kind of aesthetic game, see Julian Young, *Nietzsche's Philosophy of Art* (Cambridge: Cambridge University Press, 1992), 147; and Daniel Came, "The Themes of Affirmation and Illusion in *The Birth of Tragedy* and Beyond," in Grime and Richardson, *The Oxford Handbook of Nietzsche,* 223.

5. See Arthur Schopenhauer, "On the Vanity and Suffering of Life," in *The World as Will and Representation,* trans. E. F. J. Payne (New York: Dover, 1969), 2:540.

6. Richard Benson Sewall, *The Vision of Tragedy* (New Haven, CT: Yale University Press, 1956), 50; George Steiner, *The Death of Tragedy* (New York: Knopf, 1961).

7. Matthew 26:10 and Mark 14:6. For an overview of *kalon*, see Hans Urs von Balthasar, *The Glory of the Lord: A Theological Aesthetics*: vol. 4, *The Realm of Metaphysics in Antiquity*, ed. John Riches, trans. Brian McNeil, Andrew Louth, John Saward, Rowen Williams, and Oliver Davies (San Francisco, CA: Ignatius, 1989), 201–15. In my reading of this story, I am combining the accounts in Mathew 26, Mark 14, and John 12. The account in Luke 7 is perhaps too different to be considered a description of the same event. I will leave it to the theologians to worry about sources, redactions, and the priority of the different accounts.

8. John 12:5.

9. Matthew 26:10 and Mark 14:6.

10. Matthew 26:10–12.

11. In the account in Mark and Matthew, Judas goes to the chief priest offering to betray Jesus immediately after the anointing.

12. There is a tradition where Mary of Bethany, who is the sister of Martha and Lazarus in the account in John's Gospel, is mistakenly conflated with Mary Magdalene, a first witness of the resurrection. Mary's act of anointing is more powerful if there is no foreknowledge of the resurrection: it is a true lament, an act that only foresees death as the final outcome. What is beautiful—the disproportionate element—captures a glimmer of hope, without disclosing the possibility of a joyous outcome in what, humanly speaking, can only be a tragic situation.

13. On the moral detriment caused by the division of the sublime and the beautiful in aesthetics today, see Byung-Chul Han, *Saving Beauty*, trans. Daniel Steuer (Cambridge, MA: Polity, 2018), 1–21, 40–45.

14. Yuk Hui, *Art and Cosmotechnics* (Minneapolis: University of Minnesota Press and E-Flux, 2021), 13–45.

15. Augustine, *De musica* (Berlin: De Gruyter, 2017), 6.10.25.

16. Augustine, *De musica* 6.17.56–57. See Catherine Pickstock, "Music, Soul, City and Cosmos After Augustine," in *Radical Orthodoxy: A New Theology*, ed. John Milbank, Catherine Pickstock, and Graham Ward (London: Routledge, 1999), 247–48. Incidentally, with reference to the rhythmic theory outlined earlier, this gap or interval would be the point of difference (PoD) that folds time into rhythm, the divide in the definition of repetition as "A| V."

17. Augustine, *De musica* 1.12.20.

18. Graham Ward, "Aesthetics, Music and Meaning Making," *Religions* 10, no. 3 (2019): 1–9.

19. On the body's perception of external impulses, see Augustine, *De musica* 6.11.

20. In *De trinitate,* Augustine does use the word *harmonia,* although, technically, Ward is correct in that Augustine mentions the word as an attribution to Greek thought rather than his own, preferring to use another word, *caoptatione* (interlock), to describe concord or consonance: see Carol Harrison, *On Music, Sense, Affect and Voice* (London: Bloomsbury Academic, 1919), 23.

21. Ward, "Aesthetics, Music and Meaning Making," 8. As Ward explains, the key prefix here is "con" (with), which implies a difference-in-relation; "harmonia" implies parts integrated within a whole. Along with *consonantia,* Augustine uses the term *concordia* (especially in *De musica*) and *congruencia,* which are synonyms (with a difference—literally) for harmony.

22. A1 and A2 modes are used for didactic purposes only. Aristotle (A2), although he describes the intellect as self-motion, should not be regarded as a voluntarist figure of self-motion. His ethics—indeed, the very virtues associated with joy in his philosophy—are as much an inspiration for this book as Augustine's writings. On the mind as self-motion in Aristotle, see Michael V. Wedin, "Aristotle on the Mind's Self-Motion," in *Self-Motion: From Aristotle to Newton,* ed. Mary Louise Gill and James G. Lennox (Princeton, NJ: Princeton University Press, 1995). On Augustine and love as a motion toward the good, see Hannah Arendt, *Love and Saint Augustine,* ed. Joanna Vecchiarelli Scott and Judith Chelius Stark (Chicago: University of Chicago Press, 1996), 8–12; and Harrison, *On Music,* 47–58, 69–71. Carol Harrison notes that this "mode" of a rightly ordered love, which is one of the structuring principles of Augustine's theology, is first outlined in *De musica;* see Harrison, *On Music,* 50–51.

23. The roots of modern freedom as a self-determined will developed from late medieval voluntarist tendencies that stressed the arbitrary and inscrutable sovereignty of God's will; the tendency is already nascent in the work of Duns Scotus and William of Ockham. On the development of Aristotelian self-motion in medieval thought, see Calvin G. Normore, "Ockham, Self-Motion, and the Will," in Gill and Lennox, *Self-Motion.* On the voluntarist lineage from Duns Scotus to Schopenhauer and Nietzsche, see Hans Urs von Balthasar, *Theo-Drama II: Theological Dramatic Theory: The Dramatis Personae: Man in God,* trans. Graham Harrison (San Francisco: Ignatius, 1990) 245–48. Ironically, in recent scholarship, Augustine is often credited as a source of the modern autonomous will and its subsequent association with nihilism, particularly in connection with Cartesian notions of the self. But, as Michael Hanby has pointed out, this connection

is highly problematic and fails to take into account Augustine's cosmology (not least as represented in *De musica*), which is determined not by natural laws but by the goodness and providence of God. Augustine's idea of the will is affective, aesthetic, relational, doxological, and directed by love. Without such qualities, Augustine's concept of the selfhood would, indeed, be nothing more than the self-mastery of the stoic will that underlies Cartesian conceptions of the self. See Michael Hanby, *Augustine and Modernity* (London: Routledge, 2003).

24. This is a stereotype in Beethoven's reception history. Beethoven is much more than, and often very different from, the self-determined will of the hero; see Daniel K. L. Chua, "Beethoven's Other Humanism," *Journal of the American Musicological Society* 62, no. 3 (2009).

25. On self-motion as force in music, see Daniel K. L. Chua, *Beethoven and Freedom* (Oxford: Oxford University Press, 2019), 16–19. On the meaning of energy, force, and motion in conceptions of music in the late nineteenth and early twentieth centuries, particularly in terms of rhythm, see Youn Kim, *Body and Force in Music: Metaphoric Constructions in Music Psychology* (London: Routledge, 2022).

26. Augustine, *De musica* 6.1.1.

18
Feeling Groovy

1. Augustine, *De musica* (Berlin: De Gruyter, 2017), 6.15.4.

2. Augustine, *The Confessions*, ed. John E. Rotelle, trans. Maria Boulding (New York: New City, 1997), 9.6.14.

3. See Anjan Chatterjee, *The Aesthetic Brain: How We Evolved to Desire Beauty and Enjoy Art* (Oxford: Oxford University Press, 2014), xx.

4. On Augustine's alternative way of the melisma, see Carol Harrison, "Getting Carried Away: Why Did Augustine Sing?" *Augustine Studies* 46, no. 1 (2015).

5. See measures 12–13 and 18–20.

6. See Augustine on the nightingale in *De musica* 1.4.5.

7. On God's silent communication of truth, see, for example, Augustine's *De civitate Dei contra paganos* 11.2, 11.4, 11.29, 16.6. Also see Philip Abbott, "The Sound of Silence: Augustine's Soundscape for the Christian Empire," *Vigiliae Christianae* 76, no. 5 (2022): 537–58.

8. See Augustine, *The Trinity*, ed. John E. Rotelle, trans. Edmund Hill (New York: New City, 1991), 15:25–26.

9. On musical joy and the inadequacy of words in Augustine, see Sarah Stewart-Kroeker, "A Wordless Cry of Jubilation: Joy and the Ordering of

Emotion," *Augustinian Studies* 50, no. 1 (2019); and Abbott, "The Sound of Silence."

10. Augustine's numbering of the Psalms follows that in the Septuagint (Greek) text. In modern versions, which follow the Masoretic (Hebrew) text, Augustine's Psalm 32 is numbered Psalm 33.

11. Augustine, *Expositions of the Psalms*, ed. John E. Rotelle, trans. Maria Boulding (New York: New City, 2000–2004), 32.2.8.

12. See James W. McKinnon, "Patristic Jubilus and the Alleluia of the Mass," in *Cantus Planus: Papers Read at the Third Meeting, Tihany, Hungary, 19–24 September, 1988* (Budapest: Hungarian Academy of Sciences, 1990).

13. As Augustine makes clear in his commentary on Psalm 32, "Think of people who sing at harvest time, or in the vineyard, or at any work that goes with a swing"; *Expositions of the Psalms* 32.2.8.

14. Unlike the title of the song, the "doo-wahs" represent an improvised and wordless element in jazz that can be rendered in many other ways, such as "ba-ba doo-wah, la-la doo-dah . . . ," etc. They are not fixed lyrics but stand in for a spontaneous rhythmic embellishment akin to the *jubilus*. Hence Irving Mill's lyrics do not include these "nonsensical" responses between the lines. In fact, in the original 1932 recording, the "doo-wahs" are not sung but played by Ellington's big band (the wah-wah mute effect on the trumpets sounding remarkably like "doo-wah"). This swinging gesture was so catchy it was almost impossible for singers not to join in the fun in later recordings!

15. Augustine, *Expositions of the Psalms* 99:4. We do not know what the *jubilus* sounded like but we need to hear it as African music. It might be instructive to listen to a work song of men cultivating a peanut field in Senegal recorded by J. David Sapir in the 1960s. Sapir's description in the liner notes is similar to Augustine's description of the *jubilus*: "When the whole field is prepared for digging all the men line-up in a row, sometimes as many as fifty together. It is at this time that the men sing, all together and in rhythm to the digging interjecting shouts of encouragement and blasts from European-made whistles." "Cultivating in Peanut Field" (Bakari Badji, lead vocals), in *The Music of the Diola-Fogny of the Casamance, Senegal* (Smithsonian Folkways FE4323, 1965), track 2. Also see Paul Oliver, *Savannah Syncopators: African Retentions in the Blues* (New York: Stein & Day, 1970), 56–57.

16. Augustine, *Expositions of the Psalms* 32.2.8. I am using the translation by James McKinnon in James McKinnon, *Music in Early Christian Literature* (Cambridge: Cambridge University Press, 1987), 156–57, which picks up the element of labor more clearly than Maria Boulding's translation.

17. Augustine, *Expositions of the Psalms* 44.9.

18. Augustine, *Expositions of the Psalms* 80.3.

19. Carol Harrison, "Getting Carried Away: Why Did Augustine Sing?" (annual St. Augustine Lecture, Villanova University, November 4, 2014), YouTube video posted by villanovauniversity, https://youtu.be/xfkfRuLQ TZk?si=OKNqb6d-1lnGWl2u.

20. The identification of the *jubilus* to the melismatic ending of the Alleluia is first clearly stated by Amalarius of Metz in the first half of the ninth century. See McKinnon, "Patristic Jubilus," 69–70. On similar "ineffable" liturgical melismatic practices, see Lori Kruckenburg, "Neumatizing the Sequence: Special Performances of Sequences in the Central Middle Ages," *Journal of the American Musicological Society* 59 no. 2 (2006); and Karen Desmond, "W. de Wicumbe's Rolls and Singing the Alleluya ca. 1250," *Journal of the American Musicological Society* 73, no. 3 (2020).

21. See Augustine, *Expositions of the Psalms* 99:4–5.

22. See Harrison, "Getting Carried Away," 14.

23. See Harrison, "Getting Carried Away," 14–22.

24. Augustine, *Expositions of the Psalms* 99:4. Translation by James McKinnon in *Music in Early Christian Literature*, 158.

25. Mark Evan Bonds, *Absolute Music: The History of an Idea* (Oxford: Oxford University Press, 2014), 42–44.

26. There is a form of music theory formulated by Heinrich Schenker that can turn a vast symphonic movement into a melismatic complex. Indeed, if you look at a Schenkerian graph, it literally looks like a melismatic complex. No words are needed, since this music is "absolute." See, for example, Heinrich Schenker, *Five Graphic Music Analyses* (Mineola, NY: Dover, 1969).

27. For a modern take on musical ineffability, see Vladimir Jankélévitch, *Music and the Ineffable*, trans. Carolyn Abbate (Princeton, NJ: Princeton University Press, 2003). For Jankélévitch, music is ineffable because its meaning cannot be fixed; rather, music generates limitless possibilities and finds its true form in open-ended improvisation. Music in this sense shares with joy an open and capacious structure.

28. Braxton D. Shelley, *Healing for the Soul: Richard Smallwood, the Vamp, and the Gospel Imagination* (Oxford: Oxford University Press, 2021), 28. To experience an example of such worship, see Dr. Mattie Moss Clark, with the Michigan State Community Choir in worship at the Darnell Ishmel Gospel Music Workshop, Lansing, MI, 1989. Posted on YouTube by Darnell Ishmel, April 4, 2011: http://youtu.be/2pcM45ff5Yg. In the history of African American worship, such rhythmic forms were also widely condemned as a religious practice. It was under conditions of racial discrimination and injustice that this music staked its cultural, economic,

political, ecclesiastical, class, gender, and racial freedoms; for example, see
the chapters by Patrick McCreless, Michael O'Connor, Charisse Burton,
and Awet Andemicael on Richard Allen (1740–1850), the founder of the
African Methodist Episcopal Church, in "Part III: Singing Justice," in *Theology, Music and Modernity: Struggles for Freedom*, ed. Jeremy Begbie,
Daniel K. L. Chua, and Markus Rathey (Oxford: Oxford University Press,
2021), 201–91.

29. George E. Valliant, *Spiritual Evolution: A Scientific Defence of Faith*
(New York: Broadway Books, 2008), 133.

30. On the female ululation in funeral rites see, for example, Valerie
Hope, "Vocal Expression in Roman Mourning," in *Sound and the Ancient
Senses*, ed. Shane Butler and Sarah Nooter (London: Routledge, 2019), 61–76.
Such musical practices, like the *jubilus*, have African origins.

31. See Emmanuel Lévinas, "Useless Suffering," in *Entre Nous: On
Thinking-of-the-Other*, trans. Michael B. Smith and Barbara Harshav (New
York: Columbia University Press, 1998), 91–93.

32. Theodor W. Adorno, "Stravinsky: A Dialectical Portrait," in *Quasi
una Fantasia: Essays on Modern Music* (1963), trans. R. Livingstone (London:
Verso, 1992), 151.

33. This tragic ontology of terror and panic is most eloquently presented by Pascal Quignard, *The Hatred of Music*, trans. Matthew Amos
and Fredrik Rönnbäck (New Haven, CT: Yale University Press, 2016).

34. On the loss of listening in the bustle of the modern world and the
need to rediscover "the gift of listening," see Byung-Chul Han, *The Burnout Society*, trans. Erik Butler (Stanford, CA: Stanford University Press,
2015), 12–14.

35. See Roberto Esposito, *Communitas: The Origin and Destiny of
Community* (Stanford, CA: Stanford University Press, 2010), 12–13.

36. For a theological perspective on indwelling a music-full earth, see
Norman Wirzba, "The Witness of Praise—The Hope of Dwelling," in Begbie, Chua, and Rathey, *Theology, Music and Modernity*, 336–57.

Credits

Illustrations:
Figure 4: Beethoven-Haus Bonn
Figure 5: Beethoven-Haus Bonn, Sammlung Wegeler
Figures 6, 7, 12, 13, 14, 16, and 19: Jonathan W. Johnson
Figure 20: NASA

Index

Note: Page numbers in italics indicate figures.

and musical frequency, 280n2;
souvenirs of, 43
Pythagorean comma, 199–200, 207
Pythagorean philosophy:
balanced ratios, 50, 60, 75, 80,
83, 88, 92, 93, 112, 139, 144, 201,
227, 249; cosmic harmony, 54,
57, 62–64, 68–69, 72, 74, 76, 78,
81, 82, 84, 85, 86, 88, 90, 200,
201, 217, 225; musical theories,
82, 90, 95, 139, 144; musical
tuning, 60, 203; and the
tectractys, 239

Quartet for the End of Time
(Messiaen), 205–8, 291–92n19;
performance in Hong Kong,
209–10; preface to, 207, *208*

ragas, 140, 167, 284–85n1
reason, 4, 70, 93–94, 103, 124, 145,
189, 217, 219, 240,242,278n23:
and magic, 79–81; as instrumental reason, 86–88, 129, 144,
200, 258
recitative, 5–6
reflective judgment, 47, 131–32,
272n25, 284n33
Rehding, Alexander, 260,
290–91n7
"Rejoice Greatly" (Handel),
243–44, *243,* 252–53
relativity, theory of, 169, 286–87n12
repetition, 172, 289n9, 294n16;
linguistic, 190; in Messiaen's
quartet, 207; nonidentical,
176–81; and rhythm, 151–55, 175–85
resonance, 53, 97, 99, 113, 139, 182,
183, 233–34, 239, 258, 273n7
reward circuit, 122, 124, 127, 133,
134, 135, 137, 241, 242

rhythm: asymmetrical, 207–8,
208; and beat, 162; and blues,
155–65; bodily, 195–98; in *De
musica,* 92; of Deleuze and
Guattari, 204; and frequency,
162–63; harmonic, 159–62, 214;
of Hong Kong's fragrance, 230;
as indestructible, 291–92n19; as
joy, 196–97, 218, 228; melisma,
242–53, 254, 258, 298n20,
298n26; and meter, 162; music
as, 190; non-retrogradable, 207;
and order, 198–99; point of
difference, 176–79, 243, 294n16;
and repetition, 151–55, 175–85;
and rest, 101; in the ring shout,
156–57; self-motion, 236–37,
296n25; and timbre, 163–64; of
the universe, 256
ring shout, 156–59, *156,* 162, 163,
164, 170, 250, 254
rites. *See* etiquette (custom, rites)
ritournelles, 204, 205, 206, 207, 209
Roberts, Robert C., 122–25, 127,
131, 132, 197
Rosa, Hartmut, 273n7
Rossini, Giacomo, 192–93
Rousseau, Jean-Jacques, 188
Ruanyu Mountains, 38, 43, 49

Saïs, temple of, 21, *22,* 23
schadenfreude, 126, 281–82n15
Schaeffer, Pierre, 289n9
Schenker, Heinrich, 298n26
Schiller, Friedrich, 23, 267n2
Schoenberg, Arnold, 285n4
Schopenhauer, Arthur, 23, 25, 28,
222, 224–25, 268–69n19, 269n21,
282n22
Schreckensfanfare, 15–16, 24
science, 112